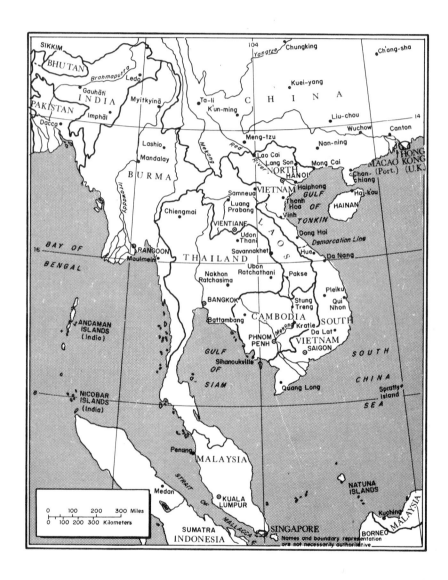

Vietnam and Southeast Asia.

The Lessons of

Vietnam

Edited by W. Scott Thompson & Donaldson D. Frizzell

London: Macdonald and Jane's

The Lessons of Vietnam
Published in the United States by
Crane, Russak & Company, Inc.
347 Madison Avenue
New York, New York 10017
ISBN 0-8448-0973-X
LC 76-20281

Published in Great Britain by
Macdonald and Jane's
(Macdonald and Company (Publishers) Ltd.)
Poulton House, Shepherdess Walk
London N17 LW, England
ISBN 0354 01092 1

Printed in the United States of America

For
Mary Carol Frizzell Vann
Susie Virginia Frizzell
James Thomas Frizzell
Ann Shipley Frizzell
Phyllis Elizabeth Pratt Thompson
Nicholas Edwin Scott Thompson
in hopes that their generations will benefit from the
lessons learned and chronicled herein.
Donaldson D. Frizzell
W. Scott Thompson

Contents

Contents

Foreword and Acknowledgments

In 1973–74, a colloquium on "The Military Lessons of the Vietnamese War" was held at the Fletcher School of Law and Diplomacy, to which a number of distinguished students of and participants in the war presented papers and led discussions on the long conflict. The range of the subject inevitably broadened to the politico-military lessons, which was the subject of a conference held in Cambridge and Medford, Massachusetts, in early May 1974, also sponsored by the Fletcher School's International Security Studies Program.

In this volume we have interspersed the papers with discussions of them which took place at the colloquium and at the spring conference, to which many of the same persons came. We have sought to present, if not a comprehensive volume, an ordered and coherent one. The logic of our outline, not the order of presentation or discussion, or even the unity of individual papers prepared by our guests, determined how we used the various contributions. We hope this has resulted in greater analytical unity than is found in the usual compendium. The reader should remember that the text seldom follows the original conversations exactly. Moreover, the participants were given the opportunity to revise their comments, though we have sought to retain the lively spirit of eight of the interchanges.

Our proceedings greatly benefited from the candor of the guests, and these same people have attempted to preserve the spirit of their contributions in the editing of their comments. We made it clear from the beginning, however, both for ourselves and for them, that we were participating as individuals, and our manuscripts and discussions cannot be taken as representing the views of the Rand Corporation, with which Ambassador Komer is associated, of or the several components of the Armed Forces or the Department of Defense with which many of the participants were then and/or at the time of publication associated.

Our thanks go first of all to our generous supporters, the Scaife Foundation, and particularly to its director, Daniel McMichael, whose counsel and lively interest in our activities have been consistently helpful. The assistance of our colleagues, Uri Ra'anan, Geoffrey Kemp—who in fact suggested the topic in the first place—and Robert L. Pfaltzgraff, was invaluable throughout the year. Student members of the colloquium and conference took this controversial subject seriously, worked hard on it, asked difficult questions, and reassured us that there is a generation coming of age willing to learn from the experience of its forebears. Richard Kessler, Karl Lautenschlager, Brian Flora, and Frank Bray, all doctoral candidates at Fletcher, gave us both substantive and technical assistance, for which we are most grateful. Joyce Jones generously and freely gave invaluable and extensive editorial assistance at several points during the project. Mrs. Jill Andrews, secretary of the program, had the awesome job of transcribing tapes, and Mrs. Nancy Hughes that of preparing the manuscript for publication. The lively interest taken by the Fletcher administration was highly important; Assistant Dean Allan Cameron, himself an authority on many aspects of recent Vietnamese history, played an important role from the start; and our Dean, Ambassador Edmund Gullion, the first American consul in Saigon and a student of Vietnamese politics ever since, whose own tireless efforts on behalf of this institution, as well as his deep interest in the subject of the colloquium, entitle him to our deepest gratitude.

DONALDSON D. FRIZZELL
*Colonel, U.S. Air Force Research Associate
The Fletcher School of Law and
Diplomacy, 1973–74*

W. SCOTT THOMPSON
*Associate Professor of International
Politics, The Fletcher School of Law and
Diplomacy*

Preface

The Lessons of Vietnam

Donaldson D. Frizzell and W. Scott Thompson

> Awareness of our limitiations should make us chary of condemning those who make mistakes, but we condemn ourselves if we fail to recognize mistakes. —*B. H. Liddell Hart*

If the Vietnam War was a frustrating experience for the United States, it was specially frustrating for those directly involved. Feelings ranged from confusion and chagrin to bitterness and anger. There had been honor in battle and solid technical achievement; there had been heroes and cowards, military successes and faliures; but overshadowing it all is the terrible fact that the whole effort was for naught. That the war raged on for two and one half years after the 1973 truce and ended in total defeat for the South Vietnamese only compounded the frustration.

There has been a backlash against the military in the United States stemming from our national frustration over Vietnam, a backlash which some see as a threat to our national security. In 1974 the Chairman of the Joint Chiefs of Staff noted that what worried him most was "the will and determination of the public at large," the public's unwillingness "to uncouple from the disenchantment of Vietnam."

In 1975, as he departed the Pentagon, James R. Schlesinger was worried about the American mood: ". . . the vitality of the nation's military establishment, for its perceptions of itself, its precision of mission, flow from a sense of purpose deriving from that larger national unity and spirit. . . . Vision and confidence have diminished; a vacuum of the spirit has ap-

peared. It has become a grave question whether national unity, combined
with freedom, still elicits a response sufficient that, in Lincoln's phrase,
nations 'so conceived and so dedicated can long endure.' "

Yet there is adequate evidence to testify that the performance of the
American units in the field was superb. The tactical capability of the
American forces was good when we entered the war in 1964 and improved
throughout the war. The failure of our military forces to bring about an
"appropriate" solution at an "acceptable" price resulted more from bad
policy and bad strategy than from technical or tactical failures. It resulted
from trying to substitute military force for effective government. It resulted
because of misconceptions about our friends, our enemies, and ourselves.
Consequently, the American people now question the utility and legitimacy
of our military commitments everywhere. We hardly need a series of such
false conclusions about the proper role of the United States in world affairs
arising from superficial analyses of our Vietnamese involvement. But this
is precisely what has happened: the American people have lost faith in
themselves and in their leadership. "There has been a trend . . . perhaps
understandable . . . to self-flagellation and carping."[1] Thus we have a
dilemma in our study of this war. There can be no "papering over" of
mistakes, but equally there must not be an overreaction to our failures,
leading to the specious conclusion that the United States must no longer
involve itself internationally where its national interests are clearly involved.

Such is the legacy of the Vietnam War. On no other war in history was
so much written with the intention of affecting its outcome. Ambassador
Robert Komer commented during one of our sessions how surprising it is
that, with all the "ink that has been spilled on Vietnam, there is really so
very little of enduring value that has been written, particularly in the way of
professional critiques of our military performance."

It may be too early for the appearance of really distinguished studies of
the war. Yet one is left to wonder if they ever will appear. During the course
of our year of study, every individual who addressed our colloquium commented on the value of getting this subject into the open. But there re-

---

[1] Michael Getler, "The Schlesinger Strategy," *Washington Post*, February 13, 1974.

mained a gap between the willingness of individuals and that of institutions to take the subject seriously. Over and over one was told in the Pentagon that the war had become a "non-subject," and certainly the discussion of it would bring few promotions. "We have put the war behind us," was a boast that was frequently heard in the centers of national defense after the debacle of spring 1975. Thus have we been pleased to see General Westmoreland's memoirs, some sections of which were first discussed at our meetings, bring the question of the war back to the center of public concern and discussion.

What sort of lessons should we look for from the Vietnamese War? It is fashionable to quote Santayana's warning that those who cannot remember the past are condemned to repeat it. This would seem to be sound advice for the prudent analyst. Yet in the face of this advice, we find a reluctance in many quarters to engage in serious analysis of the consequences of Vietnam. Perhaps there are *no* lessons, as some contend. It is possible that the United States may never again be involved in a situation that even remotely approximates the conditions of Vietnam. If this is so, then it is at least questionable if military lessons learned in this war will be germane to any future wars. It is possible that our new-found knowledge may be irrelevant.

"Another Vietnam" appears unlikely in the near future simply because the United States, having already been burned in Southeast Asia, will be reluctant to venture into similar overseas commitments. The Nixon Doctrine codified this new U.S. foreign policy posture by limiting the character of U.S. assistance: "We shall furnish military and economic assistance when requested in accordance with our treaty commitments. But we shall look to the nation directly threatened to assume the primary responsibility of providing the manpower for its defense."[2]

Professor Samuel P. Huntington goes a step further; he feels that, with Vietnam, "if we remember the past we are condemned to misread it. . . . The right lesson, in short, may be the unlesson. . . . The Vietnam problem was a legacy of Western colonial rule. . . . Vietnam was, in addition, the one

---

[2] Richard M. Nixon, *U.S. Foreign Policy for the 1970's: Building for Peace,* a report to the Congress by the President of the United States (Washington, D.C.: U.S. Government Printing Office, February 25, 1971) , p. 14.

European colony [in which] . . . Communist groups established an early ascendancy in the nationalist movement. The struggle for independence led to a divided country, a sequence of events which seems unlikely to be duplicated again in the future. Finally, the American involvement in Vietnam came at the end of a cycle of active American concern with foreign affairs which seems unlikely to be repeated for some time in the future. Every historical event or confluence of events obviously is unique."[3]

The fact that the Vietnamese War was unique does not make its lessons irrelevant. All events are, in a superficial sense, unique; it is their components that we separate out for comparison with other similar components. If there will be "no more Vietnams," there certainly will be many more guerrilla wars, counterinsurgency efforts, urban battles, problems of "costing" weapon systems, problems of unity of command in some theater of action; indeed each of the questions that we separately considered in our deliberations could be part of a different conflict environment in which the United States could well find itself involved in the future.

If indeed the real battle in Vietnam was part of an exercise in the "balance of power," as Professor Ravenal has suggested, the events of 1975 would indicate that the United States may be losing even that fight. South Vietnam, Cambodia, and Laos all fell to the local Communist forces. This would seem to be part of a shift in what Moscow calls the "correlation of forces" between the United States and the U.S.S.R. Taken in conjunction with the fundamental change in the balance of strategic nuclear forces that began during the Vietnam years and continues unabated today, the U.S. loss in Southeast Asia begins to resemble a major watershed in American history. The loss may have marked the end of an era and signaled a basic change in the international role of the United States for the future. Sir Robert Thompson has characterized this as "strategic surrender," and his suggestion cannot be dismissed idly, in view of the challenges to Western positions that appeared seemingly everywhere in the aftermath of the Western debacle in Southeast Asia.

---

[3] Samuel P. Huntington, *Military Intervention, Political Involvement and the Unlessons of Vietnam,"* a monograph (Chicago: The Adlai Stevenson Institute of International Affairs) , pp. 1–2.

Glossary

AAA	Antiaircraft artillery
ARVN	Army of the Republic of Vietnam (South Vietnam)
CIA	Central Intelligence Agency
CIDG	Civil Irregular Defense Group. A U.S. Special Forces program for organizing local tribesmen into paramilitary units for village defense
CINCPAC	Commander in Chief, Pacific
COMUSMACV	Commander, United States Military Assistance Command, Vietnam
CORDS	Civil Operations and Revolutionary Development Support. A MACV organization established to coordinate the pacification effort
COSVN	Central Office for South Vietnam. The headquarters for North Vietnamese political and military operations in South Vietnam
DMZ	Demilitarized Zone. A narrow zone along the 17th Parallel dividing North and South Vietnam
GVN	Government of South Vietnam
HES	Hamlet Evaluation System. A computerized method of rating hamlets and villages to determine the progress of pacification

JCS	Joint Chiefs of Staff
Linebacker I	Code name for air operations and mining of harbors in North Vietnam in response to the 1972 Easter invasion
Linebacker II	Code name for the intensive eleven-day B-52 and fighter-bomber air raids against North Vietnam in December 1972
MAAG	Military Assistance Advisory Group
MACV	Military Assistance Command, Vietnam
MR	Military Regions (I, II, III, and IV). South Vietnam was divided into four regions for political and military control. Each region was commanded by a Vietnamese general officer. In the 1960s, they were referred to as Corps Tactical Zones.
NLF	National Liberation Front, political arm of the Viet Cong
NSC-68	A report to the National Security Council on U.S. objectives and programs for national security, April 14, 1950
NVA	North Vietnamese Army
NVN	North Vietnam
PGM	Precision-guided munitions
PRC	People's Republic of China
RF/PF	Regional Forces/Popular Forces, paramilitary territorial forces organized for local defense
Rolling Thunder	Code name for the air operations against North Vietnam from 1965 to 1968
RVNAF	Republic of Vietnam Armed Forces

SA-2	The principal Soviet-built surface-to-air-missile system used in the air defense of North Vietnam
SA-7	Soviet-built hand-held, infrared heat-seeking surface-to-air missile first used in South Vietnam in 1972
SAM	Surface-to-air missile
SEA	Southeast Asia
SVN	South Vietnam
Tet	The Vietnamese lunar new year, which occurs in late January or early February
Tet-68	The coordinated general offensive against South Vietnam that began on January 29, 1968
USAID or AID	United States Agency for International Development
VC	Viet Cong, i.e., Vietnamese Communist
VNAF	(South) Vietnamese Air Force
Vietnam	or Viet-Nam. We have chosen to use the more well known American version in this book, although etymologists generally agree that Viet-Nam is more correct.

Checklist of Contributors
and Participants

Allan Cameron

Colonel Ray M. Franklin

Colonel Donaldson D. Frizzell

Ambassador Francis Galbraith

Professor Allan Goodman

Dean Edmund Gullion

Major General George Keegan

Professor Geoffrey Kemp

Ambassador Robert Komer

Major General Edward Lansdale

Ambassador Henry Cabot Lodge

Colonel Donald Marshall

General S. L. A. Marshall

Jerrold Milsted

Hon. Paul H. Nitze

Professor Robert Pfaltzgraff

Professor Ithiel de Sola Pool

Professor Uri Ra'anan

Professor Earl Ravenal

Major Fred Raymond

Colonel Robert Rheault

Dr. Robert Sansom

Professor Arthur Smithies

Thomas C. Thayer

Sir Robert Thompson

Professor W. Scott Thompson

Professor Francis West

General William C. Westmoreland

Stephen Young

Barry Zorthian

Admiral Elmo R. Zumwalt

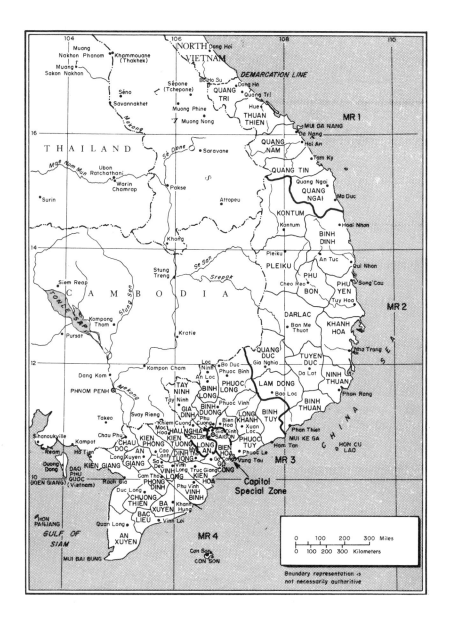

Map of Vietnam

The Lessons of

Vietnam

Chapter 1

The Strategic Background

The background to American military involvement in Vietnam has two intertwined roots. One is strategic and pertains to the developing American view concerning the distribution of forces in the world. The other evolved out of America's actual involvement in Vietnam, which followed its increased support of the French military effort after World War II. The strategic backdrop of the Vietnam War is briefly discussed in this chapter by Paul Nitze, and the proximate goals are presented by General William Westmoreland in the context of the contemporary views of national security. A brief discussion of the war in a world of interacting great powers concludes the chapter.

Paul Nitze was uniquely qualified at our conference to sketch a picture of how policy makers had thought about limited war, containment, and the special problems of Vietnam itself in the aftermath of World War II and on the eve of American involvement. As chairman of the Policy Planning Council at its high-water mark, he was the principal author in 1950 of probably the most influential national security document ever written, NSC-68, which bears heavily on the history of our involvement in Vietnam. During the 1960s he was successively Assistant Secretary of Defense for International Security Affairs, Secretary of the Navy, and Deputy Secretary of Defense.

1

The Evolution of National Security Policy and the Vietnam War

Paul H. Nitze

To talk about lessons from the Vietnam War, we must logically first deal with what the prior knowledge was and then determine what parts of that prior knowledge were confirmed or contradicted, and thus what new insights were learned by virtue of the Vietnamese experience.

The history of the evolution of basic national security policy must go back to the end of World War II. At that time, the Operations and Plans Division of the War Department was the essential focus for security strategy, having had a relatively small security strategy role during the war. Immediately after the war, the State-War-Navy coordinating committee was the body that dealt with what eventually became basic national security policy. At the end of 1947, the National Security Council was created. NSC-20, a paper on the subject of policy toward the U.S.S.R., was one of the early and important papers considered by the NSC. According to my recollection, it made the following points: In the first place, it said that the greatest potential threat to United States security was from the U.S.S.R. It then identified the nature of that threat; it put first political, economic, and psychological warfare and then the danger of the Soviet power potential. Secondly, that the risk of war was sufficiently great that it was time to make adequate preparation. Thirdly, that the domination of the Eurasian land mass by the U.S.S.R. was politically and strategically unacceptable, and that the ability of the United States to cope with the international situation could be weakened by espionage, subversion, and sabotage within the United States, by economic instability in the United States, by internal political and social disunity, by excessive and wasteful use of resources in time of peace, by a lessening of American prestige and influence, or a shrinking of the country's will to deal with its world responsibility, and lastly, by a false sense of security brought on by a deceptive change in Soviet tactics. Then it dealt with the fact that progress had been made since the end of the war in dealing with these factors but that much more had to be done. It talked about what our objectives should be and what we ought to do to put ourselves in a better position to meet those objectives. I believe that George Kennan had a large influence on that paper. The point to be made here is that there is a difference between merely laying out a policy and laying out a program adequate to implement that policy. At that time some people had the view that what we would need in the way of military capabilities were two very qualified Marine divisions, and that they would be enough to support a policy of what amounted to containment.

The next paper in this series was NSC-68;[1] that did better in getting from general objectives to the details of what the problem was and how to get from where you were to where you wanted to be. It analyzed in depth, among other things, the nature of the conflict of ideas and values between the U.S.S.R. and the United States. It dealt in detail with Soviet capabilities—political, economic, and military. It dealt with our weaknesses and strengths; it dealt with various atomic questions; it dealt with the question of negotiations, of the value and risks of negotiations in a conflict of this nature. It finally dealt with an assessment of whether or not then existing programs were adequate to meet the growing nature of the threat, and concluded that they were not. It did not lay out a program in detail as to what kind of military capabilities were needed, for, at that time, Mr. Truman was committed to a $13-billion defense budget. We had to obtain his agreement to the broad analysis before he could be expected to authorize the appropriate people to lay out a specific plan, including the numbers necessary to support the policy.

In early 1950, while we were working on NSC-68, Alexander Sachs of Lehman Brothers came to see me. He was the man who had, among other things, introduced Albert Einstein to President Roosevelt. Sachs had a

---

[1] This most famous of postwar strategic documents—largely authored by Nitze—was recently declassified. See "NSC-68 and Report to the National Security Council by the Executive Secretary," *National War College Review*, Vol. XXVII, #6, Sequence #225, June 1975, pp. 51-108.

series of charts with him and a series of papers supporting each of them. One set dealt with the Soviet doctrine of the "correlation of forces." It argued that the Soviets felt themselves duty-bound to nail down gains at any time that they felt that the correlation of forces had moved substantially in their favor. The second paper dealt with the impact on Soviet strategic thinking of the defeat of the Chinese Nationalists on the mainland and the Soviet testing of a nuclear device. This paper concluded with the judgment that these two developments would be assessed by the Soviets as a basic change in the correlation of forces calling for some initiative on their side. The third paper dealt with a map of the world showing the various crisis situations and the various places where the Soviets might move. He ended that paper with the judgment that the most likely place was an attack by the North Koreans into South Korea. Such an attack would be the least risky way for the Soviets to test the validity of their assessment. The fourth paper was a time analysis of past periods when there had been a change in the correlation of forces. How long would it take the Russians to react? His analysis led him to predict an attack by the North Koreans into South Korea by June or July of that year.

I took this analysis by Alexander Sachs seriously. But the question was: What could you, in fact, do then, in early 1950, when the Senate had just voted that Korean aid would be limited to $20 million? What we did was to supply them with some patrol boats—the main thing that the South Koreans wanted—but that was about the limit of what it was practicable to do. When the North Korean attack took place, it obviously confirmed not only Alexander Sachs's analysis, but also tended to confirm the basic analysis contained in NSC-68.

That paper was asked for by the President in January 1950. We completed it in April, so there were really only three months of work on it. I can remember the last weekend when we had finally finished drafting NSC-68. General Marshall had earlier talked to me about his judgment that the support which the American public and the Congress were then evincing for international involvement by the United States was not to be relied on in the long run. You could not count on the Congress continuing to authorize large Army and other budgetary expenditures in support of national policy. He had said it was necessary that the policies and programs that we were working on should be designed to be self-liquidating so that we could work out of them over a period of time, like the Marshall Plan. General Marshall recalled the period in the 1930s when the Army budget was, I think, $167 million, and when he had to mow the post lawn himself. It was then hard to get money for anything. General Marshall had predicted that such a period would recur. The question we debated that last weekend concerned the fact that NSC-68 envisaged a very long-range major effort on the part of the United States. Could a democracy like the United States maintain such an effort indefinitely? We argued this point for thirty-six hours and finally we came to the conclusion that there was no alternative but to try. If you gave up in advance because you were not sure that the United States would stay the course, you were lost before you started.

Another lesson that came out of the Korean War was that the most difficult situations were those where countries had been left divided by World War II—Germany primarily, but also Korea and, of course, Vietnam. During the Eisenhower administration, work on papers in the NSC-68 series continued; that was one of the main policy activities of the Eisenhower administration. Then the Kennedy administration; Mr. Kennedy was persuaded that such analyses of basic national security policy tended to limit the President's options and should be discontinued. The problem today is that since the beginning of the Kennedy administration, nobody in the United States has undertaken that kind of basic national security analysis. As a result, the evolution of policy during the Kennedy and Johnson administrations was more an ad hoc evolution in which we learned certain lessons from specific episodes, but these were not put together into a coherent structure.

The first subsequent real lesson, as I recall, came from the Berlin crisis. The essence of the Berlin problem was that it was hopeless from a military standpoint—Berlin was isolated; the Russians had much more military capability in the vicinity of West Berlin than we could possibly bring to bear there. But the essential point was that the value to the West of the defense of Berlin was far greater than the value to the Soviet Union of taking Berlin. Therefore, we could take far greater risks with respect to Berlin than the Soviets could be expected to take. It was on the basis of that evaluation that it was decided to take a firm line on Berlin.

The Berlin point bears upon the Vietnam War because it deals with the question of relative will versus relative material capabilities in a given situation. The Vietnamese policy debates, as I remember them, essentially revolved around this set of issues. The point that argued in favor of forcible intervention and support of Vietnam was that we could not stand by while a divided country was unified by force. The Berlin problem had been handled, the Korean problem had been handled, and the third one in the series was Vietnam. It seemed important not to let Vietnam collapse and unravel.

Another important point was that Mr. Kennedy had taken a great interest in insurgency and counterinsurgency, a field which had been more or less ignored up to that time. Because of that interest, there was a tendency to try to see whether something could be done as a result of the concentration upon this problem which had taken place. The countervailing argument was the question of relative will; was not the will of North Vietnam greater than that of South Vietnam and our will to support that country?

Looking at the Vietnamese problem early in 1965, I remember going to Vietnam and being absolutely horrified by the weakness of the South Vietnamese and of our positions there. The Marines had just gone into Da Nang. The position seemed to me to be militarily untenable; the Chu Lai airfield enterprise looked extremely hazardous. It seemed to me it would be the most enormous job to turn the Vietnamese situation around. The decision, however, was made to attempt it. I thought that, militarily, we did much better than I had estimated we were going to be able to do when I looked at the situation in 1964 and 1965. What is more, I think it could have worked out just the way Sir Robert Thompson has said it might have, had there not been such a serious erosion of will at home, an erosion which, in turn, strengthened the will and the obduracy of the North Vietnamese, which brings us to the next question.

We then had to ask how to maintain home support. This involved a number of different things. One of them was the economic problem. Both Robert McNamara and I thought, at the time, that once the first 200,000 men were sent in, we ought to have an increase in taxes so that we could balance the expenditures and the inflationary pressures that otherwise would result. We also thought that there should be a greater commitment of support by the Congress, and that the way you could get that would be to put a bill into the Congress asking for the power to call up reserves. President Johnson decided not to take either of these actions.

The third element was the question of the Draft Act. I remember the views of General Marshall when the Draft Bill was worked out in 1940—I had worked with him on that. He was convinced that in a democracy the draft of soldiers had to be—and be seen to be—wholly equitable. If it were not equitable, you would lose the support of the American people. The way the Draft Bill worked during the Vietnam War was to exempt students as long as they continued their studies. This was clearly inequitable and encouraged the brightest boys to avoid duty in Vietnam. It gave them the feeling that they were, in some way or other, "yellow" because they knew that they were avoiding the draft. This turned them away to things that would restore their sense of manhood; some turned violently to the radical side. President Johnson, however, was adamant against amending the draft procedures so that the selection of those who were to be drafted would be made equitably at the age of eighteen. Those three things seemed to me to be critical elements in the erosion of public support and will.

After the assassination of Ngo Dinh Diem in 1963, the political situation in South Vietnam deteriorated as control of the government passed through a succession of military regimes. By 1965, conditions were indeed dismal and into the breach at that point stepped General William C. Westmoreland. He had a distinguished military record in both World War II and the

Korean War, had been a success as superintendent of West Point, and had considerable staff experience at the Pentagon. President Johnson designated him Commander of United States Forces, Military Assistance Command, Vietnam (COMUSMACV). For reasons not entirely under his control, he came to symbolize the American role in the war, though of course his authority over American action was partial and circumscribed. In his presentation to our colloquium on December 12, 1973, part of which appears in this chapter, he was modest about success, candid about mistakes.

American Goals in Vietnam

General William C. Westmoreland

It was in a political as well as a strategic context that our nation's leaders—Democrat and Republican—decided in the early 1960s to draw the line in Southeast Asia and later more specifically to make a stand in South Vietnam. The fear of Communist expansion in a monolithic sense, "Wars of National Liberation," acceptance of the domino theory, and the failure of collective security were very real among the decision makers. President Kennedy's Inaugural Address had a profound effect on officers of the military and foreign services. The young President said:

> Let every nation know, whether it wishes us well or ill, that we shall pay any price, bear any burden, meet any hardship, support any friend, oppose any foe, in order to assure the survival and the success of liberty. This much we pledge—and more.

Popular reading at that time in the military circles included Henry Kissinger's book *Nuclear Weapons and Foreign Policy* and later General Maxwell D. Taylor's *Uncertain Trumpet*. These books developed a thesis that an essential option to nuclear war was a ready capability to fight small wars, and the judicious commitment of non-nuclear military forces could deter or defeat small wars of aggression.

Such idealistic and theoretical concepts were on the minds of policy makers when I arrived in Vietnam in late January 1964. But political chaos in Saigon was disturbing. President Diem's regime had been overthrown by a *coup d'état,* which resulted in considerable bloodshed, including the murder of Diem and his brother Nhu. A junta headed by General "Big" Minh was attempting, quite unsuccessfully, to run the country. Although things were relatively quiet in the countryside, there was strong evidence that the Viet Cong, controlled and supported by the regime in Hanoi, were taking advantage of the weak government. A few days after I arrived, the I Corps commander, Lieutenant General Nguyen Khanh, staged a successful, bloodless *coup d'état* which established him as head of the new ruling junta.

In the wake of this political upheaval, a frustrated Secretary McNamara came to Vietnam and physically embraced General Khanh to demonstrate public support for the new regime. Although it had been the policy of the Administration to reduce our advisory effort in Vietnam—1,000 men were in the process of being removed—this policy abruptly changed to one involving expansion of our advisory effort.

On March 16, 1964, Secretary McNamara sent a memorandum to the President which recommended U.S. objectives in South Vietnam as follows:

> We seek an independent non-Communist South Vietnam. We do not require that it serve as a Western base or as a member of a Western Alliance. South Vietnam must be free, however, to accept outside assistance as required to maintain security. This assistance should be able to take the form of economic and social measures but also the police and military help [necessary] to root out and control insurgent elements.

On the next day, March 17, 1964, an order signed by McGeorge Bundy, Assistant to President Johnson, stated: "The report of Secretary McNamara dated March 16, 1964, was considered and approved by the President in a meeting of the National Security Council on March 17. All agencies are directed to proceed energetically with execution of the recommendation of the report."

This policy determination set the stage for decisions that followed, involving an increased number of advisers and the eventual commitment of U.S. troops.

Following several unsuccessful coups, the Khanh-led junta was replaced by one led by General Nguyen Van Thieu and Air Marshal Nguyen Cao Ky. This bloodless ousting of General Khanh brought about the first semblance of political stability since the demise of Diem. Let me say parenthetically that I believe that, during the almost three years of intense political turmoil, we could have withdrawn from Vietnam gracefully. After that, it was inconceivable to me that we could have done so until our strategy had played its hand.

In February 1966, President Johnson requested a summit conference with the leadership of South Vietnam in Honolulu to assess the situation and the personalities involved in the Vietnam War and to formulate future policy. Present were Secretary McNamara; Secretary Dean Rusk; Ambassador Henry Cabot Lodge; the Chairman of the JCS, General Earle Wheeler; the Commander in Chief, Pacific Command, Admiral U.S. Grant Sharp; John McNaughton and William Bundy (staff assistants to McNamara and Rusk, respectively); and myself. On the Vietnamese side were Chairman Thieu, Prime Minister Ky, Minister of Defense Nguyen Van Vy, and the Chief of the Joint General Staff, General Cao Van Vien, and hosts of other officials.

Associated with the Honolulu summit meeting, a U.S. conference was convened at which Secretaries McNamara and Rusk made decisions on programs and goals. Six goals were decided upon and assigned to the U.S. mission in Vietnam as guidance for 1966. They were:

1. Attrit [decrease], by year's end, Viet Cong and North Vietnamese forces at a rate as high as their capability to put men into the field.

2. Increase the percentage of Viet Cong and North Vietnamese base areas denied the Viet Cong from 10–20 percent to 40–50 percent.

3. Increase the critical [important] roads and railroads open for use from 30 to 50 percent.

4. Increase the population in secure areas from 50 percent to 60 percent.

5. Pacify the four selected high-priority areas, increasing the pacified population in those areas by 235,000.

6. Insure the defense of all military bases, political and population centers, and food-producing areas now under government control.

Pursuit of these goals dictated the subsequent strategy and tactics of the war. Their accomplishment required aggressive operations to increase the number of people and the area under Government control, to disrupt the enemy's base areas, and to inflict maximum casualties on the enemy.

In September 1966, Admiral Sharp formalized guidance for his several subordinate commanders, specifying: "three interdependent undertakings: (1) in the North—take war to enemy by unremitting but selective application of air/naval power; (2) in the South—seek out and destroy Communist forces and infrastructure by expanded offensive military operations; (3) nation building—extend and secure areas of South Vietnam by military operations and assist the Government of South Vietnam in building an independent society (pacification)." Admiral Sharp's stated objectives were to make it as difficult and as costly as possible for North Vietnam to continue effective support of the Viet Cong and to cause North Vietnam to cease its direction and support of the Viet Cong insurgency; defeat decisively the Viet Cong and the North Vietnamese armed forces in South Vietnam and force their withdrawal; and extend direction, domination, and control by the Government of South Vietnam over all of South Vietnam.

The Strategic Framework and the Great Powers

The struggle in Vietnam was essentially an outgrowth of the U.S. policy of containment of Communism around the world. As Secretary McNamara said, "We seek an independent non-Communist South Vietnam." In the same statement he went on to say: "Unless we can achieve this objective in South Vietnam, almost all of Southeast Asia will probably fall under Communist dominance. . . . the South Vietnam conflict is regarded as a test case of U.S. capacity to help a nation meet a Communist 'war of liberation.' "[2]

Wars of national liberation, and support for them, had by this time become a point of competition between the two Communist powers, the U.S.S.R. and the Chinese People's Republic. Both were currying Hanoi's affection, and American strategy in Vietnam certainly was affected by this. But what were the attitudes and intentions of the U.S.S.R. and Red China with respect to U.S. actions? The following interchange suggests that important lessons lie here for consideration in the future.

Uri Ra'anan:
Many constraints placed upon American acts at various periods emanated from misperceptions of what either China or the Soviet Union might do. These misperceptions happened despite the fact that the signals from Peking as early as the spring of 1965, esoteric at first, and somewhat less esoteric later on, were perfectly clear—namely, that the people who were winning the struggle for power in Peking were people who were not prepared to make major sacrifices for the North Vietnamese, with the exception of some extreme contingencies which later on were outlined fairly clearly, and, I think, understood fairly clearly.

In the case of Moscow, there were many logistical difficulties for Soviet intervention, but some of us never ceased to be astounded by some of our colleagues who, at the time of the mining of Haiphong Harbor, said, "Yes, the Soviets are going to do A, B, C, D, and E," none of which was logistically likely, or even really feasible under the circumstances. Now, was there genuinely a misperception of Soviet and Chinese capabilities and intentions? Or was this used as an alibi by people who did not want to do certain things, and therefore imposed artificial constraints upon themselves?

Sir Robert Thompson:
One must go back to the Lin Piao document of 1965, which preaches self-reliance. The Chinese had no intention whatsoever of intervening in the

---

[2] Neil Sheehan, Hedrick Smith, E. W. Kenworthy, and Fox Butterfield, *The Pentagon Papers* (New York: Bantam Books, 1971), p. 278.

war to help North Vietnam win the South. Now that does not mean that the Chinese might not have intervened if there was any threat to the regime, or to the territorial integrity of North Vietnam. In other words, the Korean example. I have maintained all along that China was not going to interfere at any price, provided that the war stayed in the South. The interesting question was whether China wanted North Vietnam to win, giving North Vietnam hegemony over the whole of Indochina. In such circumstances, North Vietnam would be beholden to Moscow, both for weaponry and for economic support, because China could not give adequate economic support to the North Vietnamese. Therefore, China was being contained on its southern flank. One interesting point which reflects this is that under no circumstances did North Vietnamese troops ever go near Phong Saly, the road being built by the Chinese through Laos.

Now we come to the question of the Russians. American ambassadors to Russia have tended to be overcautious in their fears of what Russia might do in particular circumstances. If one looks back at the various things that have happened, such as fleeing Egypt in 1956 or failing to do well in the Congo in 1960, they have not been militarily aggressive when faced with possible confrontation. I have always maintained that they would not have put missiles in Cuba if Nixon had been President. I think this fear of Russian action all stems from the Cold War. The one thing Russia learned from the Cold War was that confrontation did not pay off. All that confrontation does is unite the West and make the United States very popular when Russia wants to achieve exactly the opposite results—namely, a disunited West and an unpopular United States. Therefore, *don't have confrontations.* I think that is the way the game has been played since the Cold War. Again, I would say that Russia would be, I think, quite tough, in the same way that the Chinese would, in not losing a Communist state. So many things have proved that, such as North Korea; and, if Khrushchev achieved nothing else, he at least safeguarded the revolution in Cuba with the missile crisis. We have also had Hungary and Czechoslovakia to prove it. Although they will not lose a Communist state in confrontation, they are not going to create a Communist state that way and at the risk of head-on confrontation with the United States. This is not the way they are now playing the game. This is what détente is about.

Barry Zorthian:

Without commenting on whether misperceptions concerning Chinese and Russian involvement should be regarded as miscalculation (I now have the benefit of hindsight that it was), I would note that the possibility of Chinese involvement was a very real one and a very real fact in determining policy. We not only had the Korean experience, and MacArthur and the Yalu still relatively fresh in our memories, but we had Chinese in the North—technicians, workers, whatever they were. If you will remember, in the summer of 1964, when General Khanh talked about a march to the North, we took the extraordinary step of publicly chastising our allies and saying that such was not our policy. There was a very deliberate effort to get a message through to Peking: "We have no intention of jeopardizing the territorial integrity of North Vietnam, and we are going to restrain the South Vietnamese from doing so, if they are foolish enough." So the question of Chinese involvement in the framework, at that time, was one of very real concern.

Uri Ra'anan:

We must remember the national objectives of South and North Vietnam, or, in the case of the South, national objectives imposed upon them by us. In the Korean case, the banner of national unification, carried by the North, was then picked up by the South as well, and this created a symmetry of aims between the two sides, which had a direct effect on strategy, and I would hope that it had an effect on the outcome of the war. There was also a degree of symmetry in the final outcome which was a return to the *status quo ante.*

Now, in the case of Vietnam, it was precisely that symmetry which was lacking. The banner of national unification had been permitted to remain the exclusive property of the North. The South had been precluded by our strategy from raising this banner even as a propaganda device, and certainly as an active motivating force in the overall strategy, for reasons concerning the perception and, to some extent, the misperception, of what were likely to be Soviet and Chinese responses if one went North, or if one at least raised the banner of going North.

We thus defined our objectives not in terms of defeat for the North Vietnamese, but in the more restrained terms of preventing the fall of the South Vietnamese to hostile forces, out of fear of antagonizing the Chinese and Russians. Ironically, Sir Robert Thompson noted his belief that American bombs could have killed a hundred—or even five thousand—Chinese working in Vietnam, without causing them to "blink an eye."

The formulation of our policy objective in these essentially negative terms led to an unimaginative strategy of attrition and cautious escalation which yielded unsatisfactory results in the long term.

Chapter 2

Patterns of the French and American Experience in Vietnam

Thomas C. Thayer

How does one use the evidence of history in warfare? For that matter, how do policy makers use the evidence accumulated on the battlefield of the war they are directing, to improve their strategy, to conserve matériel, to avoid deadly traps? Thomas C. Thayer, who worked throughout much of the war in the Office of the Assistant Secretary of Defense, Systems Analysis, as it was then called, devoted his time to providing one set of answers to these questions. The following paper, given in November 1973, shows how difficult it was to draw lessons from the one clear precedent for the American effort in Vietnam, that of the French in the same country two decades earlier.

Logic would suggest that there ought to be many similarities between the French and American combat experience in Vietnam. The French and the Americans, after all, fought the same foe in the same territory, although twenty years elapsed between the two wars.

Some of the similarities are obvious. Both countries committed troops to full-scale combat in Vietnam for approximately eight years. Both had trouble at home, as early support for the war ebbed and began to affect the efforts in Vietnam. Both had to start withdrawing troops from Vietnam before accomplishing their objectives, and long before all of their forces finally were taken out of combat. Neither began large-scale efforts to build up the indigenous forces until domestic pressures placed a ceiling on the availability of French and American troops.[1] Interviews with French officers also suggest that both forces were unable to send units into combat at anywhere near their full personnel strength. Both had terrible problems in finding an elusive foe and in inflicting a long-lasting defeat when they did find him. Both had identical problems with the Communists, who even turned their dud artillery shells into deadly mines.

The list of similarities is undoubtedly long, but it should not obscure the existence of many differences. For example, the scale of the American effort was probably at least ten times larger than the French effort. The Americans committed ten times as many troops; the French had no more than ten helicopters, while the Americans had thousands. The scale of the U.S. air effort was enormous in comparison.

There are many differences, and they are significant, but the question addressed here is whether the similarities were important enough to provide lessons that would have helped the Americans adapt to the new kind of war they faced in Vietnam. The approach is quantitative, because this allows for the most precise statements of the French and American experience and ought to show clearly whether the French experience could have helped the Americans.

Quantitative Analysis in a War Without Fronts

In guerrilla warfare there is no such thing as a decisive battle. —*Mao Tse-tung*

The French aptly called their war in Vietnam a "war without fronts." In such a war, and particularly in ones as fragmented and atomized as the wars in Vietnam were—with, in the U.S. case, few large battles but thousands of small-unit actions and 10,000 village, 260 district, and 44 province

---

[1] By an act of the French Parliament in 1950, the French Army could not send draftees to fight in an undeclared war, which limited the French effort to the military professionals. In the American case, the Tet offensive of 1968 led to a ceiling on the number of U.S. forces that could be sent.

wars to monitor—quantitative analysis is essential[2] to a full understanding of what was going on. In no other way is it possible to keep track of the slowly changing patterns and movements that were so characteristic of the Vietnam wars, and to relate them to the achievement of national objectives.

The American quantification of the war is often criticized as excessive and largely misleading—the body count is a favorite example. Quantification may have been overdone, but analysis of key issues certainly was not. Stress on such factors as the body count created incentive systems all of its own. But there is a difference between quantification, according to old-style rules of thumb, and analysis. The problem was that quantification became a huge effort, but analysis remained a trivial one. This is unfortunate, perhaps even tragic, because the limited analytic efforts that were undertaken yielded much useful insight into the war and into the prospects for achieving U.S. objectives, given the way the war was being fought. Unfortunately, it all had little impact.

Much of the analysis that follows is quantitative, so it is appropriate to address the problem of whether statistics from the Vietnam wars are good enough to analyze. Sir Josiah Stamp (1880–1941) has a few pertinent words:

> The government are very keen on amassing statistics. They collect them, raise them to the nth power, take the cube root and prepare wonderful diagrams. But you must never forget that every one of these figures comes in the first instance from the village watchman, who just puts down what he damn pleases.

Perhaps, but the village watchman often pleases to tell the truth, and in any case, he probably reports about the same way most of the time. So one looks for a constant bias in reporting. The individual numbers may not be completely accurate, but the trends and changes in relationships among them may tell us quite a bit about what is going on in the village and how that village compares with other villages.

---

[2] But, by itself, not sufficient. Constant reading, visits to the scene, and communication with those on the scene or recently on the scene are also critical. Effective analysis requires both—the numbers alone can mislead the analyst just as often as relying solely on narrative accounts.

This is the way to deal with the Vietnam data, which have been subject to strong criticism and have the problem of any data reported by officials whose main job is to operate and manage, not to report. The writer has concluded, after years of working with them, that much of the data from Vietnam during the U.S. involvement are good enough for systematic analysis, although their validity varies widely. For this paper the few French statistics available are simply assumed to be no worse.

Why were the wars in Vietnam so difficult to grasp? The answer lies in the character of the wars. They had no front lines, and, at first, commanders and analysts simply were unable to deal with this situation. The United States was prepared to cope with a conventional war, but not a war without fronts. Historical accounts suggest that the French had the same problem.

In a conventional war, such as in Europe or Korea, two items are needed to monitor progress: (1) What is the state of the enemy forces and of friendly forces? (2) Where is the front, and which way has it been moving? If friendly forces are stronger than enemy forces and are pushing the enemy back, then friendly forces are winning, because the objective in a conventional war is to destroy the enemy's capability to fight.

But the Vietnam wars were highly atomized struggles to influence the population in hundreds of different districts, and there were no fronts as we know them. In Vietnam only one of the two sets of data needed to keep track of a war was present, namely, order-of-battle data on enemy and friendly forces. Commanders and analysts needed a substitute for the front line if they were to understand the war and how it was going.

In the American experience, the substitute turned out to be systematic, quantitative analysis of the hundreds, even thousands of events occurring in many parts of Vietnam every day. Any given action was seldom important in itself, and at first glance no patterns were seen. Analysis, however, revealed persistent patterns and cycles. From these, analysts were able to monitor the war with surprising precision by analyzing:

Changes in the situation of the rural population

Levels of activity and forces

Trends of activity and forces over time

Locations where activity and forces were concentrated

Changes in the types and mix of activities and forces

This analysis allowed them to judge the importance of a given event or set of events to the overall progress of the war. For example, the VC/NVA offensive in the spring of 1970 was greeted in Washington as an escalation of the war by those unfamiliar with the basic trends which had been observed for at least two years. By the end of the first week, analysts were able to tell top officials that the 1970 offensive did not signify a VC/NVA escalation of the war because it was not as intense as the comparable offensive in 1969, which in turn had been less intense than the Tet offensive in 1968. The pattern of statistics showed that at that time the war was continuing to wind down even though an offensive had just been launched.

In the U.S. case, there was no shortage of data from Vietnam to analyze. Everyone was groping for understanding. Data were developed for the management of complex programs and from frustration at our continuing inability (until after Tet-68) to develop realistic assessments of the situation. Each new VC/NVA offensive (and they came on a regular cycle) knocked previous assessments into a cocked hat and credibility fell. This stimulated calls for new reporting and more data flowed in.

The extent that the French experience followed this pattern is not known to the writer, but it is apparent that the French reported plenty of statistics. The Government of Vietnam had an extensive reporting system when he arrived there in 1962, the Government of Cambodia was found to have a similar reporting system when analysts asked about it in 1971, and since both governments were heavily influenced by the French, it seems logical to assume that the French had similar reports when they fought in Indochina. However, detailed statistics from the French Archives will not be available for many years.

Limitations of space preclude a full analysis of all aspects (population, forces, operations) of the two Vietnam wars. Instead, three aspects of the fighting are analyzed:

Intensity of the conflict. The percentage of the friendly force killed in combat each year is the measurement used here. The percentage calculation neutralizes the effect of the different-sized forces and gives a better comparison of combat intensity for the friendly troops involved in each period.

The annual cycle of combat. The measurement used for the American experience is friendly combat deaths for each month of the year. Are there consistently more friendly combat deaths in some months than in others? Does the pattern stay the same year after year? For the French, comparable statistics are not available, so narrative material has been researched to provide less precise, but comparable findings.

Locations of major fighting. Friendly combat deaths by province is the measurement used for the American experience. Comparable French statistics are not available, so the French section draws from the narrative accounts, old maps, and discussions with French officers.

THE FRENCH EXPERIENCE

How, with all that military machine still intact, did we ever end up as we have?—*Colonel Nemo* (1956) [3]

Matériel inferiority in front of the enemy is not serious. What is more important is the mobilization of the people. The people must be a great ocean in which the enemy will drown itself. —*Mao Tse-tung*

Intensity of the Conflict. American military men have criticized the French strategy in Indochina as "lacking in aggressiveness, defensive, and of doubtful value."[4] A four-star general once said: "The French haven't won a war since Napoleon. What can we learn from them?" These statements raise the question of how hard the French really fought in Vietnam. The objective of this section, then, is to provide a rough estimate of the intensity of combat for the average French and allied soldier involved in the French Indochina war, and to compare it with the American experience in Korea and later in Vietnam.

From 1951 on there were two armies in Indochina fighting the Viet Minh. One was the French Expeditionary Corps. The other was the

[3] Quoted in "La Guerre dans le milieu social," *Revue de Défense Nationale,* XXII (1956), pp. 610–23.

[4] *The Pentagon Papers: The Senator Gravel Edition* (Boston: Beacon Press, 1971), I, 188.

Armed Forces of the Associated States, which included Vietnam, Laos, and Cambodia. The Expeditionary Corps included units made up of French, Algerian, Foreign Legion, Moroccan, and Senegalese troops. The French units, except for the airborne, included many Vietnamese, Laotians, and Cambodians who had been locally recruited. The French also had operational control of several "sect forces," including the Cao Dai, the Binh Xuyen, the Hoa Hao, and the Christian Militias.[5]

Detailed statistics are not available for all of these forces, so the calculations of combat intensity center on the total allied forces and their two basic components, the French Expeditionary Corps and the Armed Forces of the Associated States.

Various data suggest that the average number of full-time French and allied forces engaged in the eight-year war was about 240,000. Total combat deaths for the force were about 95,000.[6] Taken together, these figures yield an average combat death rate of about 5 percent of the force each year, or a 1-in-20 chance of getting killed. By comparison, the annual combat death rate of U.S. forces during the Korean War was also 5 percent. In the French Expeditionary Corps, the annual combat death rate was higher, averaging 6.7 percent. This raised the odds of dying in combat to about 1 in 15.

The odds were lower in the Armed Forces of the Associated States, which were organized slowly, late in the war. In this case, the combat death rate averaged about 3.6 percent per year, and the chances of dying in combat were about 1 in 28 each year. (This rate should not be taken as the combat death rate for all Indochinese troops serving with the friendly forces, because about 45 percent of the combat deaths of the French Expeditionary Corps were indigenous troops recruited in Indochina.)

The French troops took heavy casualties. Approximately 21,000 soldiers from metropolitan France were killed. The Corps probably averaged no more than 50,000–55,000 for the eight-year war. This level of casualties for metropolitan France by itself would translate into approximately 100,000 United States combat deaths in Vietnam, almost twice as many

[5] Bernard Fall, *Viet-Nam Witness, 1953–1966* (New York: Praeger, 1966) , p. 309.

[6] Bernard Fall, *Street Without Joy: Insurgency in Indochina, 1946–1963* (4th ed.; Harrisburg, Pa.: Stackpole Books, 1964) , p. 385.

as actually occurred. Thus, the casualty statistics suggest that the French fought an intense war from 1946 through 1954.

The Annual Cycle of Combat. The statistics for allied combat deaths each month are not available for the French war, so this analysis is based on historical narratives. An annual cycle of combat appears in the accounts, but cannot be identified with much precision. The cycle seems to be tied primarily to the weather, which, on average, consists of a dry season from October through April and a wet season from May through September, although some portions of Vietnam vary from this average.

In view of the difficulties of conducting major military operations during the rainy season, the dry season offered the best opportunity to go on the offensive, and both French and Viet Minh forces often conducted offensives during this part of the year. One writer speaks of it as the campaigning season: "During the 'campaigning' season of 1949–50 the French Military Command let things slide."[7] "When the rains ended in late September 1951, the compaigning season opened cautiously."[8]

Without being too precise, it is probably safe to assume that combat usually peaked from November through May and slacked off somewhat during June through October. But the evidence does not allow a firm conclusion for the French forces, because "during the rainy season, Gen. Navarre carried out a number of operations designed to improve the French position,"[9] and "no large-scale [French] operations were mounted when the rains did cease in October."[10] Finally, "by October 1952, the end of the rainy season, General Salan was not able to muster any appreciable extra numbers of French troops for offensive operations."[11] Thus the French sometimes tried to go on the offensive during the *rainy* season, and then not during the *dry* season.

[7] Edgar O'Ballance, *The Indochina War, 1945–1954* (London: Faber & Faber, 1964), p. 110.

[8] *Ibid.,* p. 157.

[9] *Ibid.,* p. 200.

[10] *Ibid.,* p. 87.

[11] *Ibid.,* p. 175.

Table 1. *Most Communist Offensives Occurred
During the Dry Season
(September 1952–July 1954)*

		Number of Offensives Underway
Dry Season	October (1952–53)	1
	November (1952–53)	2
	December (1952–53)	3
	January (1953–54)	2
	February (1953–54)	3
	March (1953–54)	4
	April (1953–54) Subtotal: 19	4
Rainy Season	May (1953–54)	3
	June (1953–54)	1
	July (1953–54)	1
	August (1953)	0
	September (1952–53) Subtotal: 7	2
	Total: 26	

The Viet Minh "offensives" from September 1952 through July 1954 seem to fit the dry-season–rainy-season cycle better. Table 1[12] collapses the two years into one twelve-month cycle and shows how many offensives were underway during a given pair of months. The table indicates that the Viet Minh offensive activity peaked during the dry season; 19 of the 26 "offensive months" were dry-season months. This suggests that the Viet Minh cycle of activity may have been well developed by the end of the war, even if the French cycle was not. As a final point of interest, the battle at Dien Bien Phu took place from March 13 to May 7, 1954, during the final weeks of the dry season.

Where Did Most of the Fighting Occur? This section is drawn from narrative accounts in the open literature and from discussions with French officers in Paris. All agree that the most intense fighting took place in North Vietnam and that significant fighting took place in what is now

[12] Calculated from data found in Bernard Fall, *The Two Vietnams: A Political and Military Analysis* (New York: Praeger, 1966) , p. 123.

Military Region I (MR I) and northern MR II[13] in South Vietnam. The most southern part of Vietnam saw less action, but there were definite pockets of Viet Minh strength.

Perhaps the best portrayal of the situation, in the absence of statistics, is shown in the maps on the next two pages. The first map attempts to portray the territory held by the Viet Minh after Dien Bien Phu fell in 1954. Two points are of interest:

1. Except for the cities of Hué, Tourane (now Da Nang), and Quang Tri, the entire area of what became MR I, plus Kontum and Binh Dinh provinces, was under Viet Minh control, although they were not able to gain title to it at the Geneva Conference.

2. Further south, the Viet Minh held the northern part of Tay Ninh Province, the Plain of "Joncs" (Reeds), Ca Mau (at the southern tip of the country), and other pockets of people and territory.

The second map shows the estimated deployment of the Viet Minh battalions on September 30, 1953. The pattern is similar: a heavy concentration of *regular* battalions in the North, reaching down into South Vietnam's MR II, with a lighter concentration of *regional* battalions shown further south.

In discussing their worst trouble spots, a French officer noted the "permanence or continuity in the centers of unrest." History and geography reveal that certain regions are traditional cradles of insurgent movements, and these later serve as preferred areas for the guerrillas. "It is in the provinces where the population has always shown itself to be proud, bold, and independent that the revolt has taken on the most acute and intense forms. . . . It is striking to compare some recent engagements with the history of certain battles which occurred during the conquest. The events were often the same and even happened at the same places." The same areas continued to be troublesome to the South Vietnamese and Americans.

THE AMERICAN EXPERIENCE

In the past four years, American or ARVN units have fallen into traps at precisely the same places French units did in 1954—traps often laid by the

---

13 Primarily Kontum and Binh Dinh provinces in MR II.

Territory held by Viet Minh after Dien Bien Phu

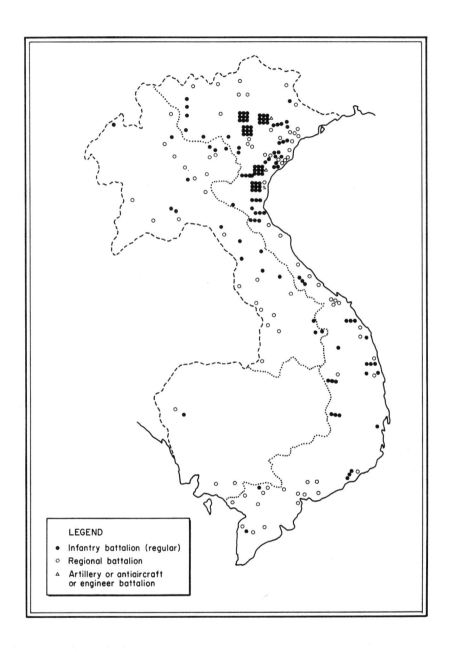

LEGEND

• Infantry battalion (regular)
○ Regional battalion
△ Artillery or antiaircraft
  or engineer battalion

Viet Minh Deployment as of September 30, 1953.

same Communist units, which succeed far more often than they should.
—*Bernard Fall*

Intensity of the Conflict. Total allied forces in South Vietnam from the end of 1964 through the end of 1972 averaged about 1.2 million, and annual combat deaths averaged about 28,000. Thus about 2.3 percent of the allied force was killed in combat each year. The chances of being killed in combat were 1 in 43 each year.

The United States lost 1.8 percent of its force each year, on average, which yields 1 chance in 55 of being killed each year. The Third Nation percentage (i.e., Australia, Korea, etc.) was even lower, 1.3 percent. The Vietnamese forces lost an average of 2.5 percent of their force each year, yielding 1 chance in 40 of being killed every year, higher than the odds for American forces.

In all cases, the percentages are well below those suffered by the French and their allied forces, possibly because those forces averaged only one fifth the size of the allied forces twenty years later (240,000 versus 1.2 million) and had vastly less sophisticated medical evacuation procedures. In addition, the support components of the American and South Vietnamese forces were a much larger proportion of their troop strength.

The Annual Cycle of Combat. Table 2[14] suggests that the basic combat cycle of the Vietnam War during the American involvement went something like this:

1. The heaviest fighting each year always occurred during February through June. May, on average, had the highest number of friendly combat deaths, followed by April, February, March, and June.

2. July was always a month of relative lull. Friendly combat deaths in July were always below those in June. In five of the seven years studied, July deaths were also below those of August.

3. In August–September the intensity of combat went up again.

4. October through January was normally a period of low combat intensity. October, on average, had the fewest friendly combat deaths and

14 Averages calculated from statistics in *Table 6, Statistics on Southeast Asia, Statistical Summary* (Washington, D.C.: Office of the Assistant Secretary of Defense—Comptroller, March 25, 1971, through January 17, 1973), pp. 1–7.

was always a lull. Friendly combat deaths were below those in September during every year studied; in five of the seven years, October deaths were also below those of November.

In summary, the basic pattern is heavy fighting from February through June, a lull in July, renewed combat in August–September, a lull in October, followed by relatively low activity until February, when the cycle starts all over again.

As in the French war, a basic determinant of the cycle is the weather. In the northern part of South Vietnam (MR I) the rainy season extends from September through January. In the southern part of the country and in the Laos panhandle (where the infiltration roads and trails were located) it extends approximately from May through September. The rain closed down the VC/NVA infiltration routes in Laos and made it difficult for them to continue their major offensive in the South. The terrain got worse

Table 2. *The Cycle of Friendly Combat Deaths in South Vietnam*
(Averages for 1966 through 1972)

By Month	War Cycle
January 2,177	
February 2,864	2,864
March 2,871	2,871
April 2,919	2,919
May 3,427	3,427
June 2,752	2,752
July 2,097	2,097
August 2,361	2,361
September 2,300	2,300
October 1,880	1,880
November 1,936	1,936
December 2,011	2,011
By Quarter	*By War Cycle*
January–March 2,637	February–June 2,967
April–June 3,032	July 2,097
July–September 2,253	August–September 2,330
October–December 1,942	October–January 2,001

and worse as they drew down men and supplies that could not be replaced until the infiltration corridors reopened in October. Thus, the best time for a major VC/NVA offensive to start was between January and April, when all of South Vietnam is dry. That is when they did start.

The cycle can be explained as follows:

1. By October the VC/NVA personnel and supplies were low. The rain stopped, and infiltration of men and supplies for the spring offensive began.

2. At some point during February–April the VC/NVA got enough troops and supplies in position to begin their major offensive of the year. The flow of infiltration continued, and gradually dwindled away as the rain started again in Laos and the VC/NVA got into the final phase of their offensive, ending it in June.

3. By July the offensive was over and infiltration through Laos had stopped. Much of the terrain in the southern part of South Vietnam was under water.

4. By mid-August the VC/NVA had regrouped enough to launch a brief summer offensive lasting into September. October brought a lull.

5. From the low point in October, the cycle started all over again. In November, infiltrators and trucks were sighted coming down the trails in Laos and the buildup for the next year's spring offensive was underway.

The cycle is important because it adds perspective to changes in the tempo of combat. Knowing that May is usually the toughest month of the year leads to less upset when activity that month exceeds April's levels. By the same token, since the infiltration cycle starts up again in October–November, it is no surprise when new North Vietnamese troops are suddenly reported heading down the trails for South Vietnam. Instead, the focus in both cases is on the level of activity, and *how it compares with similar periods of previous years.* In this manner trends can be tracked accurately if reasonably reliable data are available.

Where Did Most of the Fighting Occur? Table 3 and the map show the pattern of allied combat deaths in South Vietnam for 1967 through 1972. The pattern is a familiar one. Five provinces (11 percent of the total) accounted for about 33 percent of the friendly combat deaths. The pattern is quite stable. All five provinces ranked among the top ten provinces each

Table 3. *Percentage of Friendly Combat Deaths*
by Province in South Vietnam
(1967 through 1972)

The Five Provinces in Top Ten Every Year	1967	1968	1969	1970	1971	1972	Total Period %	Rank
Quang Tri (MR I)	12%	10%	5%	6%	7%	12%	9	1
Quang Nam (MR I)	8	10	8	6	6	6	8	2
Binh Dinh (MR II)	6	4	5	8	9	6	6	3
Quang Ngai (MR I)	7	4	6	5	4	5	5	5
Dinh Tuong (MR IV)	4	5	6	5	5	4	5	6
% of Total	37%	33%	30%	30%	31%	33%	33%	
Five Additional Provinces with Very High Combat Death Rates								
Tay Ninh (MR III)	3%	6%	10%	7%	4%	1%	5	4
Thua Thien (MR I)	5	4	2	4	2	3	4	7
Kontum (MR II)	4	2	4	3	3	5	3	8
Kien Hoa (MR IV)	2	2	3	4	5	4	3	9
Quang Tin (MR I)	4	2	4	4	3	2	3	10
% of Total	18%	16%	23%	22%	17%	15%	18%	
Ten Provinces' Total % of Countrywide Friendly Combat Deaths	55%	49%	53%	52%	48%	48%	51%	

year. Moreover, the range of percentages each year is narrow—from 30 percent to 37 percent—only seven percentage points. Stated another way, the war in these five provinces was almost four times as active as it was in the other thirty-nine provinces. The top ten provinces (22 percent of the total) accounted for about half (51 percent) of the friendly combat deaths.

All five provinces of MR I are among the top ten, as are Kontum and Binh Dinh in MR II. This is precisely the area considered to be under Viet Minh control in 1954 and where the French fought hardest in South Vietnam. In the words of Bernard Fall:

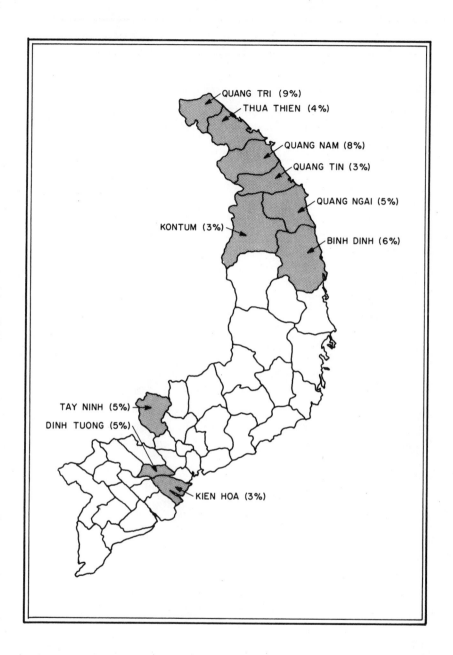

QUANG TRI (9%)
THUA THIEN (4%)
QUANG NAM (8%)
QUANG TIN (3%)
QUANG NGAI (5%)
KONTUM (3%)
BINH DINH (6%)
TAY NINH (5%)
DINH TUONG (5%)
KIEN HOA (3%)

Percentage of Friendly Deaths by Province 1967-73.

> For years communications along the central Annam coast had been plagued by Communist attacks against Road 1, the main north–south artery along the coast. The principal source of trouble was a string of heavily fortified villages along a line of sand dunes and salt marshes stretching from Hué to Quang Tri.[15]

And:

> In the plateau area of the PMS, the war also developed favorably to the Viet Minh. Anchored on the three provinces of Quang Ngai, Binh Dinh, and Phu Yen, which as Interzone V had been a Communist bastion since 1945, Viet Minh control had slowly spread to the large Bahnar, Jarai, and Rhade mountain tribes and smaller groups. Thus, they literally "hollowed out" Franco-Vietnamese areas in central Vietnam to the point where they merely covered a few narrow beachheads around Hué, Tourane (today known as Da Nang), and Nha Trang.[16]

The remaining three provinces in the top ten are further south and they also fit the French pattern. Tay Ninh was pointed out in our section on the French experience. Dinh Tuong and Kien Hoa[17] are next to the Plain of Reeds and are key provinces between Saigon and the Delta.

As to the French point that the events were often the same and even happened at the same places, the following suggests that this phenomenon persisted during the American troop involvement in Vietnam.

> On July 2, 1964, an ammunition convoy of the Vietnamese Army, shepherded by a U.S. Army helicopter, proceeded on Road 19 from the coastal town of Quang Ngai to Pleiku.
>
> It had passed An Khe without incident and at 1115 had entered the small valley which precedes the entrance to Mang Yang Pass, when its lead trucks blew up on the well-concealed land mines which barred the road. Within a few minutes the Viet Cong ambush unfolded fully and the stunned Vietnamese fought for their lives. . . .
>
> The ambush had taken place at the foot of the monument commemorating the end of G.M. 100—ten years, eight days and three hours earlier.[18]

[15] Fall, *Street Without Joy*, p. 144.

[16] Fall, *The Two Vietnams*, p. 120.

[17] The area that is now Kien Hoa Province was the prime French example of pacification success.

[18] Fall, *Street Without Joy*, p. 249.

DID THE AMERICANS LEARN MUCH FROM THE FRENCH EXPERIENCE?

In terms of their casualties, the French fought a long, tough war in Indo-china with considerable drive, although with much fewer matériel assets and combat support than the Americans and South Vietnamese had twenty years later. About 5 percent of the French and associated forces died in combat each year, equivalent to the American casualty rate during the Korean War, and more than double the combat rate of the American and South Vietnamese forces twenty years later. Moreover, the Americans served in Vietnam for only twelve months, whereas the French tour of duty was twenty-six months, which furthered the odds of being killed. The evidence suggests that the French fought hard in Indochina.

The evidence also suggests that there are striking similarities in some of the basic patterns of the French and American experience in Vietnam. Several of the similarities have been mentioned and two have been ana-lyzed. The annual cycles of combat in both wars appear to be similar, with both keyed primarily to the weather, which led to heavy fighting during the first half of the year, after the rains had stopped. The regularity of the cycle during the American experience is noteworthy. If it had been well known at the time by the Americans who served only one year and were usually unaware that a repetitive cycle existed, there might have been fewer waves of optimism and pessimism which turned out to be keyed to normal, predictable fluctuations in the tempo of the war. For example, major offenses or waves of VC/NVA activity did not occur during the last three months of the year,[19] and this was when the year-end reports of progress were being written.

The most important and startling similarities emerge when the locations of major combat are examined in both wars. The areas that caused the most problems for the French in South Vietnam were also the worst trouble spots for the United States and South Vietnamese troops twenty years later. But, in the words of Sir Robert Thompson, "the French experience

[19] Except in the fourth quarter of 1967, when VC/NVA activity rates remained ab-normally high in connection with preparations for the Tet offensive in February 1968.

in Indochina was almost totally written off and disregarded." Other ex-
perienced observers agree. Colonel V. J. Croizat, USMC (Ret.), who
worked extensively with the French and had access to their accounts of
the Indochina war, stated in 1967:

> While Mao Tse-tung, Vo Nguyen Giap, and even Ché Guevara are
> avidly read and liberally quoted, the French, who were among the first
> of the western nations to gain practical experience of modern revolu-
> tionary war, are seldom heard from outside of their own country.
> Moreover, after the United States began the rapid expansion of its ad-
> visory effort in South Vietnam in 1962, the British experience in Malaya[20]
> was often cited by Americans in Saigon as a model of how to handle an
> insurrection, but little if anything was ever said of the French experience
> in Indochina.
> What is of even greater significance is that today the United States is
> fighting essentially the same enemy and is doing this over much the
> same terrain and under the same climatic conditions. Finally, and most
> important of all, is the fact that the present leadership of North Vietnam
> is the very same whose determination and tenacity helped it to prevail
> over the French. The lessons that the French learned in the course of
> their prolonged conflict should, therefore, offer something more than
> simple historical data.[21].

Why did the Americans ignore the French experience? The answer may
lie in the relationship between the United States and France in the 1960s
and also in the attitude noted earlier: "The French haven't won a war
since Napoleon. What can we learn from them?" By 1965, the U.S. attitude toward the French was shaped by de Gaulle's withdrawal of France
from NATO and his opposition to America on a variety of fronts. "Under
such circumstances it is not surprising that American leaders looked at
de Gaulle's 1964 proposal for the neutralization of Indochina as a miscon-

---

20 For a succinct account of the Malayan effort, see R. W. Komer, *The Malayan
Emergency in Retrospect: Organization of a Successful Counterinsurgency Effort*, R-
987-ARPA (Santa Monica, Calif.: The Rand Corporation, 1972).

21 V. J. Croizat, *Lessons of the War in Indochina* (Santa Monica, Calif.: The Rand
Corporation, 1967), p. iii.

ceived anti-American ploy which would eventually result in the Communization of the area."[22]

Added to the general policy differences in the 1960s is a history of American dissatisfaction with French strategy in Indochina and particularly tense relations between the French and Americans in the period following the Geneva Conference of 1954. The attitude of the U.S. Joint Chiefs of Staff was: ". . . as a condition to the provision of those increases in military assistance to Indochina necessary for the implementation of an agreed overall military plan, the United States Government should obtain assurances from the French Government that: . . . (d) France will change its political and military concepts of Indochina to: (*i*) Eliminate its policy of colonialism; (*ii*) Provide proper tutelage to the Associated States; (*iii*) Insure that the suitable military command structure, unhampered by political interference, is established to conduct effective and appropriate military operations."[23] The French did not meet these, or other conditions specified, and "the effectiveness of the United States assistance program as an instrument of United States policy—quite aside from the outcome of the war—was thus quite low."[24]

United States–French relations became quite strained after the Geneva Conference of 1954, as the United States increased its role in Vietnam, becoming much more active on the scene, and making "life in Vietnam difficult for France."[25] In the words of *The Pentagon Papers:*

> That France and the United States would eventually part company over Vietnam might have been predicted in August 1954, when United States policy toward Vietnam was drawn. Formulae for economic, military and especially political courses of action were different from—often antithetical to—French objectives and interests. . . . It is during this period that Diem established his rule, against French advice and best

[22] Henry James Kenny, *The Changing Importance of Vietnam in United States Policy: 1949–1969,* unpublished doctoral dissertation, The American University, Washington, D.C., 1974, p. 7.

[23] *The Pentagon Papers,* I, 199.

[24] *Ibid.,* p. 201.

[25] *Ibid.,* p. 211.

interests but with almost unwavering support from Secretary of State John Foster Dulles.[26]

It is fair to ask whether the French, after the problems of the 1950s and the strains of the 1960s, would have been willing to help the United States by sharing the details of their experience and lessons learned. There is at least one piece of evidence that, if asked, they would have. Their military attaché in Saigon circa 1964 was handpicked by the French Government because of his exceptional knowledge of the English language and his distinguished record in Indochina and Algeria. He was told to help the Americans in whatever way he could. During the first eighteen months of his assignment, the only American who visited him to ask about the war was an American defense contractor of French origin.[27]

[26] *Ibid.*, pp. 211, 212. For an account of the problems of this period, see pp. 210–39.

[27] Personal recollection of the writer.

Chapter 3

The American Approach to the War

Mao Tse-tung's guerrilla doctrine for "Wars of National Liberation" is the cutting edge of many leftist and Marxist movements throughout the world. The problem for American leaders was to develop a response appropriate to guerrilla strategies. There were several models upon which to draw: notably the Philippine Huk experience and the Malayan insurgency successfully contained by the British, but more important and less used was the French experience in Indochina ending in 1954, which was discussed in Chapter 2.

How indeed does a major power approach a limited guerrilla war? How is the military input balanced with the political, economic, and psychological inputs? The probability of limited wars was implicitly recognized in the national strategy of flexible response—a doctrine that recognized a wide range of threats from nuclear war to guerrilla insurgencies. Counterinsurgency doctrines were being developed by the armed services. The U.S. Army's Special Forces, popularly known as the Green Berets, reflected the growing concern with low-level violence and limited-war strategies and tactics.

The American approach had a low profile until 1965, when a major change in strategy occurred. Starting with the Gulf of Tonkin incident in August 1964, a relentless buildup of American military power took place. The crucial question at that juncture was whether the massive intervention by the United States was necessary.

According to the argument of most of our speakers, the Americans had no choice but to intervene, if they did not wish to see the North Vietnamese and Viet Cong take over the country unopposed, so close was the regime—and its support in the countryside—to collapse. After

39

the Gulf of Tonkin incident in 1964, the Americans became increasingly involved and indeed the war took on a decidedly American character. Major General Edward Lansdale, the hero of The Ugly American *and one of the most extraordinary figures in the whole period of American involvement in Vietnam, examines some fundamental misperceptions by the Americans as they charged about, seeking to solve a primarily political conflict by military means. General Lansdale had played a critical role in the Philippines in the early 1950s, helping President Ramón Magsaysay end the Huk insurgency, before going to Vietnam for his first stint of duty. Probably closer than anyone else to President Diem, Lansdale was known to be highly apprehensive of any attempt to upset the existing South Vietnamese applecart, still more of overwhelming the country with a large American military presence.*

General Lansdale's paper is followed by an essay by General S.L.A. Marshall, a formidable student of war and a reporter of the Vietnamese War who traveled throughout the war zones in both official and unofficial capacities intermittently throughout the 1960s.

Contradictions in Military Culture

Major General Edward Lansdale

One evening in 1965, when Saigon was crowded with Americans come to wage war in Vietnam, a Vietnamese government official hosted a dinner party at his home for some Vietnamese and American officers. All were of high rank.

During the evening, a Vietnamese general started to make excuses for his early departure. The excuses promptly brought raucous cries of "General Tao Thao" from the Vietnamese guests. It was evident that the name embarrassed him. When Americans asked why he was being called "General Tao Thao," the Vietnamese explained that this was the name of a character in *The Romance of the Three Kingdoms*. From the tone of their voices, apparently the Vietnamese felt that this was sufficient explanation. It wasn't.

The point of this incident in 1965 is not that a Vietnamese general tried to excuse himself early from a dinner party. Rather, the incident is indicative of the cultural gulf that existed between all too many Vietnamese and Americans during the war in Vietnam. In the case of *The Three Kingdoms,* there is military pertinence. If there is any "military textbook" familiar to all Vietnamese of military age, that book surely is *The Three Kingdoms.*

Admittedly, most Americans find reading English translations of *The Three Kingdoms* difficult or boring. This Chinese novel from the fourteenth century, about the military struggles of third-century China, is crammed with too many characters and bloody incidents, is told in too Asian a storyteller form, to have much appeal to American tastes. On top of this, there is the further confusion of the "Vietnamization" of the Chinese characters in *The Three Kingdoms.* For example, "General Tao Thao" is the Chinese "General Ts'ao Ts'ao," the chief schemer in the Chinese classic, who used an "upset stomach" as an alibi to be absent from gatherings unfavorable to his political needs.

Although *The Three Kingdoms* is filled with accounts of battles won by wily stratagems, whose cleverness so delights the Asian readers, there is a main thread running throughout the book that related directly to the North Vietnamese in the war. This main thread teaches the dominant lesson of the book: wars and battles are fought for *political gain.* Each successful general in the book demonstrates that he has clear political objectives in mind when he embarks upon a military campaign, and uses armed force to strengthen his political moves. In other words, these Asian generals are politicians who have military skill. Whenever a general can win his objective by other means, he forgoes the use of armed force. It is the ethic taught by Sun Tzu. In more recent times, it is what Mao Tse-tung has taught.

This ethic is alien to an American military man, who is conditioned throughout his military service by the checks and balances of our democratic system, wherein civilian politicians make the political decisions which the military are to carry out. An American military man might agree with Clausewitz that war is the final instrument of politics, or have an understanding of Machiavelli's instructions about the use of force for political ends. However, the American military man's conditioning leads him to see political and military operations as separate, even compartmented entities.

The battleground of Vietnam saw the confrontation of these two, significantly different, viewpoints. The Vietnamese Communist generals saw their armed forces as instruments primarily to gain political goals. The American generals saw their forces primarily as instruments to defeat enemy military forces. One fought battles to influence opinions in Vietnam and in the world; the other fought battles to finish the enemy, keeping tabs by body count.

Oddly enough, American political leaders such as President Johnson and Defense Secretary McNamara (and Nixon and Laird later) adopted the American military viewpoint for their own behavior. Despite some political moves, such as declaring general political aims for U.S. involvement in Vietnam, limiting geographic boundaries and weaponry in the war, giving support to current regimes in Saigon, and undertaking some diplomatic actions, they made no true political use of American military power in Vietnam. Nor did they make any serious and sustained effort to turn the population of North Vietnam against the leadership of the Politburo in Hanoi, as was done in wars against Germany. Perhaps Vietnam and its people were too exotic when looked at from Washington. One can imagine that the war would have been waged far differently by U.S. forces if it had been fought in the Texas or California home areas of the

Americans ultimately responsible for the strategy on our side. It is ironic that American political leaders suffered such grievous blows in the domestic policies of the United States for their support of the U.S. military viewpoint.

Any thoughtful study of the Vietnam War, then, must take into consideration the fact that markedly different military philosophies opposed each other in that war.

The entry of U.S. combat forces into Vietnam and the ensuing struggle between them and the enemy's Viet Cong and North Vietnamese forces formed only one, intermediate part of a much longer war. To have a sound understanding of the events in the American combat period, then, one also needs knowledge of what happened before this time. Otherwise, one is like a spectator arriving in the middle of a complex drama, without true knowledge of plot or of the identity and motivation of those in the drama, and thus prone to draw faulty conclusions from what occurs.

Americans have complained about the American period of the war as having been the longest war in our history. Yet it has been even longer for the Vietnamese, who date it from the Japanese-encouraged Vietnamese nationalist uprising against Vichy-French colonial officials in 1945, the take-over of the Vietnamese movement by the Viet Minh, and subsequent combat against returning French occupation troops in 1946.

The 1954 division of Vietnam at the 17th Parallel into North and South posed a vital economic problem to the Politburo, which ruled the North. There was not enough arable land in the North for crops to meet the food needs of the people. Vietnam's true "rice bowl" was in the South, in the Mekong-Bassac region. Although the Politburo attempted to increase land tillage in the North (such as clearing hillsides for planting upland rice— which later led to disastrous flooding owing to the denuded watershed), the Politburo knew all along that it would require rice from the South for its economic well-being. In 1954, the Politburo expected to win the South politically, through a 1956 plebiscite outlined by the powers at Geneva. The South was in political chaos in 1954 and a majority of the electorate lived in Politburo-controlled territory in the North. The Politburo's hopes for a "legal struggle" for South Vietnam were dashed, however, in 1955.

A million refugees left the North and took up residence in the South, diminishing the North's electoral majority. Ngo Dinh Diem consolidated political rule in the South, ending much of the chaos there. Large segments of the rural population in the North became restive under hard "agrarian reform" programs and even students at the University of Hanoi rebelled against heavy dosages of political harangues in classrooms; the Politburo had many signs that the electorate in its territory might well vote against it in a plebiscite. (Later, open revolts broke out which had to be put down by troops.) Diem finally sealed the political road by refusing to consider participating in a plebiscite, pointing out that it was sure to be rigged by the Politburo. It seems likely that, sometime in 1955, the Politburo secretly decided to win the South by "armed struggle" instead of "legal struggle."

The Politburo had a tried and successful plan for winning a country by "armed struggle." It was Mao's Three Steps, which the Politburo had used to defeat the French. In Step One, a nucleus is positioned on the battleground to establish bases for political-military action, then working out from these bases to create its own political administration in adjacent areas, protected by its military arm, the guerrilla force, which also acts as bullyboys to ensure compliance with the political organization (a neighbor's head stuck on a stake makes a powerful argument to a villager). Step Two is to organize a political structure and conduct guerrilla operations throughout the countryside. Step Three is to transform guerrilla forces into regular forces for positional warfare, to destroy the existing government and its forces. Geographically, Mao put the steps as "first the mountains, then the countryside, then the cities." The Vietnamese Politburo had added an extra dimension to Mao's plan, when fighting the French: to undermine the enemy's home base. Agitprop work in metropolitan France led to wholesale draft evasion, rebelliousness among troops being shipped out to Indochina, a militant antiwar campaign by press, pulpit, and students, and the downfall of governments.

Step One was already a reality in South Vietnam when the Politburo must have made its decision for "armed struggle" in 1955. A cadre for political-military operations had stayed behind in the South when Viet Minh units shipped out to the North under the terms of the Geneva cease-fire of 1954; caches of arms, ammunition, and other military supplies were buried all over the South. Selected personnel from those who went North were trained as cadre and infiltrated back into the South, being given their final examination by Ho Chi Minh personally. By the time the National Liberation Front was formed in December 1960, enough progress had been made to initiate Step Two.

As 1964 ended and 1965 began, large units of regular forces were put in the field for positional warfare, not the elusive hit-and-run warfare of guerrillas. A new family of weapons was issued, using one caliber of ammunition, to replace the heterogeneous guerrilla assortment. More modern support weapons were issued. Saigon's government and forces were to be destroyed. Step Three was on.

In the first weeks of the third stage, it appeared that the Politburo had been correct in deciding that the time had come for initiating the showdown phase of the war. Two Viet Cong regiments savagely mauled ARVN units in coastal Binh Dinh Province, running them out of the countryside and forcing them to hole up in the port city of Qui Nhon. A North Vietnamese division arrived in the Central Highlands near Pleiku, apparently with the intention of moving down to the sea in Binh Dinh, cutting South Vietnam in two. Enemy forces had invested the area surrounding Saigon and, from checkpoints along lines of communication, were collecting taxes on foodstuffs and travelers en route to the capital city. To many in South Vietnam, including farm families in countryside hamlets, it looked like the beginning of the end.

At this dark hour, then, when U.S. combat forces arrived, the enemy was committed to waging a type of warfare similar to the type most familiar to the Americans—open, positional warfare by regular units, with set-piece battles. The significant factors unfamiliar to the Americans were the heavy jungle and mountain terrain where much of the initial combat was to take place and the continuing existence of both large-scale guerrilla activities and the enemy's secret political organization spread out over the countryside field of operations. Both sides had unique and difficult logistical problems in keeping their fighting forces supplied, one across a great ocean and the other by hidden overland routes; it is small wonder that so much of each side's military effort was devoted to these supply problems.

The enemy had the advantage of familiarity with the battleground, particularly in being able to distinguish friend from foe—in contrast to the Americans, who seemed almost constantly befuddled in picking out enemies from a population in the universal clothing of black pajamas, identical to those worn by enemy guerrillas. The enemy's advantage of familiarity with the scene, though, was heavily offset by the Americans' command and use of the air. While it is true that the French had used air power in their war with the Viet Minh, it had been used mostly as a supporting and secondary element for the French ground forces. This French use really did not prepare the Politburo's generals for the prodigally extensive and innovative American use of the air—such as the deployment of large units of air-mobile infantry, the frequent interdiction bombing of areas hitherto considered fairly secure in previous combat, and the almost constant servicing of troops on the field of battle by air. But, as was seen, even that was to be insufficient.

Thoughts on Vietnam

General S. L. A. Marshall

War, as Winston Churchill wrote, is a strange sea, and once embarked upon, there is no foretelling where the voyage may lead. But it is not less true, and almost invariably the case, that when the thing is badly begun, from a false and misleading premise, the blunders will accumulate—that is more likely than the possibility of a new sense of direction and ultimate recovery.

Our Joint Chiefs of Staff had voted the commitment to the Korean war unanimously. Though they did so under direct pressure from the Secretaries, it was also under the mistaken assumption that there would be a speedy termination as soon as the United States entered the conflict. That is never a justifiable optimism. So the first wasteful piecemeal moves were made, and within two weeks the illusion of easy victory had faded.

Having been personally identified with those who made the decisions, believing and saying from the first day that there was a long and tortuous road ahead, deeply troubled by the experience, I would not understand in the years that too soon followed the acceptance of a new theory of military operations by those who fashion and direct our strategy. The new theory was called "limited war."

Some of the Joint Chiefs, in particular General Maxwell D. Taylor, advocated it. Among its most vocal exponents was Defense Secretary Robert S. McNamara. Promoted ostensibly as a safeguard against the possibility of a small war getting beyond containment and mushrooming into an atomic eclipse, it postulated that a great power could conduct fighting operations with a stringent economy of force and could, in effect, buy success at the lowest possible price. I could not believe one word of it.

Running wholly contrary to the principles of war and thereby yielding initial advantage to the enemy, it threatened a repetition of the Korean miscalculation. There is only one sound way to conduct war as I read history: Deploy to the war zone as quickly as possible sufficient forces to end it at the earliest moment. Anything less is a gift to the other side. But when I felt some alarm about the drift in military thinking in high places, I continued to hope that I was misled by appearances on the surface, and we would avoid the more obvious pitfalls.

The first shock of reality came in April 1961, when I learned of the Bay of Pigs failure—an attempt at limited war and one of a series of problems that caused embarrassment for President Kennedy.

Of course, I am talking about that which is beyond final proof, but it is at least a tenable theory of our ever-deepening involvement in Vietnam that it came about because of Mr. Kennedy's disappointment over Laos, his chagrin and political embarrassment over the Bay of Pigs failure, and his outrage over the taunting over Vietnam to which Khrushchev subjected him at Vienna. Chiefs do react to personal emotions and confuse them with reasons of state. While the Bay of Pigs may not stand as a watershed in our national history, it is the case that our fortunes have steadily retrograded since.

Certainly the time factors do not run counter to the thesis. Within a few weeks after the Bay of Pigs, General Taylor was on his way to Vietnam to determine what the United States needed to do to put down Communist resistance and tip the balance toward the Diem Government. Taylor was back shortly with a long shopping list of military hardware and other essentials, of which the President bought approximately 35 percent. Yet while it is accurately said that in war half enough is never enough by far more than half, neither General Taylor nor the Chiefs nor the Defense Secretary either protested or pointed out that we were taking steps which must intensify the war, rather than quiet it, while drawing us in more deeply, with ultimate risk to our prestige and other interests. Instead, in a speech made, I believe, in Chicago in late September, Mr. McNamara boasted that we had plumbed the secret of how to defeat Communist guerrillas and would stay in Vietnam until it was done.

It was totally ill-advised, for with those words he nailed our flag to the mast. All we were programming was the beefing up of MAAG, strengthening Special Forces, and fielding a few U.S. helicopter companies to the theater. Since MAAG and the Green Berets were not new, the helicopter companies *had to be* the extra something added that would ensure victory. If the Secretary believed one word of that, he was more than a little naïve.

In the following spring—1962—I went on my only mission to Vietnam for the Department of Defense (the others were for the Army), in the company of Allen Dulles and Karl Bendetsen, former Undersecretary of the Army. Our mission was in investigate the state of our troops as to morale, discipline, supply, and the general outlook. We spent most of our days afield. To begin, we were briefed on the military situation by General Paul D. Harkins, who explained how the choppers would be used to field the ARVN companies from one fire flashpoint to another.

But when he had finished his briefing, I said, "You know it will not work. Right now Charley is making himself furtive and hard to find. But once he sees what we intend, he will conform and make himself obvious. There are too few spots approximate to their base camps where choppers can be put down. So they will draw in the ARVN to a present defense where the birds will be shot up and the soldiers dispersed before they can deploy. Ambush will follow ambush."

Harkins replied: "I can see it coming, but what can be done about it?" And to that, there was not an answer.

While troop morale was far short of high tide at that point, the MAAG advisers in the field were unusually steadfastly solid, though they could see trouble ahead. Especially alarming to me was the group attitude in the U.S. press corps. There were only about twenty-five correspondents in Saigon at the time and the main body was encamped in the Hotel Caravelle. Without exception, they were bitterly hostile to the Diem Government and hardly less so toward the U.S. Embassy and the military command. President Diem was already a walking fever; trusting no one, he had become virtually a recluse. So the newsmen were hurting for stories out of the Government, and to keep faith with Diem, our main spokesmen maintained silence about any of the affairs of the palace. The Army had no transportation for average correspondents, though when such persons as Joe Alsop or Maggie Higgins arrived, they were given the grand tour. So getting rockets from their editors' desks every day, because they were producing nothing or spinning fables out of thin air, the press corps seethed and burned. Who could blame them?

Within a few months thereafter, President Kennedy became the victim of an assassin's bullet and so did President Diem. Neither death afforded any relief from the war's steadily rising pressures, the conditions being prohibitive. Both tragedies have tended to obscure some of the larger lessons of the war, which but makes them the more lamentable. It is said that if Mr. Kennedy had lived, he would have found the way to extricate the country from a situation that would in the end make us a house divided. An idle and politically motivated conjecture, it is without any foundation in fact.

The atmosphere of Washington in that period is difficult, indeed impossible, to re-create. There were conferences almost weekly, at government expense, to gather in judgments from all possible quarters on what was to be done to carry the war to a successful conclusion. These huddles would bring together professors and self-appointed experts on guerrilla warfare from all parts of the country. The collective contribution to the national cause may have been two degrees above zero. Government was proceeding according to the notion that, if enough persons are collected, some inspired thoughts of value will inevitably flow outward. It reminds me of the Army thesis that if two half-wits are assigned to a task, you get a whole wit, whereas the mathematical prospect is, more accurately, that what comes out will be a quarter-wit. These gyrations and incantations, possibly intended to give the war a broader base of popular support, did add significantly to the bill. To that, I add that it was still a relatively popular war with the people, the press, and the Congress.

My position was that we were inviting catastrophe, and that the United States had but one of two rational choices to make: (1) it should cut clean and withdraw while its losses in prestige, power, and position would be relatively slight, and compensatable, or (2) it should move in with enough tactical force to bring off a decision. Do it right away and with no blasting of trumpets. But any course in between would be dead wrong. I was simply contending against the middle and most extravagant course.

In 1964 I warned General H. K. Johnson, Army Chief of Staff, that we should field enough fighting force to stop North Vietnam, or we should pull everything out before we truly got hurt. I recommended that eight to ten independent brigades be used, because brigades are more efficient in this type of warfare than division-sized forces. I predicted that unless we secured the defensive bases where our people were vulnerable, incidents so deeply wounding to national pride would occur that we would become fully committed regardless of the jeopardy to our main national interests.

The Joint Chiefs, who did not want the war, had accepted the notion that the main guidance would come from the White House. If they as a body are to be faulted, it is not on the score that they were in any sense warmongering, but that they would not play a strong hand in buffering the Presidential positions. While they did not abdicate, they pulled in their horns, and in that, I would say, they are reprehensible. What I had predicted to General Johnson suddenly materialized out of the slaughter of American troops at Holloway Barracks soon after the beginning of 1965. Because quite a few lives were lost and we had been nationally affronted, we found ourselves taking on a war just at the turn where it had begun to disaffect large numbers of American citizens, a significant portion of the press, and those members of the Congress who saw opposition to the war as a vote-getting stand. LBJ was in that respect a major victim of the circumstances that he had not brought about, though once he took hold, he extended his predecessor's domination of military operations and his covetousness of the decision-making powers in provinces not properly his own.

When the Holloway Barracks incident occurred and coincidentally the bombing of the U.S. Embassy in Saigon, we continued to respond with half measures, such as limited ground commitments and a limited air strike against the North.

In midsummer, President Johnson made the dramatic announcements over national TV that the First Cavalry Division (Air Mobile) would be sent at once to Vietnam, and there would soon follow a buildup of 150,000 Americans. One thing in Mr. Johnson's statement caught my ear. He said we had to think about a war that might go on for seven or eight years. It was unbelievable that he could imagine the American people sitting still for that kind of war that long.

In the following spring, I went to Vietnam and linked up with the First Cavalry Division. As a correspondent, I did my accustomed chore—the analysis of combat operations. I reported to General Westmoreland on some of my early and general conclusions. My overall estimate was that the morale of the troops and the level of discipline of the Army were higher than I had ever known them in any of our wars. There was no lack of will to fight and the average soldier withstood the stress of engagement better than ever before. But on the negative side, our marksmanship and musketry were deplorably bad, and furthermore, it was my reckoning that about one third of our losses in action were our own fault, owing to carelessness about security. We were paying an excessive price for rotation; the average captain on the line was given too little time with his company. Hardly was he broken in when he was sent elsewhere.

On another subject, I remarked that the intelligence flow in the field was a flood: there was so much paper daily that even a whiz-kid G-2 was hard-pressed to distinguish between the important and the trivial. Further in the intelligence flow, broad gaps existed between the field divisions and the Special Forces, as between both of these elements and our advisers with the ARVN. I judged that our psychological operations were, as usual, only a few degrees above zero. On the other hand, I voiced my certainty that the B-52 strikes were having a large payoff, though they were pooh-poohed by critics in the press. There had been a smashingly successful air raid against the oil refineries and storage tanks at Hanoi. The President and Mr. McNamara called Westmoreland to extend their congratulations on the first operation of that kind. They had authorized it. There was a general belief that at last the blinkers and hobbles were off—that finally we had turned the corner.

And it was all illusion—another flash in the pan. Tried once, it was dropped immediately afterward. We carried on with that more gentlemanly war in which soldiers died by the thousands. It was in that same season, by the way, that the Defense Secretary deprecated air operations against North Vietnam, saying that they added not more than 12 percent to the battlefield friction visited on the enemy, as if not understanding that in war 12 percent is a very important margin, and as if not seeing that once air operations are dropped, you have advantaged him by more than double that amount. All of this is by way of pointing out that Westmoreland was not permitted to command: sometime it may be understood that the main strategy and, in instances, major tactics were determined at the White House by a President who could pay only occasional attention to the problem. In the last month of his life, it is said, LBJ told a confidant: "I am aware of my main mistake in the war; I would not put enough trust in my military advisers." From my view, that was less a reaction to conscience than a reasoned self-criticism.

On my return to Vietnam, through the winter of 1966–67, I moved more broadly over the theater, wherever there were main operations to be reconstructed and analyzed. Morale was still high and discipline strong. We were continuing to waste too many people—our own people—out of security carelessness. The enemy was staging the same stale ambushes—there are only about ten possible patterns—and we were falling into the traps as often as ever.

But while on that point, I would make this aside: In covering forty-eight operations over there, from platoon to multi-division size, I found nothing even faintly resembling the My Lai horror. To the contrary, I was amazed that our soldiers ran such terrible risk to avoid killing civilians and many times paid with their lives for so doing. The field generals at that time felt somewhat more pessimistic than I did about bringing the war to a successful conclusion. Still, I recall General Depuy asking: "How long have we got to win this war?" I said: "Until next winter, and I will tell you why: the forthcoming general election will set up so much social and political turbulence over the war that no one up top will truly try to win it after that."

Westmoreland was then shooting for a troop basis of, as I recall, 527,000 men. He asked me to support the further buildup, and several of the field generals likewise pressed me. I said that I could not, that 400,000 was enough to serve the practical need, that if we went above that, it would result only in being torn down quickly, owing to pressures arising on the home front. I added that we should concentrate on making more effective use of the 400,000 already present. It was in the following December, 1967, that Westmoreland, with President Thieu, started the crash rebuilding of the ARVN, so that we could begin soon to displace troops to the United States, though I note in passing that Clark Clifford and other individuals have tried to take credit for these programs.

Two months later, in February 1968, came the Tet Holiday Battle of the Cities followed by the prolonged siege of Khe Sanh. These were described by our press and our people as massive and muddled defeats for our arms, and even accepted as such by the President and his counselors. They were in fact lunges of desperation and terrible setbacks for the forces of the enemy and served to bolster the confidence of the ARVN.

Then in May, Westmoreland invited me to come over again on orders to make an overall estimate of the situation for the benefit of all concerned. It was a time of high battle in the North; we were losing about 400 men killed in action per week and most of these combat deaths were occurring in the four northern provinces. There was intense infiltration by packets of NVA replacements out of the DMZ down the coastal plain and through the piedmont, and some of our commanders were straining too hard to intercept and destroy them, doing the hunting with company fronts, which offered just so many excessively broad targets. It was tactically the wrong thing.

Even so, having reported to Westmoreland on the way in, I did my summing up to General Abrams on the way out. The command had just changed. I said I was certain that the Army of North Vietnam was all but washed up. The old combat cleverness was gone; there was no longer effective deception. Combat fields were left littered with weapons and dead bodies. Camouflage was not even attempted. These signs indicated that the enemy had to be just about scraping the bottom of the barrel. Furthermore, we were picking up wounded replacements of the NVA in the Delta who were under fifteen years of age. They had been conscripted.

The offensive in the North, I said, would peter out within the next ten days. Thereafter, I would not expect the NVA to be able to mount a main offensive in South Vietnam for at least two years. I added that, without exception, I had found General Abrams' field commanders highly optimistic, whereas one year before I had found them pessimistic.

On my return home Mr. Nixon sent for me and we met on July 19 in New York. I reiterated the same general conclusions about doing it with truer economy of force: "Hanoi will be compelled to sue for truce terms in earnest by next spring. But I emphasize above all continued and systematized bombing of the North." Mr. Nixon replied: "I can hardly believe what you tell me. Only yesterday I talked with the President and the Secretary of State and all they said was hung with crepe. They see no light ahead whatever." I told him that I disagreed with that view absolutely.

Then just prior to election, as you recall, Mr. Johnson suspended bombing of the North, and that made it, as the saying goes, a whole new ball game. Following the election, I wrote President Nixon at some length. The sense of what I said was this: Your ambassador in Paris will get nowhere at the truce table. He will be treated with the same contempt as Mr. Johnson's. The one chance is to utter an ultimatum on truce talks. Give them ten days to get down to serious negotiating, under the threat of resumption of full-scale operations, which would imply bombing of the North. To make the move palatable to the American people, you can at the same time announce that you will bring back 100,000 troops this year.

We can afford to pare forces that much. Rather than a risk, it will be a saving. The political realities will compel you to start withdrawal this year in any case.

And that about rounds out what I believe should be put to you from my own narrow, personal view. The mournful title of Max Hoffman's book, *The War of Lost Opportunity,* applies to this one. Called by many a war that we should not have fought, history may give that judgment on it. Who truly knows? But once the commitment was made, the war need not have been muddled through to indecisive and nationally convulsive conclusions in a manner wholly unworthy of a great power. Termed an immoral war by some, the very title implies that there can be such a thing as a "moral war," and in that, as an infantryman, at least slightly civilized, I will never, never believe.

Chapter 4

A Military War of Attribution

General André Beaufre defines strategy as "the art of the dialectic of two opposing wills using force to resolve their dispute." At the center of the dispute over America's role in Vietnam was the question of strategy. At the level of grand strategy, the United States entered the war to honor the principle of containment and out of competition with the Communist world. The broad political objectives were a stable world order, the preservation of American power, and the projection of such American interests as free political and economic systems. An analysis of the war must look both at grand strategy and at the military strategy designed to support it; this chapter treats military strategy.

American military strategy in Vietnam was variously labeled a strategy of attrition, or one of gradualism, or as a "no win" strategy, depending on the viewpoint of the critic placing the label. General William C. Westmoreland more than any is associated with the strategy of attrition and the concomitant battlefield tactics of "search and destroy." The war in many ways became, in the popular imagery, Westmoreland's war, for which he was both praised and damned. His own analysis composes this chapter.

A Military War of Attrition

General William C. Westmoreland

In response to changes in national policy, there were basically six strategies adopted between 1954 and 1969. The first involved bolstering the South Vietnamese by sending advisers and logistical and economic support in the hope that this could stop and reverse the subversive efforts of the Communists within South Vietnam. The second was an overall strategy of gradually escalating pressure against North Vietnam in the hope of convincing the North to halt its support of the insurgency in the South. This was essentially a strategy based on bombing. The third was a base-security strategy, which was an adjunct of the decision to bomb North Vietnam but which can be called a strategy in that it represented the first commitment of American ground troops to the fighting, albeit in a defensive role. The fourth was an enclave strategy, which assumed protection by American troops of five important areas of South Vietnam but still left most of the fighting to the South Vietnamese. The fifth involved a gradual buildup of forces in the South for purposes of putting maximum pressure on the Communist structure and forces in the South, emphasizing pacification and nation building, expanding control by the South Vietnamese Government over the population, and, at the same time, escalating pressure on the North with air and naval power. The political objective was to bring the enemy to the conference table. The final strategy comprised maximum expansion of the Vietnamese armed forces, increased efforts to pacify all of South Vietnam and to build a viable nation, coupled with gradual withdrawal with or without negotiations.

The decision to launch an air campaign of rising intensity against the North was made against a background of anguished concern over the threat of South Vietnam's imminent collapse. Although the basic objective was to try to convince the North to end its support of the insurgency, another objective was to bolster the morale and strengthen the resolve of the South Vietnamese, who had long been absorbing punishment while the supporters of the insurgency enjoyed impunity.

Two basic considerations lay behind the gradual escalation of the campaign. First, a modest bombing effort might be enough to convince the North of American resolve and, if negotiations developed, might compensate for some of the leverage the Viet Cong victories gave the other side. Secondly, the fear of Chinese Communist intervention was always of immense concern to American officials. Since the Chinese had responded to earlier bombings in muted tones, policy makers in Washington deduced that a gradually increasing campaign might ruffle the Chinese less than would a sudden massive onslaught. The Administration was faced with a dilemma—mobilizing too much support for the war might produce "war fever" and cause the American people to look upon the war as a "great crusade." Nevertheless, I believe a better job could have been done in explaining the nature of our objectives to the American people and the historical background of our involvement.

The strategy of gradually escalating pressure was a new concept; the Joint Chiefs of Staff disagreed with it. It was not, to them, an early "win" policy. Most military men are accustomed to thinking in terms of terminating a war in the shortest practical time and at least cost, following a decision to fight. It is perhaps unnecessary to make the point that there is a relationship between the length of a war and its cost.

By early April 1965, it had become apparent that the new strategy, even with its adjunct of base security, was having no visible effect on the will of the North Vietnamese to continue to support the insurgency. As someone has put it, the United States was signaling Hanoi with a new alphabet that Hanoi could not or would not read. The realization that the air war alone was not doing the job—or at least would take a long time to do it—led to a belief that some new step had to be taken directly against the insurgency in the South. So long as the Viet Cong—reinforced at that point by North Vietnamese troops—continued to win, the leaders in the North, in expectation of ultimate victory, probably would endure the punishment the limited bombing campaign was inflicting.

Taking a new step against the Viet Cong clearly meant actively involving American troops, yet President Johnson and most of his advisers still shied from such a fateful step. Once committed, planes and ships could be readily withdrawn; not so with ground troops. Furthermore, how well would American troops with their sophisticated equipment perform in an Asian insurgency environment? Better to devise some kind of strategy that stopped short of unrestricted commitment, one that would further signal American resolve yet at the same time provide escape valves.

That was the thinking behind the enclave strategy whereby American troops were to take full responsibility for defense of five coastal enclaves and to be prepared to go to the rescue of South Vietnamese forces within fifty miles of the enclaves. Yet, as I pointed out at the time, it put American troops in the unfortunate position of defending static defensive positions with their backs to the sea—in effect, holding five embattled beachheads. It also left the decision of ultimate success or failure in the hands of South Vietnamese troops whose demonstrated inability to defeat the Viet Cong was the reason for committing American troops.

In the face of continuing crisis, my view, and that of the Joint Chiefs of Staff, prevailed. President Johnson's decision of July 1965 carried the United States across the threshold in Vietnam. Before 1965 ended, the United States was to have 184,000 military personnel in Vietnam, including an Army air-mobile division and a Marine division.

Based on my personal experience with the problems on the ground in South Vietnam—political and military—and considering my perception of the aims of the enemy, I anticipated in 1965 that this nation was becoming involved in a protracted war of attrition in which our national will would be sorely tried. As a student of the history of war, and remembering the relatively recent Korean War experience, I was aware of the likelihood that a limited war, fought with limited means for limited objectives, would put special strain on the body politic of a system of government such as ours.

It was in such a context that I recommended continuation of the one-year tour that had been set for advisers. It was my belief that lengthy involuntary tours would more likely bring about a hue and cry to "bring the boys home" than a tour in which the "boys would come home" after one year unless they volunteered to stay longer. Also, in anticipation of a long war, it seemed to me that the burden of service should be shared by a cross section of American youth. I did not anticipate that numbers of our young men would be allowed by national policy to defer service by going to a college campus.

I hoped, perhaps with folly, that an emerging sense of South Vietnamese nationalism and a revitalized national will in South Vietnam—manifested in a viable government and a proficient fighting force—would in the long run compensate for the inevitable waning of public support in the United States for a difficult war.

The campaign of escalating pressure through bombing North Vietnam continued in the hope that ground and air action together would prompt Hanoi to negotiate. Appropriate pauses were to be made in the air war to signal American intent and to allow time for a North Vietnamese response. One reason they could not read our signal was that the message was garbled by the loud and emotional voices of dissent on the domestic scene and sensational news reporting by the mass media.

As we know today, not until late spring of 1968 did the leadership in Hanoi agree to negotiate, and then nothing was accomplished, except the size and shape of the negotiating table, since we weakened our signal and our hand by de-escalating. But when President Nixon decided to use our available military power in a manner that truly hurt North Vietnam, negotiations began to move in a substantive way.

Behind my request for unrestricted use of American troops within South Vietnam was my belief that without these troops the South Vietnamese forces would flounder, with the result that the war would be prolonged. If the United States intended to make good its commitment in a politically acceptable time frame, that was the price that would have to be paid. The first large contingent, I believed, would be enough to halt the swift disintegration of South Vietnamese forces, blunt the main thrust of the Viet Cong offensive, and permit the construction of an American logistical base. Those objectives achieved, additional American troops, supplemented by contributions from other countries, would enable me to seize the initiative. In a third phase, the enemy would be worn down to the point where the South Vietnamese—with their manpower mobilized and their forces retrained and re-equipped—could gradually take over.

Contrary to what was written in *The Pentagon Papers* and reprinted in the press, I made no prediction in 1965 as to when victory would be achieved. Parenthetically, let me say that I did make a prediction during the question period following a speech to the National Press Club in November 1967. American withdrawals, I estimated, might begin in mid or late 1969. Withdrawals actually began in August 1969.

An understanding of the American ground strategy in Vietnam begins with an understanding of the nature of the war the enemy waged, for that always affects the nature of the riposte. The Communists in Vietnam waged a classic revolutionary war. Having created an infrastructure of hard-core political cadre and local part-time guerrillas, the Viet Cong set out to seize control of the hamlets and villages, thereby gaining dominance over a major portion of the population and a stranglehold on the towns and cities.

By the time the first American ground troops arrived, such success had the Viet Cong achieved that they had entered the third and final step of revolutionary warfare: attacks by large units of full-time soldiers—known as main forces—to destroy the Government's troops and eliminate all vestiges of Government control. Regular North Vietnamese units supplemented that effort.

As I saw the three-phase war, American combat troops were to be used at first to protect the developing logistical bases, although some might have to be committed from time to time as a fire brigade to counter large-scale enemy thrusts.

In the second phase, while gaining the initiative, the troops were to penetrate the enemy's base camps or sanctuaries. Located for the most part in remote regions, and equipped with underground shelters often connected by labyrinthian tunnels, the sanctuaries had for many years been inviolate. So long as the Communists were free to emerge from those hideouts to terrorize the population, recruit or impress conscripts, and attack Government security forces, then to retire with impunity back into the sanctuaries, there was little hope of defeating the insurgency. Invading the sanctuaries might also bring the elusive enemy to battle.

The third and final phase would consist of mopping up the last of the main forces and the local guerrillas or pushing them across the border, where we would try to contain them. All the while I was pressing for authority to pursue across the borders to destroy the enemy's logistics and disrupt their organization. We were constantly planning to capitalize on any lifting of constraints.

I anticipated that in the first two phases the job of fighting the enemy's main forces in the remote regions would fall primarily to the Americans, who were more mobile and had greater firepower. That would free most of the South Vietnamese troops to operate against the local guerrillas within the hamlets and villages in support of pacification. The South Vietnamese clearly were better suited to operate among their own people, and the arrangement would have the additional advantage of keeping many of the American troops away from a population noted for its xenophobia.

Even as the American troop buildup began in earnest in the summer of 1965, a crisis developed in South Vietnam's central provinces. Three North Vietnamese regiments massed in the wooded Central Highlands. Although that region is sparsely populated, its roads serve as a gateway to the crucial provinces around Saigon and across the narrow waist of the country into the rice-rich central coastal provinces. The North Vietnamese appeared to have two objectives: First, to push eastward to the sea to link with Viet Cong units operating in the coastal provinces, thereby to cut South Vietnam in two and isolate the northern provinces. Second, to gain undisputed control of a major segment of South Vietnam—albeit a sparsely populated segment—and there proclaim a National Liberation Front government actually functioning and controlling a portion of the South.

Hardly had America's first air-mobile division reached Vietnam in early fall when I deemed it necessary to commit one of its brigades to counter the threat in the Central Highlands. In what became known as the battle of the Ia Drang Valley, the first major engagement between American and North Vietnamese troops, the brigade drove the enemy regiments into sanctuaries across the border in Cambodia, where they could rehabilitate themselves with impunity. A similar commitment of a Marine division in two of the northern provinces provided a temporary check on the movement of two North Vietnamese divisions across the Demilitarized Zone separating the two Vietnams.

Those threats having been contained but in no sense eliminated, American forces in 1966 and 1967 fought to seize the initiative by entering the enemy's sanctuaries. These included such long-established base camps as War Zone C, northwest of Saigon; the "Iron Triangle" north of the capital; War Zone D to the northeast; and such others as the Plain of Reeds, the Rung Sat mangrove swamp, and the U Minh Forest.

Meanwhile, the Marines fought North Vietnamese units crossing the Demilitarized Zone or entering the northern provinces by way of the Ho Chi Minh Trail complex in neighboring Laos. This was the so-called "big-unit war" that garnered the headlines even though it was only a portion of the whole. At the same time, almost all the South Vietnamese forces and some American units were engaged in the populated regions, eliminating local guerrillas, opening up roads, driving main force units into the sanctuaries, protecting the rice harvest.

I had a penchant for acronyms and catch phrases, which from experience I had learned were helpful as a teaching aid with troops. Indeed, without such expressions, the troops would find words of their own that sometimes distorted the real intent. My fear boomeranged—for I was not sufficiently perceptive to anticipate the connotation that would be given to our poorly chosen phrase. I am referring, of course, to "search and destroy," an operation to find the enemy and to eliminate his base camps and logistic installations. As you know, the media and hence the public gradually came to apply the term to the overall U.S. ground strategy in Vietnam, when, in reality, it was but a tactic.

Indeed, the goals established by the February 1966 Honolulu Conference could not be achieved without such tactics. It was nothing new, but the time-tested military formula of reconnaissance in force: seek the enemy, find him, and then apply the necessary force either to destroy him or to drive him from the field. In the process, every effort was made to eliminate his base camps and logistic installations lest they serve him again in the future. The two companion operations were "clearing operations" and "securing operations," both of which were essential to pacification of the populated areas.

Given the elusiveness of the enemy in Vietnam and the jungle-like nature of much of the countryside, some of the "search and destroy" operations failed to find the enemy. Because neither the Americans nor the South Vietnamese possessed overwhelming numbers, the cordons erected when the enemy was found were often sieve-like, and many of the enemy escaped. Nor was it possible to occupy the sanctuaries or other pieces of terrain permanently, so that foray after foray had to be launched. Meanwhile, the enemy made surprise forays against us. To an impatient American public and the news media, these developments became frustrating. The public was also confused because it was impossible to follow the war by simple lines on a map as in other wars.

So, too, the term "search and destroy" fed a general American abhorrence for the destruction that warfare inevitably produces. A few graphic newspaper photographs and TV shots of American troops setting fire to thatched-roof huts were enough to convince many that "search and destroy" operations were laying waste to civilian property and the land. Yet, in reality, the operations were directed primarily against military installations—bunkers, tunnels, rice and ammunition caches, and training camps. There were exceptions, as at the village of Ben Suc in the Iron Triangle. So fortified was Ben Suc with bunkers and underground hideouts, so long had it been a Viet Cong base, so closely encircled was it by jungle, so sympathetic were the people to the Viet Cong, and so difficult was it to take the fight to the enemy without jeopardizing the noncombatant inhabitants, that there appeared to be little alternative to evacuating the population and razing the village. This evacuation was portrayed as an act of inhumanity, whereas in fact it—the evacuation—was just the reverse. There was no alternative to "search and destroy" type operations, except, of course, a different name for them. One can point to few cases, if any, in military history where victory was achieved by passive defense.

That the terrain of the remote regions was inhospitable and of the enemy's choosing goes without saying, but the helicopter and American firepower more than balanced the equation. The enemy's massing in the remote regions in a conscious effort to draw American troops away from the population was a blade with two edges. His emergence from hiding afforded an opportunity to bring to battle a foe for whom elusiveness was the name of the game. It was also preferable to engage the enemy where American firepower might be brought to bear without inflicting hurt upon the population. That factor was a primary consideration in making a stand at Khe Sanh.

It was, in essence, a war of attrition. Since the battles of the Somme and Verdun, that has been a strategy in disrepute, one that to many appeared particularly unsuited for a war in Asia with Asia's legendary hordes of manpower. Yet if one carefully re-examines the strategy of attrition in World War I, one must admit that, for all the horrendous cost, it eventually worked. Furthermore, the war in Vietnam was not against Asian hordes but instead against an enemy with relatively limited manpower. As the South Vietnamese Government's control embraced more and more of the countryside, the Viet Cong had to depend upon the North Vietnamese to make good their losses; furthermore, manpower resources were opened up for use by the Saigon regime. Although the North Vietnamese might constantly rebuild their units, they did so each time with manpower less adequately trained. Meanwhile, the continuing battle bought time to build up South Vietnamese forces and enable the Government to solidify its position in the countryside.

The losses that could be inflicted were sharply restricted by the enemy's ability to retire into additional sanctuaries in Laos and Cambodia that, for political reasons, neither Americans nor South Vietnamese were permitted to strike, except by token elements on a covert basis. Even before the major U.S. commitment in Vietnam in 1965, military leaders were conscious of this problem. One of the earliest proposals for committing American troops was based on erecting a defensive line from the Gulf of Tonkin across South Vietnam and Laos to the Mekong River alongside Thailand. Later, multiple plans were drafted to enter Laos and cut the Ho Chi Minh Trail or to destroy the sanctuaries inside the Cambodian frontier. Yet, in all cases, authority was denied by senior officials in Washington. Only in 1970, after a government friendly to the United States emerged in Cambodia, was approval granted, and even then with sharp restrictions on time and depth of penetration.

The U.S. strategy in Vietnam admittedly was geared to a lengthy timetable, even assuming no victory in the classic sense but instead an American involvement until such time as the situation would permit the South Vietnamese to take over. The building of an adequate logistical apparatus in an underdeveloped country in itself took time, and however well trained American troops were when they arrived, the final lessons must always be learned on the battlefield itself. The very essence of counterinsurgency is innovation and ingenuity, and those are ingredients that must be blended in more than one test tube before they emerge as proven antidotes.

Consider, for example, strikes by giant B-52 bombers of the Strategic Air Command against enemy base camps and troop concentrations. Those were deemed from the first to be effective, but only after long months of experiment, of developing improved intelligence information, and of devising methods to divert the planes to targets of opportunity. Only then did the B-52s become the weapon most dreaded by the enemy. The initially denied use of a riot-control chemical—CS—proved effective in driving the Viet Cong from tunnels or villages without permanent casualties among civilians. After considerable experimentation, methods were devised for using chemical defoliants to expose the enemy's jungle paths and his ambush sites along highways and waterways. Squadrons of "Rome plows"—a bulldozer with a prong at one end of the blade for felling big trees—neutralized jungle hideouts.

Special schools graduated men trained in long-range patrolling to find the enemy in the jungle and call down artillery and air strikes, reducing the need for the use of larger contingents for the purpose. World War II's obsolescent C-47 propeller-driven transport plane became a weapons platform capable of using flares to turn the night into day and of striking the enemy with 6,000 rounds a minute from each of three "miniguns." "Spooky," some troops called it; others named it "Puff, the Magic Dragon." In Road Runner operations, armored vehicles "reconnoitered" likely ambush sites with pre-emptive fire. Scout and sentry dogs sniffed out the enemy. Enemy defectors served as guides. Electronic sensors reported on enemy movements. A Riverine Force not unlike those employed on American rivers during the Civil War patrolled the inland waterways. Five-man teams lived with and trained South Vietnamese paramilitary forces. U.S. and South Vietnamese naval patrols sealed the long coastline against enemy supply trawlers.

By late 1967 progress in both the military and the pacification field was plainly apparent. Optimistic statements by U.S. officials in Saigon and Washington were common, as reflected in my speech before the National Press Club in November 1967. That there was a certain element of caution

in the pronouncements went unnoticed by most of the public. At the Press
Club, for example, I put it this way: "I am absolutely certain that whereas
in 1965 the enemy was winning, today he is certainly losing."

It was in this optimistic atmosphere that the enemy's 1968 Tet offensive
suddenly exploded on the scene. How could such a thing happen in a matter
of a few months after I had said that the enemy was losing? Even if I had
not said specifically that the United States was winning, did my words not
mean the same thing? Many people, shocked by the sudden onslaught and
by entertaining death and destruction in their living rooms every evening
with the network news, were skeptical of my and President Johnson's assurances that, even though the enemy achieved some temporary psychological
advantage, he was incurring a military defeat. That almost everywhere
except on the outskirts of Saigon and in Hué the fighting was over in two
or three days went unnoticed. Memories are short, and few recalled that
Ludendorff's troops storming across the Chemin des Dames in the spring
of 1918 and Rundstedt's divisions emerging out of the mists of the Ardennes
in the winter of 1944 were moves of desperation. When *The New York
Times* in the aftermath of Tet printed the revelation that I had asked for
206,000 more troops, it produced a seismic shock of the proportions of a
Presidential primary in New Hampshire.

The passage of time has revealed that the 206,000 troop request was
misinterpreted. Based on my own military judgment and in response to a
requirement from my chain of command, I developed a plan as a backup
for the unexpected setback or a change in policy that would call up
reserves and permit an aggressive strategy. Time has also shown that the
enemy did, indeed, incur a major military defeat in the Tet offensive. Many
of the 40,000 or so dead that the enemy lost were guerrillas or political
cadre, both much more difficult to replace than North Vietnamese regulars. South Vietnamese troops and the National Police generally performed creditably, and the reaction of the people to the violence of the
enemy's actions created an atmosphere in which the Government at last
felt strong enough to institute a general mobilization. Furthermore, damage to the pacification program in the countryside proved to be much less
than originally calculated, so that in mid-1968 a much accelerated paci-

fication program could be started. The enemy's losses caused him to break down into small units in many areas, which permitted us to do the same. The absence of a major threat from the enemy permitted us to concentrate major efforts to training and re-equipping the South Vietnamese forces. Time has also shown that the American defense of Khe Sanh, which also shocked a segment of the press and the public, was no Dien Bien Phu, but a major defeat of the enemy with little damage to civilians or property.

Whether the United States could have "won" in Vietnam—if we can use that term in relation to such a war—rested in the long run in the hands of the South Vietnamese. Yet it should be remembered that the original American goal was to preserve South Vietnam until such time as the South Vietnamese could do the job themselves. The final step took place. The Vietnam War permitted no battlefield victory in the classic sense, but an objective was established and its accomplishment spells success.

If not the strategy the United States followed in Vietnam, then what alternatives? Few have been suggested. One of the first was publicly advanced by Lieutenant General James M. Gavin in February 1966 in an article in *Harper's* magazine. General Gavin's plan was, in effect, the enclave strategy which authorities in Washington earlier had rejected, an attempt to demonstrate American resolve while minimizing American commitment.

In 1969, a former Undersecretary of the Air Force, Townsend Hoopes, in his book *The Limits of Intervention,* called for an end of what he termed "hyper-aggressive search and destroy operations." Asserting that no military victory was possible in Vietnam, he advanced a "modified enclave strategy" involving what he called "seize and hold" operations in the populated areas. That, plus a halt in the bombing of North Vietnam, he wrote, would lead the enemy to negotiate. In view of the enemy's negotiating record after General Gavin and Mr. Hoopes advanced their theories, whether either would have been successful is problematical.

Another critic, Sir Robert Thompson, also writing in 1969, appeared to base his criticism on his long—and successful—experience with the insurgency in Malaya. Sir Robert at the time believed that American preoccupation with the enemy's big units could produce no more than a stalemate. "In a People's Revolutionary War," he noted, "if you are not winning, you are losing, because the enemy can always sit out a stalemate without making any concessions." Sir Robert deemed that the proper strategy was first to create an intelligence apparatus capable of identifying the Viet Cong political infrastructure, then to concentrate the military effort, not against the big units, but against the irregulars who provided the big units their sustenance. Sir Robert's analysis of where the big units were getting their supplies was incomplete and oversimplified. In fairness to Sir Robert, it should be noted that a year after writing his book, he had modified his views to the extent that he deemed the United States had achieved "a winning position in the sense of obtaining a just peace . . . and of maintaining an independent, non-Communist South Vietnam . . . but we are not yet through."

There were, of course, two basic differences between Malaya and Vietnam. In Malaya, the bulk of the insurgents were ethnic Chinese and thus were identifiable within the population. That was not the case in Vietnam. Also, the Malayan insurgency there was no immunity for the insurgents in sanctuaries outside the country. Given the sanctuaries in Laos, Cambodia, and North Vietnam, and given North Vietnamese support, eliminating the local guerrillas would not by itself have eliminated the insurgency. It was not until Tet occurred that Sir Robert truly understood the magnitude and potential of the enemy's main forces.

We must judge past policy decisions not in the light of what we know today but in the context of the time in which the decisions were made. With the experience of a limited yet conventional war in Korea recently at hand and with the insurgent Viet Minh apparently moved North as a consequence of the Geneva accords, American advisers in the 1950s saw the main threat to South Vietnam not from within but from the North Vietnamese Army. In organizing and training the South Vietnamese forces, the Americans thus created conventional military forces much in their own image. The job of dealing with insurgency if it developed was left primarily to paramilitary forces which the U.S. conceived as necessary and supported, but when the event occurred, they were inadequate for the assignment.

From a military standpoint, it clearly would have been better to have moved much earlier against the enemy's sanctuaries in Laos and Cambodia and possibly even in the southern reaches of North Vietnam. Yet that is speaking without consideration for the political consequences. Further, if the military could have employed air and naval power in accordance with its best judgment, our strategy could have been accelerated. However, the same caution may not have been exercised and the dangers of provoking China to get more deeply involved could have been enhanced.

The Vietnam conflict was an undeclared and limited war, with a limited objective, fought with limited means against an unorthodox enemy, and with limited public support. The longest war in our history, it was the most reported and the most visible to the public—but the least understood. It was more than a military confrontation; ideological, economic, psychological, political, and nation-building problems were involved. Our national involvement in Southeast Asia became an emotional public controversy and hence a political issue. This new and traumatic experience by our nation should provide lessons for our people, our leadership, the news media, and our soldiers.

Chapter 5

The Strategy of Attrition

Colonel Donaldson D. Frizzell

Colonel Frizzell was the U.S. Air Force Research Associate at the Fletcher School of Law and Diplomacy in 1973–74 and is now the Chief of Strategic Concept Studies at the Air War College, Maxwell Air Force Base, Alabama.

Clausewitzian theory teaches that "war is designed to further political objectives and must be governed from the first to the last by those objectives."[1] Something obviously went wrong in the Vietnamese application; military force failed to yield satisfactory results as a political instrument. America adopted a traditional military strategy based on territorial control and attrition of the enemy. This strategy proved to be doubly inadequate. In guerrilla warfare, the strategic objective is control of the people, not control of territory. Moreover, success in a battle of attrition depends on the ability to inflict unacceptable losses on the enemy.[1a] The problem in Vietnam lay in finding a satisfactory definition of "unacceptable losses," the view from Hanoi and the view from Washington on "unacceptable losses" being decidedly different.

The United States approached the war in Southeast Asia with strictly limited political objectives. Denying all claims for territorial or political ambitions, the United States did not seek the military defeat of the North Vietnamese. American involvement was designed to preserve the integrity of an "independent non-Communist South Vietnam." The conflict in Southeast Asia was seen largely in terms of Communist aggression and the

---

[1] Bernard Brodie, *Strategy in the Missile Age* (Princeton, N.J.: Princeton University Press, 1959), p. 97.

[1a] Henry A. Kissinger, The Viet Nam Negotiations." *Foreign Affairs,* Vol. 47, No. 2 (January 1969), p. 212.

domino theory—hence as part of a continuing struggle with the Communists that had continued since shortly after World War II.

As the United States was soon to discover, however, the classic Cold War model did not adequately explain or fit the Vietnamese Communists nor did it adequately describe the nature of the movement that threatened the Government in Saigon. The Vietnamese Communist was correctly or incorrectly perceived to be as much a nationalist as a Communist and was an anticolonialist of considerable reputation also.

The irony was that the limited objectives of the United States were expressed in terms of an enemy too narrowly defined. The United States articulated its aims in terms of the containment of international Communism, while in reality it was taking on a variety of Vietnamese nationalism as well. The fact that the Vietnamese situation had many of the aspects of a civil war was overridden by broader strategic concerns related more to the Cold War strategy than to the reality of Vietnam. The error was not in looking upon Vietnam as a part of a global consideration, but in failing to see the overriding importance of local factors. Operating on this foundation of sand, our nation-building and military efforts were condemned to irrelevance and frustration. Our perception of the enemy was oversimplified; we underestimated the skills and determination of the Viet Cong and their North Vietnamese allies. And we were too sanguine about the ability of the South Vietnamese to build a stable and viable government capable of running the country effectively. There were dimensions of the Vietnamese problem with which our planning had not reckoned.

That the U.S. commitment was limited is further demonstrated by the fact that we did not seriously contemplate a declaration of war. Those were the days of "guns and butter" politics: the war of attrition in Southeast Asia and the Great Society at home. And "we were paying the bills out of a growing gross national product."[2] A superpower was engaged in a limited intervention to help a client state preserve its political and social integrity against a Communist insurgent movement.

On the other hand, the Viet Cong (and its North Vietnamese sponsor)

[2] Maxwell D. Taylor, *Responsibility and Response* (New York: Harper & Row, 1967), p. 37.

was fighting for what they regarded as their homeland. It was, further, an all-out struggle, a protracted struggle that might go on for years. In modern history, they had fought the Japanese and the French, achieving a brilliant victory at Dien Bien Phu in 1954. Now they were equally determined to defeat the Americans.

It should be recognized that the Viet Cong used a form of warfare very different from the classic warfare of front lines and maneuvering forces. It was a form of warfare called "People's Revolutionary War," not like the positional warfare for which the United States was best prepared. It was a type of warfare that used limited military means but was all-out in its political dimensions.

The United States was fighting in a strange land and at a distance of some 10,000 miles from our own shores. We were fighting against an enemy and in a political situation that we did not fully understand. Our survival as a nation was not an issue. On the domestic scene there was no cutback of domestic programs; there was a great reluctance to raise taxes; a decision against mobilization of the reserve forces was made; there were none of the usual belt-tightening policies associated with war mobilization. In the fighting theater we adopted a limited strategy and a stringent set of political constraints on the use of our military forces.

As previously noted, the theory was that inflicting "unacceptable losses" upon the guerrilla and main-force units would lead to an American victory. This theory suffered from a problem of definition. What are "unacceptable losses"? The United States greatly underestimated the willingness of the other side to take terrible punishment and come back for more. Time after time the U.S. and South Vietnamese forces inflicted heavy casualties upon the VC/NVA forces. The Communists suffered casualties that decimated their battalions and brigades, literally knocked them out of combat for months. There were hundreds of these battles fought and hundreds of defeats inflicted.

One of the classics involved the U.S. Marine defense of Khe Sanh in 1968. The devastation that took place around the small garrison at Khe Sanh was appalling by any standards. Two North Vietnamese divisions participated in the siege; their beginning strength was estimated at about

20,000 men. Before the two-month siege was ended, they had lost an estimated 12,000 men, while the Marines suffered 200 killed. Theodore Draper summarized the failure of "great-power thinking" to understand Hanoi's criteria for measuring losses:

> We seem to assume that a small power cannot or will not take as much punishment as a large power. But this is precisely where great-power thinking goes wrong. Great powers tend to think of "limited wars" in terms of themselves. They think of the "limit" as what it would be, in relative terms, if they were taking the punishment or in relation to the total force they are capable of using.[3]

Thus the stage was set for our frustration. U.S. forces could win a battle like Khe Sanh in a very convincing way, but could not translate the success into any kind of political advantage. Hanoi refused to change its behavior on the battleground and refused to negotiate seriously in Paris. The theory of unacceptable losses in a war of attrition did not seem to be productive in political terms. Robert Komer, who headed the pacification program after many years' experience in national security affairs, comments.

Ambassador Robert Komer:

We picked the wrong strategy. Our search-and-destroy strategy was the natural response of a hugely superior force, but it could not bring the enemy to decisive battle. This strategy of attrition failed because the enemy could control his own losses. He did it in two ways: first, by evading battle—we could always defeat the Viet Cong if we could bring him to fight, but we could rarely bring him to fight unless he wanted to—and second, he could always retreat to sanctuary and use sanctuary as his logistic base.

The only times that attrition ever worked were when the enemy attacked us, not when we attacked him. Then, of course, it became a great

---

[3] Richard M. Pfeffer (ed.), *No More Vietnams?: The War and the Future of American Foreign Policy* (New York: Harper & Row, 1968), p. 28.

killing machine. The major examples of that were his Tet-68 and follow-on offensives, and again in his Easter offensive of 1972. When the enemy attacked us we knew where he was. He was trying to kill us, so we were able to do rather well at defeating him. But most of the time he employed his classic guerrilla hit-and-run tactics even with conventional forces and we just were not able to cope with it. The enemy rarely stood and fought set-piece battles at which we would have excelled.

General Edward Lansdale:

Despite all intentions otherwise, the American period of the war became primarily one of attrition, with each side striving to exhaust its opponent. The Americans mostly had in mind giving the enemy such a bloody nose that he would quit fighting.

The war of attrition came about in subtle ways from the thinking on both sides. The thinking was not very noble. The enemy was enamored of the memory of defeating the French at Dien Bien Phu and consistently attempted similar stunning victories over the Americans—only to move masses of men onto what turned out to be killing grounds, where they were destroyed. The Americans became stuck with a bookkeeper's mentality, giving undue significance to "body count." This concept was introduced into the war by a U.S. Secretary of Defense who desired more accurate measurement of military progress and turned to electronic computers for answers—feeding in "body count" and other arithmetical factors into computer banks. (Tons of arithmetical reports were sent from Vietnam to Washington during the war, their very profusion a constant influence on military leaders to upgrade the importance of "attriting" the enemy.)

As far as its effect on the will of the enemy, American leaders might well have paid more attention to a comment made by the enemy's number-one leader in the war, Vo Nguyen Giap. Giap once said: "Every minute, hundreds of thousands of people die all over the world. The life or death of a hundred, a thousand, or tens of thousands of human beings, even if they are our own compatriots, represents really very little."

The killing in the war was far from being one-sided. In addition to the casualties suffered by our troops and those of our allies, the enemy carried its war of attrition to the civilian population in perhaps the grimmest facet of the whole struggle. Civilians in South Vietnam were the object of liquidation by the enemy. Indeed, a number of the tactical movements of enemy troops units appear to have been made primarily for the purpose of giving the enemy control of an area long enough to seek out civilian residents who were named on enemy lists and to execute them.

Thousands upon thousands of civilians died through this form of premeditated murder. Many, of course, were local officials, including those elected to village and hamlet positions. Many others, though, were so individualistic that they had been as critical of the Government in Saigon as they had of the enemy. The enemy obviously intended to liquidate all potential "class enemies," meaning those who might influence others into disagreement with the dictates of the Politburo once it had won in South Vietnam.

In this liquidation, the enemy not only followed the precedent of similar liquidation in China and the Soviet Union, but also the past actions of General Giap in 1946, when he was left in charge of the government while Ho Chi Minh and others were absent in France. Giap used his police forces to liquidate hundreds of nationalist leaders and Trotskyites, significantly and cold-bloodedly even including friends on the lists.

It can be said that we looked upon attrition to weaken the enemy's military forces, while the enemy looked upon attrition to weaken the fabric of existing society in South Vietnam. Further evidence for this interpretation of the enemy's intention came in the Tet offensive of 1968. There were not only the massive liquidations of civilians in Hué and elsewhere, but also an attempt to degrade the religious structure of South Vietnam.

As enemy units penetrated into population centers, they headed for temples and churches, where they entrenched themselves for battle with our side. This action led to fierce combat, and the consequent destruction of a noted Buddhist center and of a Catholic cathedral, as well as of lesser religious centers. There were some failures by the enemy, such as being frustrated in an attempt to occupy the Cao Dai Holy See in Tay Ninh. But the enemy's intent was plain. Peculiarly enough, this enemy attempt to degrade religion in 1968 has been generally overlooked by American observers of the war, although General Westmoreland pointed it out at the time.

Dean Edmund Gullion:
With respect to the ground war, it has been argued that General Abrams changed the nature of the war dramatically when he took over for General Westmoreland in 1968. The American newspapers have characterized "search and destroy" as a brutal strong-arm strategy and saw General Abrams' strategy as more humane, more sensitive—one of defending the citizens on their land. My question is this: Was each not right in its own time? Or putting it another way: Was it possible, the way things had gone, to have started the Abrams strategy from the beginning?

Ambassador Komer:
I was there when General Abrams took over, and remained as his deputy. There was no change in strategy whatsoever. In fact, he said he didn't intend to make any changes unless he saw that some were necessary. The myth of a change in strategy is a figment of media imagination; it didn't really change till we began withdrawing.

Barry Zorthian:
I would endorse the concept that Westmoreland's tactics were proper for his time and that General Abrams' were appropriate for his.

I think you have to bear in mind the military situation that prevailed in late 1964 and early 1965, when the American forces were introduced. American forces came in because the Vietnamese forces had virtually collapsed. Through that long and dismal campaign of 1964, battalion forces disappeared; the police had virtually disappeared. While divisions existed on paper, Westmoreland faced a very real need for building a new Vietnamese Army. He was also faced with some very real restraints and restrictions on that effort. The M-16 was not given to the Vietnamese until almost 1968, partially as a result of a decision in Washington to limit our production. Other equipment was in fairly limited supply, and there were major problems in training and developing combat skills and leadership in the South Vietnamese Army. So Westmoreland had a choice between a collapse of the South Vietnamese and the use of U.S. combat forces. The North Vietnamese and the Viet Cong had virtually cut the country in half from Kontum through Binh Dinh Province. He either had to let the Western side go, which obviously was not acceptable to the United States, or use U.S. combat battalions. Initially, when he was criticized very heavily for using these forces, he was employing tactical air support and helicopter mobility to put out fires wherever and whenever he could. He had only a limited supply of U.S. troops.

I would remind you that American forces at that point came in primarily to defend U.S. installations. That was the initial rationale for American entry into the war—later it extended much further. In July 1965, the critical decision was made in favor of a large-scale U.S. involvement. At that time the Vietnamese Army was not ready—it wasn't really ready until almost 1968. It was a gradual thing, of course, and they kept taking on more and more responsibility. Where main-force units were not involved (as in the Delta, where there was only one American battalion stationed) it was primarily a Vietnamese effort.

Where there were main-force units involved, we had no choice but to use American troops. When General Abrams took over after the mobilization of the Vietnamese following Tet, he had the luxury, if you will, of undertaking a different type of war, and very wisely he did. But I think Westmoreland has been criticized quite unfairly at times—and I do not mean this as an absolute judgment that there weren't errors in his tactics—but unfairly at times for overuse of the American forces and for underdevelopment of the Vietnamese forces. The circumstances, it seems to me, just did not permit as much of that as we all would have liked.

Professor Francis West, of the Naval War College, is a Marine veteran of the War and was later special assistant to Secretary of Defense James Schlesinger. Here he describes American strategy as one of "grinding the enemy down."

Professor Francis West:
I would like to answer Dean Guillion's question about the strategy by asking what the strategy was that sent our ground forces there in the first place. We have talked a lot about what different aspects of it were, but I

have not heard anybody try to articulate what our ground-war fighting strategy was. I think you can begin in 1965 by acknowledging that the GVN was beaten, and then you put yourselves into General Westmoreland's place. You can ask what the dominant constraints were when he decided to get into the war. There were two and the military accepted both: first, the fact that the Communists had geographic sanctuaries and that we were going to fight the ground war only in South Vietnam, and second, the concept of gradualism. Having accepted those two things, having agreed with the political leaders to fight the war under those two constraints which they would now reject, the military really had four options. The first option was the classic one—destroying the political leadership of the other side along with its ground forces. But that was rejected because of the constraints. That left three options.

The first of these was to fight a counterforce war of attrition in the South. The second option was to take over and rebuild the South Vietnamese forces, as Robert Komer has described it. The third was to control the territory—that's really not controlling the population, but controlling the territory where the population is, and simultaneously hoping either that the South Vietnamese get better or that you grind down the opposition. I can't submit that either General Westmoreland or General Abrams made a definite decision among these three options.

It also became a very decentralized war. To understand how we fought the war, you literally have to look at each division, because each division commander was allowed, by both General Westmoreland and General Abrams, enormous latitude in what he chose to do. As a result, if one asked, "What did the division commanders do?" I think that one can understand their decision making being driven by two forces.

The first is what one can call "satisficing"; that is, there was no way that a *division* was going to *lose* in Vietnam and every division commander knew it. There was no way that the North Vietnamese could ever decisively beat the United States on the battlefield. Now this greatly affected the style of how we fought the war because we never had the pressure of having to worry about *losing*. For example, if you were a battalion commander, you really had a 30 to 50 percent chance of being relieved of command because you failed. If you were a division commander, however, you had less than a 5 percent chance of being relieved of command, given your resources.

The second thing that I think affected our decisions on a decentralized level was organizational incentives. General Keegan, the Air Force Chief of Intelligence, has referred to it as being concerned with the civilian management from the top and with a "Catch-22" reporting system. But I think we cannot excuse the services from concern about organizational health: that the Army and Marine Corps recognized that they were in competition, which would affect their structures after the war; that the Air Force and the Navy recognized that they had better generate sorties and make it look good if they wanted those air squadrons going after the war; and that the Air Force had to be very careful about how it handled the Army in terms of close air support. I think that there were a series of organizational incentives within the services which affected what we decided to do on the ground.

Add all that up, and ask, "What did we decide to do?" It really was a seesaw between the attrition strategy of counterforce on the one hand and trying to hold territory on the other hand. If you tried to resolve that by asking, "Where did we really allocate our resources?"—although there is evidence that indicates it varied markedly from division to division—it comes out about fifty-fifty overall. We tried to do counterforce attrition on the one hand and territorial control on the other.

If you look at the classic examples, you come up with some terrific myths. For instance, most people believe that the Marines were much stronger in pacification and territorial control than they were in fighting the war of attrition. In actuality, when you look at what the Marines really did, it turns out that they fought a harder pacification than the Army, but they also fought a harder counterforce war, measured in terms of the number of dead, etc. Although we shy away from it, we did decide to fight the war of attrition—that is how we fought that ground war, when it finally comes down to it.

If one asks what the difference is between what General Westmoreland did and what General Abrams did, I am not sure that anyone could really make the case of saying that a great difference existed. I think that another myth was perpetrated on the American public following the Tet offensive. Tet-68 occurred and we all drew a lesson—we had lost the war and we were going to get out. When did we get out of the war? Four years later. Four years later we had ended up spending more money after Tet-68 than before it, and having just as many casualties. This allowed General Abrams to do things that General Westmoreland could not do, because the public, at this point in the war, believed that the war was going to end. I think there is a great irony in terms of how the press reported that whole phenomenon. From the viewpoint of the military, perhaps we lost a great opportunity in 1968. In 1968, United States morale at home was totally shattered, but as Ambassador Komer pointed out in Vietnam at the time, if we had really gone out and fought that war in 1968, and had kept bombing, that war could conceivably have been quite different.

Some look at Khe Sanh as a symbol of how we fought that war, which is unfortunate. We were out there simply to kill North Vietnamese and do nothing else. We used our infantry as bait. We used technology to kill them. It is the exact opposite of what one would expect of our infantry. Marines love to tell the story about being surrounded and saying, "Good, the bastards are not going to get away this time." In Khe Sanh, the Marines were like a turtle, because even the military was affected by what had happened to us politically, and they really did not take advantage of the military situation.

I think that 1968 was a lost opportunity for military strategy, but if you look at the drift of the war over time in terms of how we used U.S. forces on the ground, I think it comes out to one thing—there was a steady war of attrition between us and anybody who got in our way. Ultimately the results of that were twofold. First, thanks to the great decision making of the North Vietnamese Communist Party, the destruction of the indigenous Viet Cong occurred—because the Viet Cong tried to stand up to us in battle. Secondly, we ground down the North Vietnamese to the degree that the South Vietnamese, who did improve, achieved a level of rough war-fighting parity. The U.S. strategy was, in the end, a strategy of continuous attrition. The hypothesis that General Westmoreland and General Abrams had two different strategies does not hold up if you look at the way U.S. infantry resources were allocated.

Ambassador Komer:
If you are talking about grinding the enemy down, then the fact remains that, in eight years of trying to grind down the enemy, from 1965 up through 1972 to the end, we were never able to inflict unacceptable losses on the enemy, losses sufficient to drive him from the field. We were never able to erode his will the way the attrition strategy in World War I finally sapped the Germans or as in certain aspects of World War II. I think we cannot, in drawing lessons, get too far away from what we did as opposed to what perhaps we should have done, which is also a legitimate area for inquiry.

Sir Robert Thompson:
You don't quite want to make the judgment that you never got them to a point where it was hurting. They, in fact, got themselves to that point. I think that by the end of the 1972 invasion they were *really* hurting as far as manpower was concerned in their forces inside South Vietnam. It was one of the reasons they had to negotiate: they were about to lose territory which they had gained, because they could not possibly have held it with what they had left. I saw stupid remarks in the papers like: "The crack NVA Seventh Division poised for an attack on Saigon." That division was down to 1,750 demoralized men who could not take a district town and did not. The North was in a position where it did not dare commit a division in that situation to any sort of an offensive battle, because they were getting close to the point of annihilation for some of their units. I do not say that was general right through the country, but I would just be a little bit careful about saying, "Look, we haven't attrited them." As a result of the 1972 invasion, which they initiated, and the B-52's around An Loc and Kontum and everywhere else, the casualties they took were enormous.

When we knew that the 1972 invasion was coming, I asked General Abrams what his estimate was of what Giap was prepared to spend in terms of lives. We both thought this out and the figure we came to was 60,000.

We had been involved in that war for a very long time and we were 100 percent off. Giap spent twice that much. But it was *his* spending and he brought the attrition on himself. At that point the attrition was getting very, very close to grave dangers for the North.

Throughout the colloquium and at the conference, there was general agreement that the U.S. strategy could fairly be characterized as mainly a strategy of attrition. As might be expected, however, there was considerable disagreement on the efficacy of such a strategy and on the degree to which it was successful. Thomas C. Thayer does not agree with those, including Sir Robert Thompson, who hold that the war of attrition was winnable. His critique of the attrition strategy is based primarily upon the 1965–69 period, however, and not on the later period when many of the objective factors had changed considerably.

We Could Not Win the War of Attrition We Tried to Fight

Thomas C. Thayer

The dominant US/GVN strategic thrust from mid-1965 through at least 1969 was to grind down the VC/NVA organized military forces by attrition. As General Westmoreland, commander of U.S. forces in Vietnam for much of the period, says elsewhere in these pages: "It was, in essence, a war of attrition." He also quotes what became the more or less standard formulation of the attrition objective: "Attrit, by year's end, Viet Cong and North Vietnamese forces at a rate as high as their capability to put men into the field." This was always stated as one of several goals, but, at least until late 1969, it was always considered the most important one.

But after several years the war was acknowledged to be a military stalemate. Why was this? Why did the attrition strategy fail? After all, on the face of it, the allies had all the military advantages. They outnumbered the VC/NVA forces by as much as six to one, and they had far superior mobility, firepower, and combat support. Yet the allied forces could not destroy the VC/NVA forces, despite their attrition strategy. Quite the contrary—the estimated VC/NVA force level at the end of 1972 was higher than in 1965. The forces were weaker, but intact.

It was becoming apparent as early as late 1966 that the U.S. military strategy of attrition was in trouble. The objective of "attriting" the VC/NVA forces at a rate equal to or greater than their ability to infiltrate and recruit new troops was not being achieved. This theme is evident in Secretary of Defense Robert McNamara's statements of November 17, 1966, in his draft memorandum for the President: ". . . the data suggest that we have no prospects of attriting the enemy force at a rate equal to or greater than his capability to infiltrate and recruit, and this will be true at either the 470,000 U.S. personnel level or 570,000."[4]

The VC/NVA forces survived because North Vietnam had enough manpower to rebuild the VC/NVA units after each offensive. Furthermore, the VC/NVA were able to control their casualty rates to a great extent, by controlling the number, size, and intensity of combat engagements, and could therefore limit their losses to what they could afford.

By the middle of 1967 it was clear that the availability of North Vietnamese manpower and the willingness to send it South would prevent the allies from winning the war of attrition. After more than two years of American troop involvement, the number of NVA troops in South Vietnam was less than 2 percent of the North Vietnamese male labor force, and less than 3 percent of the male agricultural force. By comparison, the U.S. forces in Southeast Asia at that time amounted to about 1 percent of our male civilian labor force.

After the 1968 Tet offensive, statistical analysis again suggested that manpower reserves in North Vietnam were sufficient to meet 1968 requirements and could even support a higher level of mobilization without significant shortages, although there would probably be some strains in the

4 *The Pentagon Papers: The Senator Gravel Edition* (Boston: Beacon Press, 1971), IV, 369, 370, 371.

labor force. The analysis also noted that, if North Vietnam mobilized the same percentage of its population as South Vietnam, its full-time military force would double in size.

Another set of calculations after the 1968 offensives suggested that, at the loss rates of the first half of 1968 (the highest of the war), available North Vietnamese manpower would be exhausted in about 30 years and Viet Cong manpower in 3.5 years. The Viet Cong and NVA together appeared able to last about 12 years.

The analysis was crude, but it does give some idea of the VC/NVA's potential staying power in the face of loss rates so high that they never occurred again. It also suggests that the Viet Cong forces *could* be attrited. Indeed, by the end of 1972 most of them were gone; only 20 percent of the VC/NVA forces were estimated to be Viet Cong. The rest were North Vietnamese troops—even in traditional Viet Cong units.

The foregoing were all very rough estimates based on the best data available in 1967–68. But they have turned out to be roughly right. They accurately foreshadowed the allied inability to win the war of attrition.

A second major reason the VC/NVA forces were able to survive the allied strategy of attrition was that *they were able to exercise considerable control over their loss rates and thus keep them from going beyond the limits they could afford.* They did this by deciding when and where large-scale combat would occur—they held the initiative in this respect.

Our vastly superior forces found it difficult, despite repeated offensives, to pin down and defeat an enemy who chose to evade combat. A key aspect of the VC/NVA's ability to avoid combat was their use of sanctuaries in North Vietnam, Laos, and Cambodia, which remained off limits to US/GVN ground forces for political reasons until 1970–71.

The following analysis assumes that:

1. The ability to control casualty rates is a good measure of military initiative in South Vietnam.

2. To win the war of attrition, the allies must hold the military initiative. Specifically, the tempo of allied offensive operations must control the tempo of VC/NVA combat deaths; if allied operations increase, VC/NVA deaths must rise accordingly, whether they want them to or not.

A statistical analysis after the 1968 offensives indicated that the VC/NVA had much more influence over fluctuations in both their combat deaths and U.S. combat deaths than did the allied forces. It concluded that the VC/NVA held the basic military initiative in South Vietnam because they could alter the combat death levels by changing the frequency and intensity of their attacks.[5] Changing the tempo of allied operations had little effect.

The very strong relationship between VC/NVA attacks and U.S. combat deaths was interpreted to mean that if the VC/NVA desired to increase U.S. casualties, at the cost of increasing their own, then they could simply step up their offensive operations and their willingness to fight U.S. forces whenever the opportunity arose. The lack of a similar relationship between casualties and any of the allied activity indicators was interpreted as a lack of casualty control by U.S. forces as long as they persisted in a policy of maximum pressure on VC/NVA main forces at all times.

A later study used the same statistical correlation technique to see whether the earlier relationship continued to hold after the Tet offensive in 1968. When the July 1968–November 1969 period after Tet-68 was compared with the January 1966–June 1968 period, the relationship between VC/NVA attacks and allied combat deaths *declined* substantially. The correlation between U.S. combat deaths and U.S. battalion and larger-unit operations *increased* as dramatically. This was taken as a sign that the military initiative in terms of control over U.S. combat deaths had been shifting to the United States after June 1968, as we shifted away from an aggressive, maximum-pressure strategy. However, the VC/NVA ability to control fluctuations in their own deaths remained high.

The correlation between VC/NVA attacks and *their own combat deaths* did not change much after the 1968 offensives. This suggests that there was little change in the VC/NVA's ability to alter their level of combat deaths by changing their level of attacks. Before 1968, they could presumably control about 85 percent of the fluctuations; after 1968, they

5 Attacks include all VC/NVA attacks (large, small, and by fire) and are used here as an indicator of the level of the VC/NVA willingness to fight and to take casualties.

seemed to have some control over about 75 percent of the changes,[6] enough to frustrate the allied attrition strategy.

The correlation between VC/NVA attacks and U.S. combat deaths changed significantly in the allies' favor after the Tet offensive. Before and during the offensive, the VC/NVA seemed to control about 85 percent of the fluctuations in U.S. combat deaths by changing their level of attacks and willingness to fight. Afterward, they could control only about 20 percent of the variations in U.S. combat deaths.[7]

In short, the VC/NVA no longer exerted the control over U.S. combat deaths that they did before, though they still retained considerable control over their own combat deaths. Put another way, the VC/NVA still lost large numbers of troops only when they were willing to, but they could no longer increase U.S. and allied combat deaths easily when they wanted to.

The following conclusions emerge from the analysis. Up to and through the 1968 offensives, the VC/NVA maintained a fair degree of control over fluctuations in their combat deaths and those of the allies, particularly of U.S. forces. By increasing their willingness to take casualties (signified by a rising attack rate), the VC/NVA could increase allied casualties, or, by reducing the attack rate, they could limit their own combat deaths.

The allies, on the other hand, appeared to have little control over changes in their own combat deaths or those of the VC/NVA. This is interpreted to mean that the VC/NVA held the military initiative in South Vietnam through June 1968, at least in terms of casualties.

However, after the Tet offensive in 1968, the initiative shifted somewhat. The U.S. forces gained considerable control over both their own combat deaths and those of the Communists, although the latter's ability to retain control over fluctuations in their own deaths remained high.

---

6 All percentages are based on the R^2 coefficients derived from statistical correlation analysis. The R^2 indicates the degree of relationship between the variables; that is, the proportion of total variation in one variable explained by the other. An R^2 of .50 indicates that 50 percent of the variation in one variable can be explained by variation in the other. In this case, the R^2 are .84 and .77, respectively.

7 R^2 were .87 and .22, respectively.

The results seem to say that major fluctuations in VC/NVA losses were still fundamentally determined by their willingness to fight, but that the U.S. forces learned how to step up their operations and fight much more efficiently when the VC/NVA stepped up their attacks.

A second reason why the initiative may have shifted toward the allies is that losses of trained VC/NVA cadre and personnel, particularly during the 1968 offensives, apparently lowered the fighting effectiveness of the Communist forces in South Vietnam. The results of the accelerated pacification campaign in the second half of 1968 and the further gains made without stiff opposition until 1972 both testify to the serious beating the VC/NVA cadre and units took during the Tet offensive. Largely because of these losses, Hanoi apparently elected to conserve and rebuild its forces during 1969–71, while awaiting U.S. withdrawal.

But even the shift in initiative was not enough for the allies to drive the VC/NVA forces from the field and win a clear-cut victory. The VC/NVA military forces were weakened significantly in the years following 1968, but they remained strong enough to launch a major offensive in 1972 and, though defeated, came back in 1975 to win control of all of South Vietnam.

How did they do it? In terms of total military manpower, the allies always outnumbered the VC/NVA forces by at least 3 to 1, and the ratio approached 6 to 1 during 1969–71. But the cutting edge of fighting forces is made up of the troops in maneuver battalions, and allied superiority falls away sharply on this basis. Instead of outnumbering VC/NVA forces by almost 6 to 1 in 1970, the advantage falls to 1.6. Moreover, the ratio remains fairly steady during the 1965–71 period, instead of rising as the total manpower ratio does. And it actually shifts to an allied *disadvantage* of 0.8 to 1 in 1972.

The comparision is revealing because the maneuver forces are the principal forces available to each side for combat and their size imposes a limit to offensive activities.

Furthermore, the commitment of some of these forces to defensive missions further reduced allied offensive capabilities. For instance, the allies had large and continuing needs for combat forces to secure military bases, lines of communication (roads, canals, etc.) , and populated areas.

An analysis of force allocations in January 1968 suggests that only 40 percent of the allied maneuver forces were available for offensive operations during that month.

Of course, allied offensive forces could be increased by shifting units from security missions back into offensive operations, and this happened, especially during VC/NVA offensives, but there was always a risk of leaving the population unprotected. The RVNAF's ability to shift forces to where they were needed was always severely limited until late in the war, when the territorial forces had become numerous enough and strong enough to take over most of the security missions.

The VC/NVA's strategic situation was quite different. They did not have to use many of their regular forces for defensive missions. They had no cities to defend, and their base areas and lines of communication were not held and defended by large numbers of troops. They also had the advantage of sanctuaries up to 1970–71. Most of the VC/NVA regular forces were free to engage allied forces as they saw fit, as long as they did not incur heavy losses too frequently.

Given the commitment of regular forces to security missions for much of the war, the remaining allied forces held no significant advantage over the VC/NVA forces that could potentially be committed against them. The force ratio in this situation ranged from an allied advantage of 1.2 to 1 to an allied *disadvantage* of 0.7 to 1. Stated another way, the VC/NVA potential sometimes outnumbered the allied maneuver forces by 1.4 to 1, measured on this basis.

The two sets of combat-force ratios given above are not precise—far from it. They are based on the best data available, some of which are rough estimates. However, the findings deserve serious consideration, because, even if the ratios are wrong by 50 percent, they still say that the foxhole-force ratio did not favor the allies nearly so much as the total manpower figures suggest. The data may be rough, but the findings seem roughly right, and they do help explain why the allies were unable to win the war of attrition.

The comparisons do not tell the whole story, because the allies enjoyed overwhelming superiority (or so it seemed) in firepower, logistics support, and rapid movement of troops. However, there is evidence that the VC/NVA were able to fight in a way that nullified many of the allied advantages.

One such way was for the VC/NVA to mass their forces to exploit favorable opportunities while tying down allied forces by using small forces[8] to attack and harass outposts, roads, waterways, and the population. In this way the VC/NVA tied down some of the allied forces in order to gain an advantage against others. Such a strategy, combined with the use of night operations and thousands of standoff attacks by fire, went a long way toward neutralizing allied advantages. The cost in VC/NVA lives was high, but controllable, and the allies were not able to turn their decisive resource superiority into a decisive military advantage.

By the end of 1968, the futility of the attrition strategy had become evident to all, as expressed in the summary of responses to National Security Study Memorandum 1—"The Situation in Vietnam":

> There is general agreement with the JCS statement, "The enemy, by the type action he adopts, has the predominant share in determing enemy attrition rates." Three fourths of the battles are at the enemy's choice of time, place, type and duration. CIA notes that less than one percent of nearly two million Allied small unit operations conducted in the last two years resulted in contact with the enemy and, when ARVN is surveyed, the percentage drops to one tenth of one percent. With his safe havens in Laos and Cambodia and with carefully chosen tactics, the enemy has been able during the last four years to double his combat forces, double the level of infiltration and increase the scale and intensity of the main force war even while bearing heavy casualties.[9]

Finally, late in the summer of 1969, the attrition strategy ceased to be the prime objective stated by MACV. It was superceded by Vietnamization, which reflected the U.S. decision to withdraw from the war gradually.

[8] More than 90 percent of all reported VC/NVA ground assaults were by units estimated to be smaller than a battalion—even during the peak combat years of 1968 and 1972.

[9] *Congressional Record,* Vol. 118, No. 76 (May 10, 1972), p. E4978.

Professor West took some exception to Mr. Thayer's quantitative approach to the matter of attrition.

Professor Francis West:
What Thomas Thayer is really telling you is that, on the margin, U.S. casualties or enemy casualties can be explained according to enemy initiative. This is on the margin, which does not tell you about the bulk of activity that goes on day to day, but only about fluctuations above the steady state. One gets an entirely different look at it by observing the absolute number and what happens on a day-to-day basis. Looking at the history of the Vietnam War, one would have to conclude that we did have the initiative and that the war of attrition "worked" in the short run. The problem with saying they could fight forever is that physically, of course, they could. The problem is: Has there ever been a nation that has chosen to fight an offensive war until it literally killed itself off? The answer to that is: Of course not. So what one has to ask is: What do we know about the human will? At what point does a nation say "enough is enough" in terms of attrition? We know that the North Vietnamese went at least as far as the Germans and the French did during World War I, but we also know what happened to the nations of France and Germany after World War I.

So I submit that an analysis could have been done which would have shown that the North Vietnamese could have continued the war forever. But that is only the physical factor. One must also ask what was the psychological factor—the will to fight—and that is what was hurt by attrition.

Chapter 6

Rear Bases and Sanctuaries

In this war the rear bases of all the major contenders have been the subject of a series of major controversies. American troops were introduced into Vietnam initially in 1965 to protect U.S. bases in the South. The whole question of in-country and cross-border sanctuaries used by the Viet Cong and the North Vietnamese was debated for years. The bombing and ground attacks into Cambodia and Laos were aimed at rear bases and supply lines. The bombing of North Vietnam was aimed at the strategic rear areas of the North Vietnamese Army.

Hanoi used the immunity of sanctuary in Laos and Cambodia to cover its land lines of communication to the South. The only weapon that the United States could bring to bear on the Ho Chi Minh Trail was the airpower of the Air Force and the Navy. This chapter will discuss sanctuaries and rear bases and some of the unique problems that occur in limited war when rear bases are either attacked or granted immunity because of constraints or miscalculations.

Ambassador Robert Komer:
The availability of sanctuaries in Cambodia, Laos, North Vietnam, and base areas in remote parts of South Vietnam forced us to try to win the war in the South. The alternative would have been to invade the sanctuaries, which we did not want to do, primarily because of our fear of a Soviet or Chinese Communist reaction. But we could, and did, pulverize the enemy's lines of communications. I once suggested to Admiral

Zumwalt that the single most cost-effective thing done by any American military service in Vietnam was the blockade of the coast of South Vietnam. Up until about 1965 the bulk of the supplies that came to the Viet Cong from Hanoi did not come down the Ho Chi Minh Trail. They came by sea, which is the most efficient way of delivering supplies and support. The American Navy, with Vietnamese support, blockaded the entire, marvelously indented, coast. They blockaded, not to keep the people on shore from getting out, but to keep the people who were out from getting in, and they were notably successful. We forced the enemy to give up their chief line of communication and to develop the Ho Chi Minh Trail complex.

This they did more successfully than we ever believed they could. Since the Ho Chi Minh Trail was in the mountains and jungles, we had to employ a different method of interdicting this overland line of communication. Being constrained not to use ground forces in the sanctuaries, we chose a massive cumulative application of air power. Again, this was a traditional Europe-oriented use of military force, unsuited for the task, which failed to destroy the enemy's will or capability to reinforce in the South. In fact, we could not even interdict Hanoi's supply or reinforcement sufficiently to prevent them from mounting several major offensives. We dropped millions of tons of bombs on the Ho Chi Minh Trail and could not stop the flow.

Now, everybody talks about the way in which we were constrained. The Air Force and Navy were constrained against the targets in North Vietnam, but there were very few constraints with respect to the Ho Chi Minh Trail. We invented some pretty fancy things and we could not stop the supplies from coming down. I argued that, at least, we were preventing them from sending so much down that they could swamp us. But we could never completely interdict the line of communication. We could not prevent the enemy from bringing sufficient forces to the South and resupplying them at levels sufficient to frustrate our military aims. So when the generals say, "The politicians held us back," I say look at the cumulative amount of ordnance we dropped on the enemy—over eight million tons, or three times the total amount of bombs we dropped on Japan and Europe during World War II.

Sir Robert Thompson contends that the rear base for both sides is the same in a war of insurgency. Both sides are attempting to draw their strength from the same population, territory, and set of resources. In the next section he presents an interesting analysis of U.S. strategy in various periods of the Vietnam War as it was related to the rear-base strength of the Viet Cong and the North Vietnamese. Beginning with the 1968 Tet offensive, the strength of the Viet Cong began to wane. The Cambodian operations of 1970 effectively ended the immunity enjoyed by the Communists there. Our most effective denial of sanctuary came in 1972, when the United States put together a comprehensive strategy of interdiction, beginning with closing the North Vietnamese ports and rail lines and extending throughout their logistics systems to the front lines. The eleven-day bombing campaign in December 1972, which ended the American phase of the war, brought U.S. strategic bombers to bear on the North Vietnamese rear-base areas in a telling way.

Sir Robert Thompson:
The subject of the military lessons of the Vietnam War is a serious one. All sorts of phrases come out, such as "There were no front lines," "You did not know whether you were winning or not," "The war was unique," and "In any case, it was unwinnable." One should be wary of making these premature judgments, which I do not think will stand up to the scrutiny of history. Of course, there are differences in all wars, and in the Vietnam War itself there were plenty of differences through what I would call the four phases of the war: the early phase from 1959 to 1964, the second phase from 1965 to the Tet offensive of 1968, the third phase from 1969 to 1971, and then the fourth phase, which was for the most part a conventional war.

I want to talk about this war in terms which I have not used before and which I have not seen anyone else write very much about—that is, to go back to three very simple, straightforward aims of war, and to look at these in the perfectly simple situation of two countries fighting each other without anything else involved. Now, these three aims, in their normal sequence, have always been, firstly, to defeat the enemy's main forces in the field; secondly, to disrupt the enemy's rear base; and thirdly, to break the enemy's will to resist, or, of course, on the other side, the enemy's will to attack. Now, the first and second of these are only important in their contribution to the third. Unless you achieve the third, you do not win a war. The first alone—that is, defeating the enemy's main forces in the field—is not enough, and, in any case, it is secondary in importance to the second aim of disrupting the enemy's rear base.

There are plenty of examples of this. I am very fond of a report by Marshal Villars to Louis XIV after the battle of Malplaquet, which he lost. He wrote, "If God gives us another defeat like this, Your Majesty's enemies will be destroyed." The better, and more recent, example, of course, is clearly the 1967 Arab-Israeli war. I can remember that I happened to come to the United States at that time. I was going out to the Vietnam training center in Hawaii. I was met by a well-known professor, who said, "Wasn't that an incredible victory?" I said, "Look, it wasn't a victory. The Israelis won a battle, but they haven't won the war." He said, "What do you mean?" I said, "The other side does not have to treat. The war isn't won. It has not produced a result." So you can defeat an enemies' main forces in the field, but you do not necessarily get a result from it. You can see that from World War II, where you had, for example, the United Kingdom with its main forces in the field defeated, going out through Dunkirk. You saw the second aim being applied—the attempt to disrupt the rear base of the United Kingdom, the German bombing of the United Kingdom—but neither of them quite enough to achieve the third aim of breaking the will to resist.

Now, if we apply the three aims that I have mentioned to insurgency, the sequence of these aims changes immediately for both sides—for the insurgent and for the government. It is the rear base which becomes the priority for both of them, and the reasons for this are quite simple. Right from the outset, the battle is taking place within the rear base of both sides, and they both have the same rear base. The second reason why defeating the main forces in the field should not be the first aim is that neither side can defeat the other side's main forces in the field. As far as the government is concerned, at the beginning of the insurgency, the insurgent does not have any main forces, and even halfway through, those main forces are probably too elusive to be defeated. When they are finally strong enough, they have probably reached the position where it is the government's main forces that are collapsing, and they are not collapsing because they have been defeated in the field. They are collapsing because of a loss of will within the country.

I have said before, as a basic principle, that the military aim of a government in the insurgent phase must be to destroy the enemy's underground organization, not his guerrilla units. The guerrilla units are a secondary priority. Equally, on the government's side, the government's aim with respect to its own rear base must be to secure its main base areas within the country *before* they become threatened by the insurgency. Now, of course, that whole situation changes, or becomes a great deal more complicated, when we have elements of an outside invasion from the North Vietnamese, as we had from 1964 onward, and when we had intervention by an outside power, the United States, from 1965 onward.

I was very critical of United States strategy during the period 1965–68 because it concentrated primarily on the defeat of the North Vietnamese Army's main forces in the field, that is, those that were inside South Vietnam, and on the disruption of North Vietnam by bombing. Neither of those tactics—and I am doubtful whether they ever could have succeeded at that stage of the war—got anywhere near breaking the North Vietnamese will to resist. They also had another effect. They did not threaten the rear base of the Viet Cong inside South Vietnam at all. The Viet Cong, therefore, through that period, to all intents and purposes had almost a free run and were in a position where *they* were threatening the rear base of the South Vietnamese.

The initiative of the war at that time thus lay entirely with the North Vietnamese. They were dictating the pace of the action because they had rear bases, they had sanctuaries, they could come in, they could fight when they wanted to, they could pull out. If there was a degree of

disruption of their supply lines, it might mean that they could not put
a regiment back into South Vietnam next week, but they could do it
three weeks later, and that did not really make very much difference.
They could maintain the scale of the war they were fighting and put
you into a position of doubt as to whether you could maintain the
scale of the war that you were fighting. This is where I think I am
possibly misunderstood by many military people, and certainly misunderstood by General Westmoreland, when I say "priority" as compared with "major effort." Now, I understand full well what North
Vietnamese regiments, battalions, and divisions mean, and that those
had to be held and dealt with. That required a major effort, but
we still come back to what is your priority policy during this stage. Your
priority policy must be to defend or, better still, to improve your own
rear bases while trying to attack the enemy's rear bases. My own feeling
about the whole situation at that time was that you had reached a state
of perpetual motion. It could have gone on forever at that sort of pace,
provided you were prepared to keep it up. The whole thing was changed
by the Tet offensive, which, after all, was carried out on Hanoi's
initiative.

Now, there is one point I would like to raise about the Tet offensive
as compared with the invasion of 1972, which I have been quite unable
to work out in my own mind. Were they compelled by anything to
launch the Tet offensive? I understand very well that they were compelled to launch the invasion in 1972, but I do not know quite what it
was that compelled them to start the 1968 offensive. All the emphasis in
what they said and what they wrote was based on a mass uprising in
Saigon. That was what they were expecting. What they got, of course,
was a mass uprising in the United States, and there was nothing really
to show in what they said that they expected to get that. Certainly one
can sum up that offensive by saying that militarily it was a dreadful
defeat for them, but psychologically it was an extraordinary victory.
Certainly it destroyed the Viet Cong militarily—that is, the Viet Cong
regular forces and the Viet Cong regional forces, which the North
Vietnamese had the good sense to put into the front of the offensive, and

it was the Viet Cong who took most of the casualties. In other words, the Viet Cong were no longer a possible regional rival to the NVA in South Vietnam. Exactly the same sort of thing happened to the Khmer Communists in Cambodia.

Fortunately, the Tet offensive did not all that seriously disrupt the South Vietnamese rear base. In fact, arising out of that offensive, we had a far greater mobilization of the South Vietnamese than had ever been seen before. It also created, which I certainly did not see at the time— but I would like to state quite definitely that Ambassador Komer was one of the few people who did understand—it created a complete vacuum in the countryside. The Viet Cong were not in it, and the Government was not in it. They had all come back to the towns, and the question that then arose was: Who could get back to the countryside fastest? But the offensive had also achieved a psychological victory in the United States. It caused what was almost tantamount to the abdication of an American President, and it led to the opening of talks. The moment you open talks, you are immediately admitting that you are going to make concessions. Moreover, it also called a halt to the bombing. Therefore, it removed completely the only threat there was at that time to the North Vietnamese rear base.

Probably the most notable achievement of the North Vietnamese throughout the war was the manner in which they were able to defend their rear base by negotiations and diplomacy. Consider the Laos Agreement of 1962. It gave them free run down through Laos and Cambodia, and it kept the United States out of Laos. True, you used various means of going back into Laos, but there was theoretically a total restriction on American action in Laos: That was the whole purpose of the Agreement. The war in the South could not have been pursued as it was if the North Vietnamese had not had a free run down the Laotian panhandle. At the same time, because of Sihanouk's stand on neutrality and nonalignment (that is, with four North Vietnamese divisions on his soil) , and because enough was said about it, the United States was prevented *at that time* from taking any action.

I have mentioned that the talks halted the bombing in 1968. Compare that with the opening of talks again in September–October 1972, when, as a gesture of goodwill, the United States halted the bombing again, in October 1972. Goodwill offerings like that make no impression whatever.

Many of the previous mistakes were corrected through the period 1969–71. Take Vietnamization, which meant that you were restoring and improving South Vietnam's rear base: Pacification was doing that in part, but it was equally, of course, destroying the rear base of the Viet Cong on the other side, *inside* South Vietnam. Do not forget that every bit of populated ground that you get back is a double gain. It is a win to you and a loss to them. The effect of that pacification program through 1969–71 caused a swing in the balance of manpower and support for the Government within the country. It was fascinating, for one could go around villages in a province like Kien Hoa which were defended entirely by ex-Viet Cong. You could see the switch that had resulted from these programs. You had really started to take away their rear base inside the country and had turned it into a part of the South Vietnamese rear base.

One point I should perhaps have made earlier. It was terribly difficult, I believe, to be in Washington, or even sitting in Saigon, and think in terms of who controlled what. Was this ours or was it the Viet Cong's? Most people gave it up and just said, "There are no front lines." That is not entirely true. When you went down to districts, everyone knew where the front lines were, and who controlled what. What you could not do was to put it on a national map, at least not in any way that made any sense. When going around at district level, everyone understood exactly how far you could drive down a particular road, whether you could go into a particular village, and so on. Everyone knew where the front lines were.

In addition to the rear base inside South Vietnam, we began to get a change on the other rear bases. I personally regard the incursion into Cambodia in 1970 as one of America's truly effective acts. First of all, it closed the port of Kompong Som (Sihanoukville). It meant that the whole of their supplies for Military Regions III and IV, which had previously been coming in through Kompong Som, had to come down the Trail. I happened to be in Washington just after that, and I saw Dr. Kissinger. He asked me, "How long do you think this has gained us?" I said, "At least a year, probably eighteen months, and quite possibly two years." He said, "Everyone in the Pentagon, State Department, and CIA is telling me it has only gained us three months." I said, "That is not possible. Some of this stuff is coming from Europe on Russian and other ships: they cannot possibly in that time frame do a switch of supplies and beef up the Ho Chi Minh Trail to put all that stuff down the Trail within a matter of just three months."

But it had more effect than that, of course. It was a warning shot that Cambodia was no longer off limits. It became off limits to you, but it was not entirely off limits to the South Vietnamese. I regret to say that subsequent South Vietnamese expeditions into Cambodia were not exactly successful, but they did have some effect, just as Lam Son 719 into southern Laos quite definitely had an effect, because here were what had previously been absolutely secure bases now liable to attack. Before this they had not needed one man with one gun to defend them! Now they did have to think in terms of these rear bases having to be defended.

I said earlier that I could understand the invasion, and why they attacked in 1972. At the end of 1969, I said that if these programs then being carried out in South Vietnam continued as they were going, then, by 1972, North Vietnam would have no alternative but to invade. The result of successful Vietnamization and pacification was that by early 1971 the North decided that the only thing left was to invade.

Here we come to a completely different phase of the war. Coming back to my three aims of war, here, at last, was an opportunity where either side could defeat the other side's main forces in the field. By 1972 that was possible for the first time. It was a close thing for the South Vietnamese, and it was a fairly close thing, too, for the North Vietnamese. But the North's rear bases were now really open to attack.

There were also two distinctions on the effect in particular of the bombing in the North in 1972 as compared with the previous period, and on the timing of the mining of Haiphong. Here you had the North conducting a conventional invasion with modern weaponry—130-mm. guns, T-54 tanks, and so on. You cannot refuel T-54 tanks with gasoline out of water bottles carried on bicycles. It has got to come down in trucks, and in trucks in quite large numbers. In other words, for the first time there really was a target for an air force. Another distinction was that, at this stage, the Air Force had what it needed to do it with, which was the laser bomb. Consider the Thanh Hoa bridge: I have not been able to get an exact count, but I am told that somewhere between 800 and 1,000 sorties were flown on that bridge between 1965 and 1968. Commander John McCain told me that he thought that ninety-five planes were lost and it was not even hit! This time, the first four Phantoms with laser bombs got it. Now the rear base of the North Vietnamese in the North was really being hit. The mining of Haiphong took place on May 8. Quite obviously, it was not going to affect the battles that were then taking place in South Vietnam. That week was the height of the battle of An Loc and Kontum, and, of course, it was right at the height of the battle north of Hué. But the actual mining itself was too late to affect those battles. The mining was going to have a later effect, and that later effect was going to come in several months.

We therefore had reached the stage by about July 1972 where the North was suffering positive damage and its rear base was for the first time truly threatened. The first thing that hit the North in July 1972 was that Quang Tri was recaptured. Who would have believed in May that the South Vietnamese could have turned around and, with three divisions against six North Vietnamese divisions, recaptured Quang Tri? That was a very, very strong message to the North. The point was, of course, that the North's divisions, by this stage, had suffered heavy casualties indeed. In fact, the number of men killed and disabled by July–August 1972 has been estimated in the region of 130,000. The South Vietnamese had not suffered anywhere near such heavy casualties, and whether by luck or coincidence or good planning, they had 80,000 men coming through their training centers during that summer and all units were back to strength in July and August 1972. The Marine and airborne divisions in the North were certainly kept right up to strength.

What did this mean to the North? It meant that the South Vietnamese were in a position to carry out counteroffensives—not just something really major like Quang Tri, in the one area where the North Vietnamese Army could put its major forces and supply them most easily—but they could also start conducting counteroffensives in the Central Highlands, at An Loc, and so on. I have no doubt at all that if the war had gone on—if it had gone on without any peace talks—by October or November the South Vietnamese would have taken Loc Ninh back. It would not have been any problem to them by that time. It only needed 5,000 men to go in by helicopter, and they would have had it with the air support they were getting. So the North could see that it was about to lose all the ground that it had taken in the South. It was also suffering heavy damage in the North. And whereas a certain amount of arms, ammunition, gasoline, and so on could still come in through China, they could not get enough *food* in through China for North Vietnam. This point was proved in 1973, after Haiphong was reopened, when they had to import one million tons of grain—a three months' supply on their current ration. Hanoi could see that situation coming by the end of 1972. Their rear bases were really under attack and the South Vietnamese rear base, at the same time, was in good shape. In my view, on December 30, 1972, after eleven days of those B-52 attacks on the Hanoi area, *you had won the war. It was over!* They had fired 1,242 SAMs; they had none left, and what would come in overland from China would be a mere trickle. They and their whole rear base at that point were at your mercy. They would have taken any terms. And that is why, of course, you actually got a peace agreement in January, which you had not been able to get in October.

Now, let us just look at that peace agreement. Here we come back again to the whole business of rear bases. That cease-fire agreement restored complete security to the rear bases in North Vietnam, in Laos, in Cambodia, and in the parts of South Vietnam that it held. It subjected the South Vietnamese rear base again to being absolutely open to military attack. That is what the cease-fire agreement actually achieved.

Chapter 7

Psychological Factors

It was not until the Tet offensive of 1968 that the disparity between Hanoi's and Washington's views of "unacceptable losses" was highlighted. It was not until Tet that the United States began to understand that the outcome of guerrilla warfare is determined as much, if not more, by political and psychological factors as by military considerations.

The Tet celebration of 1968 was shattered on January 31 when the Viet Cong and the North Vietnamese Army launched an all-out, countrywide offensive in South Vietnam. The leadership in Hanoi evidently felt that the South Vietnamese were ripe for revolt and would rise up to smash the Saigon regime and the Americans. This proved to be a miscalculation; what resulted, assessed against conventional criteria for military success, was a disastrous Communist military defeat. But politically the Tet offensive had a vastly different meaning. The North Vietnamese succeeded in using psychological weapons against both the American public and the Vietnamese people—a double victory that fostered their political objectives, in their judgment, far more than military defeats had hurt them. For their military losses were acceptable to them and they had succeeded in demonstrating that no one in South Vietnam was safe or secure. By doing so, they undermined the South Vietnamese Government. Unable to demonstrate that they could provide security to the people, the Government was unable to sustain the loyalty and backing of the population. Thus Hanoi had successfully exploited fear to political advantage.

Public confidence in the United States also eroded rapidly. Tet-68

107

greatly accelerated the growing credibility gap between the U.S. Government and the general public. General Giap's offensive drove a wedge between optimistic public pronouncements and the realities as seen on American television. In spite of the generally good performance of the ARVN, the war began to look hopeless and irrational to the American people and to American leaders. In Washington, the net effect of Tet was to convince our leaders that success in our goals in Vietnam could not be attained by military means.

Many military men believe that we should have vigorously followed up the Tet-68 military success with increased pressure, diplomatically and militarily. The Viet Cong cadre had been decimated: there were over 30,000 killed in the first two weeks of the offensive. After Tet there was a golden opportunity to exploit the weakness of the enemy. Instead, Washington reacted with an investigation into charges that American forces had been taken by surprise in the coordinated attacks. There was an opportunity at this point in the war to convert military success into meaningful political gain. Instead, our resolve obviously wavered, we began to fold our hands and started looking for a way out of the war.

The extent of North Vietnam's psychological victory in the United States became apparent on March 31, 1968, when the President of the United States announced that he would sacrifice his political future in exchange for peace talks. The stock market reached a new high. The stage was set for the American withdrawal from the war.

We had hoped to bring Hanoi to the peace talks by making the war too costly for them to continue. After all, conventional wisdom held that a superpower could obviously outlast a small nation like Vietnam. But conventional wisdom failed us in the same way that conventional strategy had failed. Losses in Vietnam became "unacceptable" to the United States first.

In this chapter we examine three components of psychological forces in the war: as they affected the battle for the "hearts and minds" of the South Vietnamese, as they affected the North Vietnamese in their international context, and finally as they affected what turned out to be the critical variable—the American public.

Barry Zorthian:
Candidly, I would have to say that we had no major successes in the political-psychological area. We had some limited ones, at various times and of varying impact. *Many* people recognized the importance of undertaking programs and adopting policies that would achieve a favorable response from the population in Vietnam *and* the population overseas. I think if we look at this psychological area in the broadest terms possible, involving both world reaction (including the U.S. domestic reaction) and reaction within Vietnam, we would all acknowledge great shortcomings.

Some programs had a positive impact. Land reform eventually had some effect. Some of the agricultural programs were helpful. Our health programs at times had some effect. The evidence for these limited claims lies in the considerable response achieved at times in the Chieu Hoi "returnee" appeal and in the "Phoenix Program," even though the latter was criticized in later years for some of its tactics and techniques.

However, the desire of the Vietnamese for justice and personal freedom was never really accepted or pursued. In terms of impact outside Vietnam, for whatever reason, our own inadequacies or North Vietnamese skills or a combination of the two, we ended up with little official support, little public support, though behind the scenes there was a certain amount of endorsement of what we were doing in terms of pure strategic considerations.

If we are going to distill lessons of Vietnam, an evaluation of the "whys" of all this is very important. Part of it is that the psychological aspect was not as integral to our efforts as it should have been. As a structure, as an institution, our whole mission effort out there never quite absorbed this, never quite made it essential or basic to our efforts. If you talked about psychological operations, the concept really ended up being a leaflet-dropping Chieu Hoi type of program—press conferences on one side and perhaps a few programs that got some limited support—but it was always something to set off on the side for the so-called "psychological warriors," not something for the mainstream of a mission to worry about.

I think that the relationship of psychological operations to the rest of the mission was better in Vietnam than in any earlier war. We had more participation than in the past. We moved closer to what was desirable, but I am suggesting that we never moved close enough. I do not think the psychological organization or its head—the director of the Joint U.S. Public Affairs Office (JUSPAO) in this particular situation—should be the final authority. The head of the mission must be. The political factor in this kind of a situation is at the very core of the operation, not out in the periphery. This was, I believe, something we never really achieved.

The whole subject is very complicated, of course. For example, there were problems of organization which were never solved. We never quite bridged the gap between the words we were saying and the reality we were living with.

Ambassador Komer:

We did have one qualified political-psychological success in Vietnam, particularly during the period 1968–71. We managed to wean the bulk of the rural population away from tacit or active support of the Viet Cong to at least passive support of the nationalist side. I have never been clear in my own mind how much that was due to our efforts, though we tried with a wide range of programs, from land reform to rural economic revival. But how much did what we did make the difference, as opposed to what the enemy did—what General Lansdale described as the systematic enemy campaign of terror directed against the rural population? And then the Tet offensive, in which they attacked the people in the cities and outraged most of the population of South Vietnam?

Moreover, while we may have weaned the rural population away from support of the other side, and their nationalist revolution failed, we never were able to translate this into positive and active rural popular support for the Government of Vietnam. We tried that, too, and a lot of people here were involved in that effort at the grass roots and at the top. In the last analysis, I am inclined to think that it just was not "do-able." Here I am reminded of Barbara Tuchman's verdict on our attempt to prop up the Nationalist Chinese in World War II. You remember that in her book she ends up saying that we Americans could not do this because it was just not anything that Americans could do. We simply could not change the face of China and make Chiang Kai-shek into a reformer. The basic forces were against us. However much we tried with Diem, with his various successors, and with the most successful, President Thieu, we were never able, ourselves, to generate a counterattraction in Saigon that ever had the charisma, the capability, the administrative effectiveness, call it what you will.

Major Fred Raymond:

My viewpoint and remarks should be considered perhaps as coming from one of the weeds down there at the grass roots. The problem for a District Adviser was the *chung toi* syndrome in U.S. planning and action instead of *chung ta*. We are talking "we" in the more restrictive sense of the Vietnamese *chung toi* we—*the Americans.* Nothing could get done ultimately at the grass roots unless it was planned, coordinated, and implemented in a *chung ta*—or totally inclusive we—sense. I am not pretending to make any moralistic recommendations on whether or not we should have been in Vietnam, but a plea that if we ever get into something like this again, where we have people out there at the end of the line in a country like Vietnam, let's set it up right—either we go in and run it, as in the Haitian experience, or else let's just provide the wherewithal.

Our efforts—judging from my three tours as a Popular Force Motivation Adviser and twice as a District Adviser—resulted in some concrete and worthwhile contributions both to Vietnam and to our experience and expertise in foreign-policy planning and implementation. But I think my retrospective afterglow is clouded by a sense of guilt that I could not get many things accomplished—at least with the customary efficacy and dispatch—that my previous military training and experience had imbued in me as necessary if the mission was to succeed. This feeling is tempered, however, by the knowledge that the American sense of haste, outweighing the necessity for planning and coordination, permeated our own organization at higher levels as well. As witness to this, the transition from a Special Forces "A" Team to a MACV District Advisory Team at Ha Tien in 1967 left both myself and the District Chief in a state of shock when we found ourselves left astride a critical border-infiltration area with only a 60-mm. mortar as indirect fire support and the District Team without the rudimentary household necessities, such as beds, stove, refrigerators, etc. Only the ultimate intervention of the Corps Senior Adviser in directing the lateral transfer of some assets from Special Forces to the MACV team resolved our plight. Control, or at least coordination, of programs and operations conducted by various military and civilian agencies continued to be a problem throughout 1967–68. The "feel" I got was that while these actions were probably rather well thought out and coordinated at top levels, they then went directly down through the various individual agency channels without being closely coordinated at intermediate levels. This resulted in a constant chase at the district level, trying to find out what was—and was supposed to be—going on.

Stephen Young:

There is one point which is absolutely critical and which must be understood by all if our Vietnamese experience is to be properly evaluated. We Americans did find the target, we did do the job: we put together Vietnamese nationalism and American power to defeat the NVA and rally mass support for the nationalist government in Saigon. It started in late 1968 and Ambassador Komer put it together on the American side.

Two words say it all—villages and nationalism. The new decentralized pacification program which began in the fall of 1968 opened up the Saigon power structure for the emergence of nationalist leaders at the local levels. In the background stood the changes brought about by President Johnson's insistence on a constitution for Vietnam and elections thereunder. Americans laughed at Vietnam's democracy because they only looked at the generals in Saigon. Few, if any, paid attention to new leaders and coalitions emerging at the village and provincial levels. The necessity of holding elections forced the generals to open up the system a bit. Fortunately for all of us, the Tan Dai Viets were ready and able to move in and open a wedge so that more and more could follow. When the opposition Buddhists entered a slate for the Senate election in 1970, the strategy of electoral accommodation had mobilized the people of South Vietnam behind a non-Communist, constitutional government in Saigon.

Komer's new concept of pacification—guns, money, and power to the people—gave the villages a new and vital role. Local community leaders could take the initiative on behalf of local aspirations. They now had the power to stand up for what they felt was right in their heritage and their national tradition. As the failure of the Tet offensive showed, the Vietnamese people when left to themselves rejected the Communists. Village communities proved to be a natural ally of a nationalist government in Saigon. At the same time President Thieu made an alliance with the Tan Dai Viets to begin an expansion of his political base. The Tan Dai Viets (whose political theorists had inspired the constitution adopted in 1967) were able to play the role of broker between Thieu and his administration and the villages and other nationalist groups.

Now Komer's new management structure for pacification, the Central Pacification and Development Council, made the Vietnamese Government work. Central administration was linked to the villages in common effort along the lines specified by the eight goals of pacification. This re-created an organic national community unknown in Vietnam since the reigns of the great kings Le Loi and Le Thanh Ton in the 1400s. The deep well of nationalist loyalty was tapped at last. Komer's successor, William Colby, also deserves praise. He fostered a very sophisticated decentralized political process which sustained and encouraged the growth of this new nationalist momentum. Colby designed the pacification programs to stimulate self-sustaining cycles of patronage and voter participation at the village and provincial levels. Our village credit program, the local revenue improvement program, the people's groups program, all placed resources at the command of local citizens. The central government reached out and incorporated the population into its political community. Hanoi was denied the people of South

Vietnam. Thus in 1974 we had a situation where Hanoi's sole political asset in South Vietnam was seventeen NVA divisions. The tables were turned and a "People's War of National Liberation" had been defeated. It took us too long and cost far too much, but we had helped the South Vietnamese build a nationalist political community.

Could psychological operations ever have been more than marginally successful against a totalitarian enemy? An interesting dialogue on the question of the North Vietnamese regime's accountability ensued on this point. "The costs to General Giap of such operations," General Edward Lansdale commented, "could be disregarded because his regime had no accountability."

General Edward Lansdale:
There were no political costs in the war to the leaders in Hanoi. We never really attempted to use our vast communications resources to make Giap and other Hanoi leaders politically accountable for their actions in the war. This small clique, the Politburo, brought ruin and tragedy to millions in Vietnam. Yet we never tried to arouse feelings among the Vietnamese or among Americans or among others in the world against this small clique of leaders—as we did against the Kaiser in World War I and again against Hitler in World War II. For some baffling reason, we accepted the self-portrait of Ho Chi Minh as a benevolent old "uncle" who was fond of children—and of other Politburo leaders as speakers for a people they did not permit to have opinions. So we let their claims to leadership go unchallenged while their people suffered and died—and while first President Johnson and then President Nixon were challenged grievously by highly vocal portions of the American public, despite the fact that North Vietnamese leaders were elected to leadership through Party back doors and rigged, totalitarian elections.

Vietnam and the Vietnamese perhaps were too foreign for a politico like Johnson to understand. If the war had been in Boston, or in Texas, or in California, a little clique of politicians such as the Hanoi Politburo would have been hit hard with all political shrewdness and knocked out.

Sir Robert Thompson commented that the North Vietnamese not only were not accountable to their own constituents, they never became accountable to world opinion. But General Lansdale responded that there was a relationship there, and if we had tried to make them accountable to world opinion, we might have been able to get at their own constituency, which was never challenged. Allan Cameron expressed the view that it was a mistake to assume that the North Vietnamese could not be considered, or be made to be, accountable.

Allan Cameron:
They definitely were accountable—to the Soviet Union in particular and to China in a large degree. Everybody forgets that in 1963 the Soviet Union "broke" relations with the North Vietnamese as far as it was possible for them to do it. They pulled every man, every blueprint out of the country. We were unable to exploit it. The North Vietnamese had to go to Canossa, which they did in February 1964 after a *tremendous* internal debate. Le Duan of the Hanoi Politburo had to go to Moscow and get on his knees—almost literally—at which point, for the first time, the Soviet Union endorsed the North Vietnamese effort.

A second aspect of the tragedy is attributable to what I think was a running misperception of the internal politics of the North Vietnamese regime which lasted at least until the death of Ho Chi Minh. We assumed that, if Ho Chi Minh died, it would fall apart, for we had, as an article of faith, the notion that Communist regimes always have succession crises.

Professor Uri Ra'anan:
Our side regrettably became implicity stuck with the concept of fighting for partition. The other side, sometimes implicitly, more often explicity, appeared to be fighting for unification. It could be said that this is very nice but quite unrealistic because of the constraints that made it impossible to accompany and orchestrate a Southern unification slogan with a Southern military campaign aimed at the land conquest of the North.

It is not a very close analogy—simply an illustration—but it was quite conceivable for the West Germans, with devastating effect for a number of years, to employ the slogan of German unification entirely in their favor and entirely to the damage of the other side, in spite of the fact that it was not accompanied by any military moves whatsoever for the conquest of East Germany. It would not have been beyond the realm of credibility, I believe, to have placed South Vietnam in a position where it, too, was fighting, at least implicitly, for unification.

There was a broader audience of the war, which reacted to the initiatives of both sides. Ambassador Francis Galbraith, for many years the American Ambassador to Indonesia, commented on Sir Robert Thompson's concept of rear bases.

Ambassador Francis Galbraith:
I have been very impressed by the fact that we had the will of the Southeast Asians with us: I specifically mean the people in the vicinity of Vietnam, who wanted us to prevail and wanted us to stay. In contrast, our allies in Europe, particularly, varied from disapproval to indifference, and I have always thought that this had a fairly important effect on the public opinion of this country. I wonder if we could have convinced the Europeans that their own attitudes did have these effects on our public opinion. In other words, could, conceivably, the notion have

been conveyed in some way that this was in the national interest of the various allies and in that way strengthened our own conception?
Sir Robert Thompson:
Here I think you ran into a problem. France is a subject by itself, because the French were in a very ambivalent situation. I would say that one of the errors that President Johnson made was in choosing Paris for the peace talks. Warsaw would have been much better.

If you take my own country, you were fully supported by the Macmillan and the Douglas-Home Government. In 1970, when you went into Cambodia, Michael Foote, who became a Minister of Employment, on a motion to adjourn the House—a necessary formality—condemned the American invasion of Cambodia. This was at the end of the Labour Government's administration of 1964–70. The Foreign Secretaries, Michael Stewart, George Brown, and so on, were, at all times, right behind you. Mr. Wilson, rather like the French, was ambivalent on Vietnam, as he was on any other subject. Now, this vote of censure got some mileage in the U.S. press. Do you know what they raised out of 600 members of the House of Commons for censuring the United States? Sixty-five. One tenth voted for it. The Conservatives abstained because this was an internal Labour row. The Labour Party voted, I think, somewhere like 260 or 270 to 65 against that censure motion. So your stand there was supported in the United Kingdom. Of course, it has been influenced now by what you have done and what the situation is.

In this discussion, as we have already seen in earlier ones and will see still more of later, there was one point of view that started from the fundamental question of American constraints. Professor Earl Ravenal states the position very clearly.

Professor Earl Ravenal:
The question that immediately must be raised is: What is causing what? That is, if the psychological factor was the critical element on which

the North Vietnamese were able to play and that factor inhibited the requisite degree of American effort, is this a constraint or is this a variable situation?

~ In other words, which is the tail and which is the dog?

The psychological factor can be regarded as a variable in the sense of another front of the war: a campaign to fight through manipulation in terms of either your own public opinion or the other side's. In the sense of a variable the psychological factor may be helpful but not critical. However, if in the model it is considered to be a constraint, then it becomes critically important. If it is a constraint, then the largest lesson that we have to learn from Vietnam is that we can never again, as a nation, attempt this kind of thing.

The large question is: What kind of a model do you have and what kind of conclusions do you draw from it? I would tend to say that an attempt to manipulate or regiment American opinion or sentiment in order to conduct this kind of lengthy operation in peripheral areas of the world again, is either going to fall on its face or it is going to entail another kind of crisis which, in turn, is going to present problems, and be a most divisive situation. That is, it will entail a constitutional crisis. I daresay that, when faced with those alternatives, probably the American people, given that trade-off, will prefer the comfort of a relatively unrestrictive political system—free expression, a rather weak central government, and all the other nice things that go along with it, to which we have been accustomed since 1789. What is going to suffer is our ability to undertake efforts of this kind.

I completely agree about the central importance of the psychological factor, but I think that it is an absolute constraint and it is never going to be sufficiently manipulatable except at the peril of our basic constitutional set of relationships, and therefore, it may be well for us, to use a military image, to withdraw to a different kind of perimeter.

Was the constraint so absolute? Mr. Zorthian pointed out that, "with all the shortcomings, all the criticisms, all the bad press, up to Tet, some-

thing like 46 percent of Americans nonetheless supported the Vietnam effort. Nor did the other 54 percent oppose it, as there was a large portion of 'don't knows.' It was only with Tet that public support here collapsed." Partly the problem was one of presentation, as Sir Robert Thompson goes on to argue.

Sir Robert Thompson:
It is a bit tough on an Englishman to tell you how to handle the internal domestic politics of your own country. I know you used to do it to us. I do think that the presentation of the war was deplorable. One of the reasons is that I do not think many of the people who were trying to explain it knew what they were trying to explain, which makes it doubly difficult. After all, a war of this nature is very confusing. Honestly, and with all due respect, when I came back from that area to the United States, how many people could I talk to on the subject without having to make a single explanation, without even having to quite finish the sentence because you knew what it is about? You could not do that in the United States. What I have been saying here would be Greek to the United States public.

It is of more than passing interest whether North Vietnam had achieved a "subjective" or "objective" triumph. Did they intend, with Tet, to elicit such a response in the United States—or did it surprise them too? Sir Robert Thompson had argued in his presentation that they did not expect such.

Mr. Zorthian:
A lot of these things are worth long debate. But the one thing I just cannot let go by is the suggestion that the North Vietnamese, or the

VC, never conceived of the Tet offensive in terms of a major impact on the U.S. public. I suggest that one of their major targets in the Tet offensive was U.S. public opinion. Yes, they did talk about a mass uprising in Vietnamese cities. Yes, they did indoctrinate troops in that regard. But they hardly expected a mass uprising in the American Embassy, and it was through the attack, through coverage of the war by the press, that they achieved a very dramatic victory in the United States. In turn, that led to a collapse of U.S. support, or whatever U.S. support for the war there was left.

Sir Robert Thompson:

My only point on that one is that you have to go back to their documents on it. Where, in their documents, did you see it put as number one— "This is going to overthrow President Johnson" or whatever? No, all the way through, the one thing they were saying at that time was that there would be a mass uprising in the cities. It had no effect, and I have never seen them prophesy what you attribute.

Ambassador Komer:

If we were not winning, or at least if we were not winning in objective terms, why did the VC and Hanoi change a winning strategy up to that point? The classic Maoist strategy is to win the countryside and deprive the enemy of its popular base.

Sir Robert Thompson:

That is still a point that I do not completely understand. I understand why they did it in 1972, but I still do not understand why they undertook the Tet offensive in 1968. Mark you, I accept everything that's been said about its effect, but why did they change doctrines? Why did the NVA persuade the Khmer Communists (KC) to attack Phnom Penh in the summer of 1973 while American bombing was still available, and so on, and take very heavy casualties indeed? What exactly went on behind the scenes on the other side—we have not really fathomed. These people can think like that: the North Vietnamese may well have been very happy to see the KC defeated. After all, in 1968, the Fifth Division and the Ninth Division were VC divisions, and you do not hear anyone calling them Viet Cong divisions now.

Ambassador Komer:

Let me ask for comment on a hypothesis, that far earlier than we, Hanoi and the Viet Cong saw that the stalemate was ending, and that by sheer weight and mass or whatever, we were beginning to gain the upper hand. This could be a justification for the radical change in a strategy which was involved in the Tet offensive of 1968.

Sir Robert Thompson:

What I cannot be sure of there—and none of us can—is the timing of their decision on this. One fascinating feature was the fact that the whole of the Viet Cong in MR III and MR IV were armed with AK-47s in a matter of five to six months, from Kompong Som. This changed the whole military balance of firepower. Maybe it was that infusion of weaponry that influenced their decision.

Dean Edmund Gullion:

I wanted to bring up the question of the press. Why did we not get a better press? Could anything have been done about it? Was the press available to the missions to do something with it that was not done, or was the press being controlled at home by the publisher?

The home and in-theater relationship is interesting. Various psychological and press-relations problems stem from the fact that the reasons for the war were never declared at a high level, by the President—by any President. It was presented to this country as something we were doing in order to give the Vietnamese the right of self-determination. That is not worth it. Four Presidents did not really do it for this reason. They did it, rightly or wrongly, because a perception of this had a great effect on the alliance systems of the free world and in accordance with some of the doctrines enshrined in the early papers that Mr. Nitze talked about. Without that kind of a declaration and without the mobilization of this country—putting it on an emergency footing—everything was bound to happen and it did happen. In other words, there was a travesty, of allowing people from this country—journalists and others—going off and sojourning in the capital of the enemy, giving it all sorts of aid and comfort, while GIs, Americans, in that same country, with access to television and radio, wondered, "What the hell am I doing here?"

It may be that there was nothing one could do with the press. But thirty years or so of dealing with the press in stressful situations in Third World countries makes me wonder.

Mr. Zorthian:

The subject is obviously a terribly involved one. Everyone is going to have a somewhat different evaluation. Dean Gullion earlier put his finger on one of the factors of the problem: the whole issue of gradualism in Vietnam. While we were in a guerrilla-warfare stage and in an insurgency stage, there was some very sharp criticism of the way we were executing our missions, but even the most critical press—and I refer to David Halberstam or Neil Sheehan, for instance—thought we should be in Vietnam doing what we were doing. It was not until later that they turned against the entire involvement.

If we could have moved forcefully at that time and perhaps won the war, the attitude of the press and of the American public in due course might have been quite different. But then, could we have won it in any different way? Could we have achieved those same objectives with much less division at home? In a guerrilla situation we might have, or, perhaps, with an all-out effort, rather than the gradual effort we adopted. The sore would not have festered. Herman Kahn used to say that there were many ways of winning the Vietnam war; there was only one way of losing it, and we figured out that one possible way!

Given the situation and the nature of the war; given the way we backed into it, and the personality of LBJ, and his interaction with a largely skeptical press corps; given the openness of the war; given the lack of censorship, and the letdown the press felt in the Harkins period and then subsequently on a number of our "claims"; given the lack of a well-formed military attitude and structure, and even a State Department attitude and structure, to deal with a very active, very large press in this kind of a situation: given all'that, the amazing thing is not that the press was critical, but that they stuck with us so long. Obviously, there are exceptions—there are some notable ones who were critical from the start—but by and large the press was fairly responsive to our effort in the middle years. This was the result of a lot of work on the part of

many people in our mission. It is fashionable now for everyone to say that the press was lied to in Vietnam and nothing good was done with the press. Many people worked very assiduously with that press and, I think, got some results. Doubts grew, a lot of things happened, and then the North Vietnamese, fighting very skillfully to attain their psychological objectives in the Tet offensive, undermined many of our stories.
Sir Robert Thompson:
I am a bit worried about some of the debate. It seems to me that what you are saying on the political and psychological side is that you cannot do it but the other side can. Here we come back to the accountability. I do not believe that they are as insensitive as you make out. The Russians would not have let Solzhenitsyn out if they had not been very sensitive. I am quite sure that the North is sensitive to world opinion and that it would have had an effect. But how do you answer this question? How can a lady like Mary McCarthy get up on BBC television as late as 1971 or 1972 and say, "There is no verifiable evidence that the Viet Cong ever intentionally killed a woman or child." Of course, there was a "wet" liberal interviewer who did not challenge it. If Dennis Duncanson had been there, he would have destroyed her argument, as he did to Frances FitzGerald. How can this happen? Perhaps because we were only giving out our reports, and we were not giving out what the Viet Cong and Hanoi were saying in their documents, in their prisoner reports, in the interrogation reports, what was coming over their radio for internal consumption, and so on. No one focused on this at all, on what their ministers were saying in the North, on what their aims were, but it is all there, it is all documented.
Mr. Zorthian:
But we did books on it. Douglas Pike's book, *Viet Cong,* did not come out of thin air. The trouble with the Mary McCarthy issue derives from her reputation as a writer and her one visit to Vietnam. You and Europe accepted her much more as an expert than anyone in the United States. She should not have been on the BBC to start with.

Chapter 8

Air Power: Mixed Results in the Early Years

The United States entered the war in Vietnam with a great deal of confidence in its air power. Airmen of the Army and Navy had been the heroes of World War II. In the Cold War, air power was the vanguard of nuclear deterrence and provided the potential shock power of flexible response. Air power had saved Berlin during the blockade, and American fighters had defeated the MIGs over the Yalu in Korea by a margin of ten to one.

All four services had developed formidable capabilities in the air. From the U.S. Army helicopters to the U.S. Naval Carrier Task Forces to the strategic bombers of the Air Force, air power was held in high regard and promised decisive results.

But the use of American air power became a contentious issue in this war. Controversies over bomb tonnages, targeting policy, effectiveness, and the prisoners of war were among some of the more prominent issues. No one was very happy with the progress of the war by 1968—the war had become a vital election issue. The costs of the air operations were very high and there was a furious debate raging over the use of American air power in Southeast Asia; this debate spilled over into our discussions.

General Edward Lansdale:
It is evident that the enemy was surprised by the air power of the Americans, for there were some cruelly bloody lessons before the enemy learned not to be so open to attack from the air. For example, a North

Vietnamese regiment confidently dug positions on a hillside which commanded the surrounding terrain but was exposed from above, commenced a battle from this supposedly advantageous position, and then was quickly destroyed by napalm delivered by air. Other enemy units were caught on the march in the open, took only rudimentary dispersal and concealment precautions after the appearance of aircraft, and paid heavy prices in casualties when quick-reaction forces hit them from the air. Headquarters, support, and rest areas in more remote jungles were hit by the cratering heavy bombs from B-52s, for which their too shallow bunkers and underground systems were ill-prepared.

The enemy's lessons about American air power were learned, however. It became customary for the enemy to prepare the ground for battle long in advance, with porters bringing in supplies via hidden routes and burying the supplies in ground caches awaiting the time of battle, to ensure that resupply during combat would not be stopped from the air. Forces en route to battle made increasingly effective use of cover from aerial observation. Permanent posts went deeply under the surface into complex burrows containing headquarters, hospitals, barracks, mess halls, storage for ordnance and quartermaster supplies, and repair depots. New antiaircraft weapons and tactics were introduced, including sophisticated Soviet weaponry. In battle, enemy tactics called for heavy fire to interdict potential landing zones for troop aircraft. Air bases were the target for suicidal sapper commando raids and hit-and-run operations by heavy-weapons teams (using such weapons as mortars and rockets), all designed to destroy parked aircraft and air crews on the ground.

The United States, however, was able to keep up its combat pressure from the air throughout the war. One of the enemy's strategic failures was in not knocking out our air bases and not halting our construction of new air bases throughout South Vietnam. From the sporadic nature of enemy attacks, and despite the savagery of some of them, it was evident that the enemy, in following Mao's dictum on the waging of a "people's war," simply had not given a high enough priority to this objective. The air mobility of U.S. military power prevented the enemy from ever taking and holding enough ground in South Vietnam to establish a rival capital to Saigon for providing visible evidence to the world that the NLF was the true "wave of the future" in South Vietnam. As it was, the enemy had to make continuing and constant use of sanctuaries across the border in Cambodia, a gift from our self-imposed political decision to limit the geographical boundaries of the war, which allowed them to ready units for combat and rest them up afterward.

The other side of the coin about U.S. use of the air in the war, though, was the psychological and political ineptness with which we carried out the bombing of North Vietnam. We started out soundly and then dropped political astuteness for a military rationale of necessity that was politically disastrous. Our continued bombing of North Vietnam, which we stated was to stop the movement of men and matériel to South Vietnam, was exploited brilliantly in psychological terms by the Politburo in Hanoi. The presence of U.S. aircraft over North Vietnam gave visible veracity to Politburo claims that it was leading the people of Vietnam in a struggle against an invading foreign power, the United States, just as it had led them against those other foreigners, the hated French colonialists. In Churchillian style, the Politburo portrayed the North as a set-upon David fighting a bullyboy Goliath, the United States, and thereby was able to rally the North Vietnamese into grimly determined war efforts, while enlisting the sympathy of much of the world, including many Americans at home. As Le Duan of the Hanoi Politburo put it in a dialectical aphorism, the Politburo used "the strategy of exploiting contradictions in the enemy camp." If the United States claimed to be in the war to help the Vietnamese people, this was demonstrated to be false by the U.S. action of dropping bombs to kill so many noncombatants in North Vietnam. Attention was skillfully and tellingly diverted from the military rationale.

The initial bombing raids against North Vietnam were clearly labeled as retaliation for enemy actions against the United States in the Gulf of Tonkin and South Vietnam. As retaliation, they were psychologically understandable at home in the United States and to the world. If we had not dropped this political concept, and substituted a military rationale, the war would have progressed far differently. Consider what might have been if each U.S. bombing raid was plainly identified—to the people of North Vietnam (by radio and leaflet drop) and to the world (via the press) —as reaction to specific acts of aggression in South Vietnam ordered by Hanoi's Politburo, with the firm promise that when these acts of aggression stopped, then our bombing would stop also. We could have warned people to evacuate potential bombing areas while explaining to them that the bombs would drop only if the Politburo ordered cruel acts against their fellow Vietnamese in the South. This would have put excruciating pressure on the Politburo to cease and desist its aggression, pressure coming from the people of North Vietnam (whose support was vital to the Politburo), the Politburo's Communist allies, and the world. It would have been our way of "exploiting contradictions in the enemy camp."

As a footnote to these comments about the importance of U.S. use of the air in the war, it should be noted that Hanoi's Politburo tacitly acknowledged that importance after the cease-fire in South Vietnam. It worked hard at building air bases in areas its forces occupied in South Vietnam. Evidently, the Politburo was readying its forces to contest the unique aerial advantage our side had during the American period.

Dissatisfaction with the Air War

Colonel Donaldson D. Frizzell

In April 1968, a partial bombing halt restricted air operations to areas south of the 20th Parallel (or to the southern third of North Vietnam). The air war over the North was wound down while at the same time the flow of war materials and supplies continued to move through the port facilities at Haiphong. The Joint Chiefs of Staff still favored bombing the harbor facilities and mining the harbor in order to choke the flow of supplies to the North Vietnamese from outside sources. General Earle G. Wheeler, Chairman of the Joint Chiefs of Staff, recommended a course of action based on "new principles," which included "mining the harbors, bombing dikes and locks, and invading North Vietnam with land armies."[1]

The desire of the JCS to escalate the campaign against the North attests to their judgment that the restrained bombing policy was not yielding satisfactory results. The new principles, calling for the blockade of North Vietnam, bombing of dikes and locks, and a land invasion, were an admission that the limited strategy was not working. The Chiefs' dissatisfaction was shared by Secretary of Defense McNamara, who came, however, to the opposite conclusion. He said that the bombing had not produced noticeable results upon the POL (Petrolium, Oil, Lubricants) supplies; the transportation system was still functioning; morale appeared to be good; and most essential economic activities continued. McNamara wished to see the bombing campaign ended.[2]

Numerous reasons have been offered to explain this apparent "failure" of air power to bring about a conclusive result in Vietnam in this early phase. Some argue that the expectations of our leaders and the American people were unrealistically high. Major General Robert N. Ginsburgh cites the fact that since World War II "air power has often been billed as a potentially decisive element."[3] Thus the public expected and was led to believe that the bombing operations in Vietnam would bring the war to an early conclusion. "They assumed that air power would be as decisive a factor in Southeast Asia as it was against Germany and Japan in 1944 and 1945."[4] General Ginsburgh further argues that these misconceptions occurred because people did not recognize that air power was being employed in a different way in this war.

[1] Neil Sheehan, Hedrick Smith, E. W. Kenworthy, and Fox Butterfield, *The Pentagon Papers* (New York: Bantam Books, 1971), p. 578.

[2] *Ibid.*, pp. 554–55.

[3] Major General Robert N. Ginsburgh, "Strategy and Air Power: The Lessons of Southeast Asia," *Strategic Review*, I, No. 2 (Summer 1973), p. 22.

[4] *Idem.*

We were not using classic air doctrine at all. This was not an air campaign in the sense that air power was used in World War II or even in Korea. Air power was applied in a consciously restrained and deliberate way; the purposes were tailored to a new graduated strategy and were responsive to a set of overriding political considerations.[5]

We employed our air power in a limited way, but held on to our rather unlimited expectations of what it might accomplish. If military advisers made a mistake in this war, it was in failing to recognize that air power cannot have the desired results if it is applied in an environment that is inappropriate for its use. Further, it cannot succeed if it is employed in a manner that strongly mitigates against its ultimate success.

It is interesting, at this point, to re-examine the objectives of the bombing campaign. Expectations were voiced at two levels: there were official objectives and there were also unstated objectives or hoped-for results. In November 1964, Ambassador Maxwell Taylor proposed air strikes on the North as a means to bolster morale in the South, encourage political stability among the Saigon leadership, improve the counter-insurgency campaign, and persuade the North Vietnamese to stop its aid to the Viet Cong and force them to cease their efforts to overthrow the Saigon Government.[6] Also in November 1964, William Bundy circulated a "Draft Position Paper on Southeast Asia" prepared for a National Security Council select committee. It stated that a carefully graduated, systematically applied program of air strikes could cause Hanoi to yield and seek a negotiated settlement. Though not explicitly stated, there was at least an implication that these results could be expected within two to six months.[7] Bundy's expectations were even more ambitious than Ambassador Taylor's.

In 1967, President Johnson said that our goals were to back our fighting men, to deny the enemy a sanctuary, to punish the North Vietnamese for violations of the Geneva accords, to limit the flow of supplies and

5 Ginsburgh, "Strategy and Air Power," p. 22.

6 Sheehan et al., The Pentagon Papers, p. 372.

7 Ibid., pp. 374–75.

men moving from North Vietnam, and to raise the costs of the infiltration substantially.[8]

Although disappointed in the progress of the war and supporting further escalation, General Wheeler made the following statement in 1967 in support of the bombing efforts:

> The bombing has been achieving the limited purposes it was designed for. The bombing has denied North Vietnam a sanctuary. The bombing is exacting a heavy penalty against North Vietnam's already strained human and material resources. Bombing has increased substantially the number of men and tons which must be dispatched from the north to get one man or one ton into South Vietnam. It has apparently caused them to resort to the shorter supply routes across the DMZ and contributed to their reduction of major scale operations within South Vietnam.[9]

Comparing the limited objectives as stated by President Johnson and the results as assessed by General Wheeler, one would conclude that the early bombing of the North had accomplished its goals. This view certainly has credence and has been supported by other observers. General Ginsburgh, for example, said, "In my view, air power was quite effective, in achieving these circumscribed objectives."[10]

The problem is that this approach does little to explain the dissatisfaction of the Secretary of Defense and the JCS with the progress of the war in 1967 and early 1968, and with the effect that the bombing campaign had on that progress. While the very limited objectives stated by President Johnson were indeed articulated as the official objectives, it may be that they were understated somewhat as a hedge against uncertainty. It seems proper to assume that our expectations and hopes were

[8] Ginsburgh, "Strategy and Air Power," p. 22.

[9] General Earle G. Wheeler, "Selected Statements on Vietnam by DOD and Other Administrative Officials, July 1–December 31, 1967," reprinted in *Background Information* (Washington, D.C.: Office of Information, Office of the Secretary of the Air Force, October 1968), p. 8.

[10] Ginsburgh, "Strategy and Air Power," p. 22.

higher than those stated objectives and that the disappointment expressed in 1967 was measured against a set of expectations that were quite different from Johnson's stated objectives.

It is apparent that there was not a universal agreement on the objectives for the bombing or for the expectations that the United States had for its efforts over the North. In a study conducted for the U.S. Senate, Robert E. Biles focused on goals for the 1965–68 period of the war:

> The objectives to be gained by bombing North Vietnam have varied during the course of the war, but can be summarized as follows: (1) to reduce the infiltration of men and supplies into South Vietnam, (2) to make North Vietnam pay a high cost for supporting the war in the South, (3) to break the will of North Vietnam, (4) to affect negotiations for an end to the war, and (5) to raise U.S. and South Vietnamese morale.[11]

Three of these goals parallel the official objectives put forth by President Johnson in 1967. But there are two others in Biles's list that are of a higher order. "To break the will of North Vietnam" and "to affect negotiations for an end to the war" are rather more serious and difficult missions than raising friendly morale or enemy infiltration costs. There is also a crucial difference between stopping the flow of supplies and men along the infiltration routes, as some observers seemed to expect, and merely raising the costs of infiltration for the enemy.

When the effectiveness of air power through 1968 is weighed against the set of higher expectations, it does not measure up. And it would appear that the higher objectives were in fact the operative ones at the time, hence the obvious frustration and disappointment of Mr. McNamara and the Joint Chiefs.

There are many analysts who believe it was a mistake to undertake the bombing of North Vietnam in 1965 at all. Sir Robert Thompson, for instance, in analyzing the strategy of North Vietnam, concluded

---

[11] Robert E. Biles, "Bombing as a Policy Tool in Vietnam: Effectiveness," U.S. Senate Committee on Foreign Relations, Committee Print (Washington, D.C.: U.S. Government Printing Office, 1972), p. 1.

that North Vietnam was an unsatisfactory target for a bombing campaign. In order to be successful, bombing would have to deprive North Vietnam of critically needed resources. Thompson concludes that the few industrial, economic, and transportation targets available were really not critical to their effort. The principal North Vietnamese asset was manpower. "It was the one target which the Americans could not attack either by bombing the centers of population or indirectly by bombing the Red River dykes."[12] Even trying to attack the population directly would have been difficult because the North Vietnamese population is fairly well dispersed and, given the degree of control that the Politburo has over the population, could be dispersed even further.

Thompson felt that there were many reasons why the bombing of North Vietnam was a counterproductive policy as conducted in 1965: (1) It greatly expanded the scope of the war; (2) legally, it escalated the war, creating the POW issue and legitimatizing North Vietnamese infiltrators as POWs; (3) the bombing turned the war into an anti-American crusade for the people of North Vietnam, enabling Hanoi to mobilize the whole country; (4) it justified dispatch of NVA units to the South; and (5) it created a common bond between Russia and China in support of North Vietnam, this in spite of the Sino-Soviet rift.

In a sense the proponents of air power had been "hoist on their own petard." The use of air power in an independent campaign not directly related to the ground war is fully in keeping with the established beliefs of U.S. air power proponents. It traces its historical roots from Cold War deterrence missions through the successful strategic bombing campaigns of World War II, back to the theories and writings of General Billy Mitchell and General Giulio Douhet after World War I.

These theories are not, however, based on the kind of limited warfare, limited commitment, and limited objectives that were present in the Vietnamese conflict. They are based on a kind of all-out war in which the continued existence, the central interest, of both contenders is at stake.

[12] Sir Robert Thompson, *No Exit from Vietnam* (New York: McKay, 1970), pp. 58–59.

The air war has been criticized by many factions and on numerous grounds. Dean Edmund Gullion expressed the frustration of many when he said, "My feelings can be summed up in a resentment and rejection of the approach of gradualism. I think that in diplomacy and in war, as in courtship, there are two factors that count—timing and energy. It seems to me that our course in Vietnam, for whatever reason it was done, fell short in both timing and energy. There were lags in perception, lags in execution, lags in intelligence, and lags in keeping the home front coordinated with the forward front." Colonel Frizzell further analyzed the dilemma of gradualism in the air war.

Colonel Frizzell:
In the fall of 1964, William Bundy headed an interagency working group "to draw up various political and military options for direct action against North Vietnam."[13] In a position paper coordinated with members of the group, Mr. Bundy laid out the concepts for our strategy. He described a projected program for increasing military pressure upon North Vietnam. He visualized a graduated sequence of actions, made up mainly of a series of progressively larger air strikes, the weight of which would be adjusted as the situation developed. The campaign would be designed to make it clear to the North Vietnamese that our behavior would be keyed to their activity in the war, that we were fully prepared to apply more pressure or less pressure as dictated by developing events.[14]

The U.S. decision for a policy of restraint was taken after careful consideration of the alternatives and indeed seemed logical enough at the time. A restrained policy was to be expected of a great power when engaged in a limited war. General Maxwell Taylor participated in the deliberations in 1964 when the decision was reached. He explained the rationale behind the policy of gradualism:

13 Sheehan et al., *The Pentagon Papers*, p. 322.
14 *Ibid.*, p. 375.

The purpose of rational war is to break the will of the adversary and cause him to adjust his behavior to our purpose, not necessarily to destroy him. . . . We wanted Ho and his advisors to have time to meditate on the prospects of a demolished homeland. . . . Thus, in bombing North Vietnam we limited our operations to low-intensity attacks, restricted as to type and location.[15]

As a military strategy, gradualism had many shortcomings. Admiral Thomas H. Moorer said it resulted in "committing our forces piecemeal with initial employment at low intensity and, subsequently, increasing the tempo in a slow and deliberate fashion."[16] We restricted our force as to type of targets, with many important targets not included on the approved lists. Important areas of the target system were off limits to our fighter-bombers, which effectively put many targets beyond reach. The level of attack, the frequency of attack, and in many cases even the tactics used were restricted.[17]

Gradualism allowed the North Vietnamese time to build up their air defenses once the bombing began. This resulted in much higher losses. It granted significant sanctuaries to the enemy around Haiphong and Hanoi and along the Chinese border. It allowed them time to disperse their people, supplies, and industries and gave them time to mobilize civilian labor teams to repair damaged facilities.

As the bombing of only selected targets was continued at a low level of intensity, the North Vietnamese were able to build alternative facilities and multiple modes of transportation and to look for additional supply sources. Air power has its greatest impact when it can take advantage of the principles of mass and surprise. Our campaign over North Vietnam from 1965 through 1968 was short on both counts. It was deliberately not massed and because it went on for so long the advantage

---

[15] Maxwell D. Taylor, *Swords and Plowshares* (New York: Norton, 1972), p. 403.

[16] Admiral Thomas H. Moorer, "The Decisiveness of Air Power in Vietnam," *Supplement to the Air Force Policy Letter to Commanders* (Washington, D.C.: Air Force Office of Information, November 11, 1973), p. 7.

[17] *Ibid.*, p. 7.

of surprise was soon forfeited. "Gradualism forced air power into an expanded and inconclusive war of attrition."[18]

Politically, gradualism failed to have the desired effect on the North Vietnamese. Ambassador Taylor said after his tour in Vietnam that it suggested a lack of decisiveness to the Hanoi leadership. Gradualism, punctuated by repeated bombing pauses, encouraged the enemy to persevere.[19] The net result was that our restrained strategy and re-strained application of power caused a marked prolongation of the con-flict, reduced it to an indecisive war of attrition, sharply increased U.S. losses over the North, and contributed to the growing disaffection with the war at home.[20]

If strategies of restraint and slow escalation will not work against a determined enemy, when then are the alternatives? It seems that we are faced with what General Taylor calls the "dilemma of limited war."

> Should . . . a President employ military force swiftly and decisively and risk the international consequences, or should he proceed tentatively and incrementally and risk a prolonged war on the Vietnam model? Neither is an attractive choice, but the only other is the do-nothing option which offers the prospect of a progressive attrition of our interests.[21]

If faced with this difficult delimma in the future, we must critically and carefully evaluate the political and military environment, critically examine our own national interests, and devise a strategy which will avoid the pitfalls that we created for ourselves in Vietnam.

In contrast to the general policy of gradualism, the events at Khe Sanh during the 1968 Tet offensive were fast-moving and militarily decisive. The battle for Khe Sanh was a brilliant tactical success for U.S. air power

18 Moorer, "The Decisiveness of Air Power in Vietnam," p. 7.

19 Taylor, *Swords and Plowshares,* p. 404.

20 *Idem.*

21 *Idem.*

as 5,000 U.S. Marines defended a small plateau in western I Corps against 20,000 North Vietnamese. The NVA stood still, exposed their position, and laid siege to the Marine outpost—thinking that another Dien Bien Phu would be achieved. They did not reckon that the United States had learned the tactical lessons of Dien Bien Phu and was determined not to repeat the mistakes of the French. Firepower, control, airlift, and target intelligence made the difference.

In an effort organized under the Seventh Air Force in Saigon, aircraft from all the services were employed against the encircling North Vietnamese divisions. In the end, the North Vietnamese were destroyed and the U.S. Marines prevailed.

Major General George Keegan discusses how the planning of Khe Sanh was handled.

General Keegan:

I suppose that in many ways I played a major planning role in the defense of Khe Sanh. The situation came on a Sunday morning when Westmoreland turned to my boss, General William Momyer, and said, "Spike, Khe Sanh has become a symbol. It is of no importance to me, but it has become of great psychological importance to the United States. It is related solely to the Dien Bien Phu syndrome and the target is the soft underbelly of the United States. Spike, if I lose Khe Sanh, I am going to hold the United States Air Force responsible."

Westmoreland had no other choice. He had deployed his forces and his troops to defend the cities. He knew an attack was coming. He knew the Tet offensive was imminent, and he had done the best he could to protect what he considered most important to South Vietnam—the population base.

The Air Force faced many difficulties in overcoming the manner in which air-ground coordination had been established in South Vietnam. The Air Force role had been confined by the Army to airlift and the provision of reconnaissance and fire on call. It was the first war in the

Air Force's history in which the Air Force was not directly involved in the daily development and maintenance of a data base on enemy ground-force dispositions. Hence the Air Force was suddenly faced with establishing overnight a capability to locate the enemy on the ground and to bring him under fire unilaterally.

General Momyer and I moved swiftly to set up an intelligence-gathering and targeting structure along with AAA suppression, airlift and airborne control of all Army, Navy, SAC, and tactical air assets. The intelligence techniques were those of World War II and Korea. We took the tools we had, including our own (Army-managed) air reconnaissance, along with our newest cameras, and proceded to locate the hidden, foliage-covered enemy. We used all of our exotic technology, never before used effectively—infrared detection means, communications, intelligence, ground sensors, prisoner-of-war documents, and interrogations. With the active assistance of radio finding techniques, we were able to pinpoint every company and battalion of the two divisions that were deployed.

We were assisted with some excellent strategic and tactical advice provided by French survivors of Dien Bien Phu. Using sand-table models, they spelled out in detail what was wrong. Within days we knew that airlift would be crucial, as would the suppression and interdiction of AAA; night tunneling would have to be stopped with napalm.

In short, we reviewed the lessons, learned of the pitfalls, and set in motion the tactics, control, and integrated intelligence not previously applied to the air-ground war in South Vietnam. Every source—diplomatic, clandestine, documentary, sensor, and reconnaissance—was used. The results were fed to a command center where we recorded where every bomb went, where every unstruck target remained, and where every antiaircraft gun was located. We policed the application of fire by the Army, the Navy, the Marine Corps, and the Air Force. We created a controlled environment that permitted us, in six weeks, to destroy each of the enemy's battalions. Khe Sanh was held.

The lessons relate to unity of command and integration of intelligence. Khe Sanh was a microcosm of what can be done when you are thorough, unify your command, integrate the management of the elements that support that command structure, and permit directed fire against an identified force in a precisely known place.

Ambassador Robert Komer:

I just wanted to make a point about the importance of seeing our use of air power in Vietnam from a quantitative perspective, not just from the operational viewpoint of General Keegan, who spoke mostly of what we used to call "air operations against the North." We dropped over eight million tons of air ordnance in Southeast Asia. But I think the vast bulk was dropped in South Vietnam and on the Ho Chi Minh Trail and in the Laotian panhandle. In other words, the vast bulk of our air operations was not against North Vietnam, but was interdiction of their lines of communication to the South and close air support in South Vietnam. This is where most of the ordnance and the great bulk of the money was expended. And those operations were not under anything like the kind of political or civilian restrictions that the operations out of country were. In fact, we had more air power than we had targets. So there was no lack or inhibition on the use of air power against the Trail or against the enemy in the South, and that was where the bulk of the air effort went.

None of what I am saying is, in any way, critical of General Keegan's point. I am just saying that there was another large part of the war. In the case of Khe Sanh we might not have known where the enemy was, but we sure as hell knew where we were, and he was attacking us! That was made to order for the use of air power, which we used tremendously effectively. But when you are talking about air power, be sure not to confine the discussion to the out-of-country operations, because that was not where all the money and the effort went.

General Keegan:

That is a valid point. We have often used our air power inefficiently. Khe Sanh was an exception. We have frequently used our air power, in terms of tonnages and weapons, against the least effective and efficient target area that was open to us. We have used it against the most nonproductive targets, the most difficult to find, and those that had the least impact on the battle in the long run. Some of the reasons for this were political. Our intelligence was inadequate, as was our ability to integrate all sources of intelligence for details of the enemy's logistics system. But the Air Force's intelligence means and functions since the 1960s had passed to the control of CIA, NSA, the Defense Intelligence Agencies, and other bodies—thus compounding the problem of acquiring tactical intelligence. Other reasons were doctrinal and reflected concern over other services usurping Air Force missions after the war. Finally, the Air Force's "effectiveness" often forced it into chasing trucks rather than blocking their entry points into South Vietnam, thanks to the constraints imposed on us.

General Keegan was also asked about the tactics of the air campaign and about lessons learned. His comments ranged across all the years of American involvement, from the Kennedy years to the eleven-day bombing campaign of December 1972.

General Keegan:
I doubt that you could find any two officers in the Air Force who would agree on what the relative lessons were. I am struck by the relevance of Robert Komer's observations. National objectives were ill defined. Little thought was given to the cost in men and treasure of restricting the Air Force to the least effective spectrum of targets. I think it was good that the young of this country raised their hands and said, "We've gone far enough." I hope that in the years to come, the leadership in this country will think more carefully about committing itself to open-ended conflict in which the costs to society have not been thought through carefully.

With regard to general objectives, strategic doctrine, tactics, and technology, I would recall an observation of Walt Rostow's when asked, informally, how the Kennedy administration had arrived at its great strategic perspectives, guidelines, and framework for the policies which evolved. He said, "Well, it wasn't nearly as studied as you might think.

A group of us got together for a few days at Camp David and we talked loosely and generally about the future and we expressed our hopes. Those hopes became the statement of strategic objectives." In many respects, I think the approach into Southeast Asia was just as superficial. We must understand the limitations and capabilities of air power, the role of new precision-guided weapons, and learn to balance our selection of objectives with full appreciation of the capabilities of the men and the systems that we intend to use. And we must be aware of the human, material, and psychological costs.

Doctrinally, if I could sum up close air support and ground-air coordination, I don't think you will ever find a soldier in the U.S. Army or Marine Corps, for that matter, who is ever satisfied with the quality of air support that he gets. Nor are you likely to find an airman who is equally satisfied with his ability to perform. Having said that, and looking back on my involvement in past wars, I would judge that our airground coordination doctrines have probably reached as high a level of competence as is likely. However, technology will improve the precision of fire. We are twenty-five years ahead of the Soviets in our airground coordination of fire.

Interdiction worked about as we expected. I know of no responsible airman who has ever judged publicly that the Air Force could do more than impede maybe 10 to 15 percent of the flow of the enemy's logistics. Our weapons were not adequate to the task. Our reconnaissance and our intelligence were totally inadequate to the task. The enemy was operating in a hidden mode. It took a lot of technology to find him. But we could seldom localize with precision. I think the best answer in the future is the Ranger battalion.

Having said that, though, I would like to observe that the Air Force long since had lost the ability to plan and support, with intelligence, interdiction operations. Years ago, the mission of targeting was taken away from the Department of the Air Force and passed to the Defense Intelligence Agency, where it has simply died. The assessment analysis of enemy logistics (economic impact) has fallen to the CIA by default. So the Air Force entered this war with very limited tools for assessing logistics flow in depth, and yet one of the Air Force's principal missions is to impede the flow of logistics into the battlefield. By 1968 we were a little smarter. Sensor technology contributed. However, sensors never accomplished what they were designed to do. They did not locate targets. But they did give us an advantage. In northern Thailand we built a multimillion-dollar center with a great array of computers and communications—with a brilliant staff of technicians.

Such a facility could never have been justified to support intelligence. However, we quickly learned to use this great and costly facility to do logistics analysis.

We converted the mission to an intelligence mission. We integrated communications intelligence. We exploited captured documents. We took everything the Army could give us on the character of enemy movement. Then we used the sensors and the computers to discipline our knowledge of how the enemy moved. We computerized our new data base and developed a significant logistics input-throughput-output model of enemy logistics. We undertook to measure every pound of supplies the enemy put into his net. A reporting system was developed to determine consumption for road repair, feeding, active defense, and the like. We were thus able to determine net input into South Vietnam. We were thus better able to direct our interdiction, when to anticipate the ebb and flow of enemy combat. We then were able to determine the real impact of interdiction.

In 1968, for every ten pounds that entered through the panhandle of Laos, something on the order of one pound reached South Vietnam. It went into food. It went into antiaircraft fire. It went into road repair and construction. It went into survival along the Ho Chi Minh Trail. It went into the medical evacuation of an enormous number of casualties. It soon became clear that tactical interdiction was having a far greater impact than was appreciated in Washington. Regrettably, the record is buried in tons of archives.

General Abrams was the first, I think, to sense the impact air power was having upon the intensity of NVN ground combat. But despite General Abrams' vigorous support of integrated use of tactical and strategic air power to impede the flow of logistics, the intelligence mechanism used to defend Khe Sanh was soon dismantled.

There are some useful strategic targeting lessons also. Air power can be made to penetrate any defensive environment that science, technology and man develop. Air power, properly directed, properly equipped, properly planned, can penetrate any target system, however dense, no matter where. There will always be a price. It will be affordable—provided the doctrine of gradualism is abandoned and the direction of battle is left to the professionals. The tragedy of Vietnam is that the target system evolved in Washington was the most inept of any war in which modern air power has been committed. Contrary to the judgments held by 99 percent of our defense analysts and political leaders, I for one came out of that war convinced that a bombing campaign like Linebacker II—an eleven-day campaign with B-52s, fighter-bombers, F-111s operating at night at two hundred feet, and jamming—could have brought the war to a close as early as 1965. North Vietnam could have been isolated from the battlefield in a matter of weeks and North Vietnam's wherewithal to fight in the South would have been reduced to such proportions that the ground defenders could have managed far more easily than they did. I continue to believe that North Vietnam since 1965 has been nothing more than a transmission belt for Soviet and some Chinese military matériel to which the North Vietnamese have added human cannon fodder.

A word about communications. Our ground, naval, and air forces have paid an enormous price for their near total lack of communications discipline. The enemy always knew where we were, what we intended to do and when. Except in Linebacker II. The enemy knew everything there was to know about us. They knew when we were going to strike, where we were going to strike, under what conditions—ground, air, or naval. That permitted him to make do with but a fraction of the assets and resources we required to operate with.

This kind of information permitted the enemy to achieve results out of all proportion to relative commitment of firepower. Still, the costs of the NVN were far higher than any Caucasian army could long sustain.

Sir Robert Thompson:

I had the privilege of being briefed by General Vogt on Linebacker II, and I certainly regard it as the most effective plan of war ever waged in eleven days. This is one of the points I made previously—you had the war won; you did not have to do it again. But you had to be in the position to say that you could and would do it again, and this, I think, is what the Air Force now has, what it did not have in 1965 or 1966: the techniques that can achieve a situation in which, because you have the capability—and if you have the credibility and can convince people that, if it is necessary, you will use it—you then have no risk. It won't happen.

Professor Allan Goodman:

With respect to the puzzling period between October 1972 and January 1973, you have told us that we nearly lost the war, but at the point when we were on the verge of peace we were also on the verge of winning the war. Was the pursuit of détente and the desire not to press the unilateral advantage we were gaining in Vietnam so overwhelming that Kissinger and Nixon were not aware of your assessment of the situation, not aware of the fact that if we had persisted, for example, we would have achieved far more than we got in the Paris agreement? How strong, in particular, was our desire to show the Russians that we would not press the unilateral advantage in Vietnam by seeking a settlement that was less to our advantage but consistent with a settlement grounded in détente?

Sir Robert Thompson:

I would have accepted the cease-fire agreement you got, though you could have got a better one. You could probably have got a withdrawal of North Vietnamese troops out of South Vietnam. I won't press that one. However, you could have got Article 7 and Article 20 enforceable, with respect to Laos and Cambodia. Then the whole agreement would be enforceable.

Professor Goodman:

But not because of détente.

Sir Robert Thompson:

How much do you make of détente? Does it mean that every time Dr. Kissinger moves into the scene, because of détente, it is the Americans or, much worse, the American ally who is going to have to make all the concessions?

The Impact of the Air Effort Probably Outweighed Many of Its Benefits[22]

Thomas C. Thayer

Thomas Thayer continues the analysis of air operations with some data on the costs and effectiveness of the bombing of North Vietnam and Laos. This air campaign in some ways might be called strategic bombing but is usually referred to as an air interdiction campaign. Air interdiction has been and continues to be a controversial subject. Interdiction is often characterized by the term "isolate the battlefield" and therein the problem may lie. Most air and ground commanders do not expect that air interdiction will isolate the battlefield in any total sense of the word. Experience in World War II, Korea, and Vietnam demonstrated that interdiction is very effective when enemy forces are massed (as for an attack), when the battle situation is fluid (the enemy is not dug in), and when the enemy's consumption of supplies and equipment is high (as when he is forced into sustained combat). When these conditions do not pertain, air interdiction can be expected to limit the enemy's options and capabilities substantially but usually will not result in his outright defeat.

Air interdiction is often judged against a criterion of 100 percent isolation of the battlefield. Occasionally air power may be able to cut off all lines of communication, but these occasions will probably be rare and surely will not occur in a war conducted with numerous sanctuaries,

[22] This analysis focuses on U.S. and South Vietnamese (VNAF) operations by fixed-wing combat aircraft in Southeast Asia, including the B-52s. It does not cover helicopter operations or the operations of the fixed-wing aircraft (C-130s, etc.) which moved troops and supplies.

limited strategies, and rigidly constrained rules of engagement. There are important lessons in these discussions for both the proponents and the opponents of the U.S. air interdiction campaign against North Vietnam.

It is not often realized how large a role US/GVN air operations played in the attrition strategy. The bulk of these air operations was broadly directed at supporting the attrition strategy in South Vietnam and along the Ho Chi Minh Trail.

The air operations with fixed-wing combat aircraft in Southeast Asia were enormous in size and cost. U.S. and South Vietnamese fixed-wing aircraft flew more than 3 million combat sorties in South Vietnam, North Vietnam, Laos, and Cambodia during 1965 through 1972. The costs ran into the billions:

1. The full program budget costs were probably about $14 billion for the three-year period of Fiscal Years 1969–71.

2. The incremental[23] costs of bombing North Vietnam in 1968 were probably about $2 billion.

3. In mid-1970, it was estimated that the incremental costs of the U.S. and South Vietnamese fixed-wing combat air operations in South Vietnam and Laos had been more than $3 billion in Fiscal Year 1970.

4. Hostile and accidental losses of U.S. Air Force and Navy fixed-wing aircraft in Southeast Asia cost at least $5 billion.

The total costs of the air effort are not readily available, but the cost estimates given above are enough to indicate that this was the largest and costliest air effort in the history of warfare.

The tactical air operations performed two primary missions—close air support and interdiction of troop and supply movements.

The objective of close air support is to furnish fire support to the troops on the ground quickly when they need it. However, only a small

---

[23] Expenditures over and above what would have been spent on the forces in peacetime.

proportion of the sorties were needed for this purpose. Less than 10 percent of the fixed-wing air strikes in South Vietnam were flown to support allied forces in contact with VC/NVA forces.[24] Another 25 percent responded to a request for an "immediate" strike on a target of opportunity (e.g., VC/NVA troops, an occupied base camp, an antiaircraft site). Most of the remaining sorties (two thirds of the total) were planned twenty-four hours or more in advance and they struck known or suspected VC/NVA locations, roads, and supply storage areas.

Extrapolating from these figures, it seems likely that no more than 25 percent of all the attack sorties flown in Southeast Asia were closely linked to combat taking place on the ground or to a freshly sighted target.[25]

This suggests that most of the enormous tactical air effort in Southeast Asia concentrated on interdicting supplies and, occasionally, personnel movements.

The results of the interdiction campaigns are best illustrated by the U.S. air operations in North Vietnam and southern Laos. These two target areas together consistently accounted for about half of the sorties, but the distribution between them shifted each time the rules of engagement changed. When North Vietnam could be bombed, most of the sorties went there. When it couldn't the sorties shifted to Laos.

The shift into Laos is seen clearly in 1969, after the November 1968 bombing halt in North Vietnam. When North Vietnam was fair game again in 1972, the sorties shifted back into it from Laos. In 1973, when Laos and North Vietnam were both off limits, the available sorties simply swung into Cambodia until the bombing there was halted.

Thus, the distribution and rates of out-of-country interdiction sorties apparently depended more on the number of sorties potentially available from the aircraft in the theater than they did on strategy or considerations of relative sortie effectiveness among the target areas.

---

24 Only 4 percent of the Southeast Asia total.

25 The pattern for artillery fire is the same. In FY 1968 and FY 1969, except for the Tet-68 period, about 70 percent of all U.S. artillery rounds were fired in situations of light or inactive combat, as judged by the reporting artillery unit.

Probably the best analogy is a fire hose, running under full pressure most of the time, and pointed with the same intensity at whichever target is allowed, regardless of its relative importance in the scheme of things.

In the words of Senator Stuart Symington: "In fact, as the general just said . . . orders were that if you do not need the planes against Vietnam, use said planes against Laos."[26]

The important question, however, is not how the sorties were allocated, but how effective they were.

As often stated, the objectives of the operations in Laos, North Vietnam, and later Cambodia were:

1. To impose a ceiling on VC/NVA combat activity in South Vietnam by reducing the flow of supplies below amounts required to support high activity levels, the primary concern being the VC/NVA ability to launch an offensive serious enough to upset Vietnamization.

2. To promote a settlement by imposing a meaningful cost on the North Vietnamese in terms of their matériel and human resources (to be meaningful, the costs must be at or near maximum levels which the North Vietnamese are willing to sustain).

All of the estimates of supply flows down through North Vietnam are uncertain, and among the least certain are the amounts estimated to have been destroyed by air strikes. Nonetheless, extensive analysis suggests the following tentative conclusions:

1. The VC/NVA probably received about 70 percent of their supplies for operations in South Vietnam from sources *inside* the country. About 15 percent was estimated to come from North Vietnam over the supply routes through Laos, target of the primary air interdiction effort.

2. About one third of all supplies shipped into southern Laos were estimated to have made it into South Vietnam through 1970. The rest were estimated to be destroyed by air strikes, consumed in transit, or stockpiled in Laos. After 1970, the allies may have done better owing to

26 U.S. Senate, Subcommittee on United States Security Agreements and Commitments Abroad Hearings, October 20–23, 1970, p. 713.

the truck-killing C-130 gunships that were so effective operating at night, but the VC/NVA still managed to move enough supplies and manpower South to keep the war going and to launch another major offensive in 1972, although the most intense fighting was supplied largely through North Vietnam across the DMZ.

3. Apparently there were plenty of supplies to ship, because the estimated flow of imports into North Vietnam was twenty times the size of estimated supply shipments from North Vietnam into Laos.

These conclusions seem to suggest that the more than 1.5 million sorties flown in the out-of-country interdiction campaign did not choke off VC/NVA combat activity in the South. They probably did impose a ceiling, but it was pretty high.

What about the second objective, to impose a meaningful cost on the North Vietnamese? Here, too, the apparent results are not very encouraging. The data suggest that the air operations probably did not impose critical matériel costs on North Vietnam, since its allies paid for most of the resources destroyed. North Vietnam's estimated foreign aid during the three years up to 1970 was two or three times as large as the costs of keeping its forces in South Vietnam, Cambodia, and Laos supplied and replacing the damage in North Vietnam caused by the bombing.

The results indicate that Secretary of Defense McNamara was correct when he stated in November 1966: "A substantial air interdiction campaign is clearly necessary and worthwhile. . . . But at the scale we are now operating, I believe our bombing is yielding very small marginal returns, not worth the cost in pilot lives and aircraft."[27]

When the political impact of the bombing is added to its other costs, the effectiveness of the way the air war was conducted is open to question. Indeed, the military themselves kept pointing out how political constraints impeded the optimal use of air power. But these constraints applied mostly to North Vietnam and Cambodia. No comparable re-

[27] *The Pentagon Papers: The Senator Gravel Edition* (Boston: Beacon Press, 1971), IV, 374. Statement was made in a paper of November 17, 1966.

straints existed in South Vietnam and along the Ho Chi Minh Trail, where the vast bulk of the sorties were flown.

Mr. Thayer agreed with many of our other contributors that North Vietnam was merely a conduit for supplies moving from overseas sources through the North Vietnam ports and thence into Laos, Cambodia, and South Vietnam. With this nearly unlimited input at the top, there was very little that could be done to create a real logistics crisis for the Viet Cong, particularly since they controlled the level of military activity and hence their own levels of consumption.

Bombing of the Ho Chi Minh Trail, which wound through North Vietnam into Laos, Cambodia, and back into South Vietnam, was only a partial solution. Bombing of these lines of communication could not cut off the movement of all supplies into the South. Nevertheless, interdiction along these jungle roads was substituted for the more comprehensive approach advocated by General Wheeler and others in 1965. That air and naval power could be used effectively to deny the enemy his objectives was demonstrated in 1972 with the mining and bombing of North Vietnamese ports and rail lines from China. The United States learned its interdiction lessons during the war and adjusted its strategy to accommodate to the realities of the situation. Changes in U.S. strategy are discussed in more detail in the next chapter.

Chapter 9

Air Power and Negotiation in 1972

Colonel Donaldson D. Frizzell

> One of the lessons of the Vietnamese conflict is that rather than simply counter the opponent's thrusts, it is necessary to go for the heart of the opponent's power: destroy his military forces rather than simply being involved endlessly in ancillary military operations. —*James R. Schlesinger,* April 1976

In 1972, the United States was presented an opportunity to engage and destroy the enemy's military forces in the field and with reason to go for the heart of the opponent's power as we sought first to contain the Easter invasion and second to bring the North Vietnamese to the peace table. Colonel Donaldson D. Frizzell felt that U.S. air power successfully blunted the Communist military drive and was instrumental in bringing them into serious negotiations.

By the winter of 1972, the American people were thoroughly disillusioned with the war in Southeast Asia. Critics sharply questioned the legality of U.S. intervention there and the rationality of continued U.S. involvement. For that matter, the role of the United States in world affairs was under intense fire from many quarters. The nation suffered as the American people tried to reconcile their frustration over the war, their responsibilities as a superpower, and their disillusionment with military force as an effective instrument of national power.

America had shed its blood and spent its treasure on this war, had put its reputation on the line and come up empty-handed. Vietnam presented a huge military commitment with no payoff.

The North Vietnamese mounted a major offensive against the South in March 1972. By then, there were few ground combat troops left in Southeast Asia. The South Vietnamese fought back, providing the manpower on the ground; the United States responded with its air power and a fundamental change in strategy.

This chapter will briefly discuss the evolution of U.S. policy and strategy from 1965 to 1972 and will show how air power was used under the umbrella of a new and more effective strategy to help bring about the "peace" settlement of January 1973. This discussion seeks to show the relationship between choice of strategy and efficiency of military force and to highlight the role that military strength can play in the resolution of certain difficult international situations.

EVOLUTION OF U.S. STRATEGY—1968 TO 1972

In the earlier days of the Vietnamese War (1965–68), the United States had followed a policy of gradual escalation and slowly increasing military pressure in an attempt to force Hanoi to desist in its efforts to take over South Vietnam. The military strategy was based on a theory of attrition in which the more powerful United States would wear down its weaker opponent.

After the Tet offensive of 1968, the United States concluded that its strategy was not leading toward a satisfactory solution. We changed our course from one of increasing military pressure to a policy of de-escalation, Vietnamization, withdrawal of U.S. forces, and a stepped-up negotiation effort.

The attrition strategy of the earlier period had been unsuccessful for a number of reasons. First, it tended to ignore the political weaknesses of our South Vietnamese ally and placed most of the emphasis on a military solution. While "Americanization" of the war between 1965 and 1968 may well have been necessary at the outset, it only worsened the political and military weakness of our ally. The trend toward more

American control took the war out of the hands of the South Vietnamese. This contributed politically to the Viet Cong effort because it bolstered their case that the Saigon Government was weak and ineffectual. It made it easy for them to brand the Americans as imperialists and interventionists. "Vietnamization," which began in late 1967, was the cure for this problem. Between 1967 and 1972, the war effort was gradually shifted from American to local control. In 1972, the war in the South was handled by a revitalized South Vietnamese Government. Saigon fought its own ground war with its own people and, so long as external aid continued at adequate levels, did well. The armed forces of South Vietnam had received extensive training and new equipment and were a more effective fighting force.

Success in the battle of attrition depended upon our ability to inflict "unacceptable losses" upon the enemy. This presented a definitional problem because the concept of "unacceptable losses" had different meanings for Washington and Hanoi. As it turned out, losses became unacceptable to the United States first. We had seriously underestimated the casualties and matériel losses that Hanoi was willing to absorb. By 1972, with this lesson in mind, we knew we faced a tough and determined enemy; we knew we had to optimize our strategies and tactics to take full advantage of our assets.

In the earlier period, we handicapped our own ground forces by granting wholesale sanctuary in Cambodia, in Laos, and across the DMZ. This made meaningful attrition in the ground war nearly impossible because the enemy forces were permitted to slip away for rest and refitting at their leisure. The Cambodian and Laotian sanctuaries were now denied (ARVN and U.S. troops first attacked Cambodia in 1970). A new strategy in 1972 would put heavy pressure on North Vietnam as well.

Hanoi's war matériel originated in the Soviet Union, China, and several East European countries. North Vietnam was the conduit for the supplies, which came in through the major ports and down the railroads from China. The United States had taken no military action prior to 1972 to shut off the flow of matériel into the war zone. We had tried to conduct a campaign of attrition by closing off the bottom of the funnel in South Vietnam. General Westmoreland's "search and destroy" operations, though very effective in a tactical sense, had not been able to deal with the steady flow of infiltrators and war supplies that continued to stream into South Vietnam. The 1972 strategy cut off these imports.

After allowing Hanoi to import war matériel freely, we had tried to deal with the problem by destroying some of the matériel after it arrived and by interdicting the lines of communication from Hanoi-Haiphong to the combat zone in the South. The bombing operations from 1965 to 1968 (Rolling Thunder) were meant to do this job. Rolling Thunder was inadequate for this task. It was not conceived as part of a comprehensive interdiction campaign but was a highly restricted and selective program that was designed gradually, and in a very controlled manner, to apply increasing pressure on the North Vietnamese. This concept of gradually increasing pressure had not stopped the flow of supplies nor had the pressure ever been great enough to bring Hanoi into serious negotiations. In 1972, gradualism was abandoned. It had robbed air power of its effectiveness by violating the principles of concentration and surprise. The net result was to decrease the effectiveness of air power seriously while at the same time driving up U.S. losses.

THE EASTER INVASION OF 1972

By late 1971, Vietnamization had moved along well and U.S. ground forces neared completion of their withdrawal. Most of the active fighting shifted out of South Vietnam into Cambodia and Laos. The fortunes of the Viet Cong and the North Vietnamese had steadily declined following the Tet offensive of 1968. In that fight, the Communists lost over 40,000 men, including most of the Viet Cong cadre. This had reduced their influence in the villages and rural areas, helping South Vietnam's pacification program penetrate former Viet Cong-held areas.[1]

---

[1] Richard Egan, "Nixon Confident on Latest Bombing Raids," *National Observer*, January 8, 1972, p. 3.

The assault into Cambodia in 1970 by the combined American and South Vietnamese force substantially weakened the Communists by depriving them of their traditional sanctuaries. It disrupted their lines of communication, forcing them to develop new infiltration routes for operations in South Vietnam.

In December 1971, the Communists escalated the air war with a sharp buildup in activity. The number of surface-to-air (SAM) sites in the southern half of North Vietnam was doubled. MIG fighters moved south to airfields along the Gulf of Tonkin. From these bases, MIGs attacked U.S. Air Force fighters operating over northern Laos in support of the Laotian Army and in southern Laos over the supply trails. It was the first time that Hanoi's fighters had operated outside North Vietnam on such large scale.

The missile and fighter activity against U.S. aircraft was part of a general increase in Communist activity that Defense Secretary Laird felt was not in keeping with the "understanding" between Washington and Hanoi.[2] The United States retaliated by hitting North Vietnam with more than 1,000 bombing sorties on December 26–31, 1971. *The New York Times* reported:

> Ninety percent of the bombing of North Vietnam during the last five days was concentrated on enemy supply dumps and antiaircraft positions near the entrances to the Ho Chi Minh Trail. . . . Other attacks were made on MIG fighter plane bases between the 18th and 20th parallels.[3]

Reaction from the anti-Vietnam, anti-Nixon forces was swift. " 'Sheer madness,' exclaimed Mayor John V. Lindsay of New York. A 'desperate attempt to salvage a wrecked policy,' said Senator George McGovern of South Dakota."[4] It was apparent that the war in Southeast Asia was still alive as the year 1972 opened. Neither the problem nor the criticism had abated much, as the war lingered on.

[2] Egan, "Nixon Confident," p. 1 ff.

[3] "Report U.S. Raids Hit Supplies," *The New York Times*, December 31, 1971, p. 3.

[4] Egan, "Nixon Confident," p. 1 ff.

The year 1972 was destined to be a fateful one for both sides, but this was not immediately apparent. The Paris negotiations were hopelessly deadlocked. The United States was pursuing its Vietnamization policy, withdrawing U.S. forces while working hard to build up the Saigon Government and the South Vietnamese armed forces. U.S. air power was still present and active in the area but at a reduced level.

The Communists were not getting any closer to achieving their objectives in South Vietnam and were beginning to worry also about their Chinese and Russian friends. The United States and the Soviets were moving toward détente and an agreement was expected soon at the SALT talks. The rapprochement between Communist China and the United States had stunned the world and must have made Hanoi wonder if the United States and China had a new understanding concerning Southeast Asia.

Out of this set of political and strategic factors came the decision by Hanoi to launch a major offensive in the spring of 1972. The buildup of antiaircraft forces in the area north of the DMZ and in Laos showed an increasing concern by Hanoi with protection of its supply lines to the South and was a portent of things to come.

During the early months of 1972 there was a record stockpiling of supplies in the South. After returning from a visit to Indochina on January 31, 1972, General Westmoreland, by then U.S. Army Chief of Staff, predicted a major Communist offensive within a month. Intelligence reports said:

> . . . the flow of trucks along the Ho Chi Minh Trail in Laos is at record levels, with each truck carrying about four tons of supplies. In two nights . . . American gunships damaged about 200 trucks a night.[5]

There was also evidence of significant troop movements, and intelligence data revealed that three North Vietnamese Army divisions had moved into positions along the Laotian–South Vietnamese frontier. Another division was reported in a position just north of the Demilitar-

---

[5] William Beecher, "Any Enemy Offensive Expected to Be Long," *The New York Times*, February 11, 1972, p. 14.

ized Zone near Laos. Additionally, an estimated 50,000 replacement troops were "strung out along the infiltration pipeline" leading through Laos into South Vietnam.[6]

The buildup was quite apparent and was being carefully watched. Most observers expected the heaviest attacks to come in the northern provinces of South Vietnam (Military Region I) and in the Central Highlands around Kontum and Pleiku (Military Region II). The attack was expected in February because "conventional wisdom was that the Communists planned to embarrass President Nixon during his historic visit to Peking," scheduled for February 21, 1972.[7]

No major attack came in February. The buildup continued and speculation mounted as the month of March went by also. Meanwhile, the U.S. Army continued its withdrawal plans, with an eye toward meeting President Nixon's announced May 1, 1972, troop ceiling of 69,000 men.

The invasion came on March 30 with a vengeance. A U.S. Air Force historical document contains this statement on the Communist invasion:

> The reason for the continued stockpiling in Southern NVN, the DMZ, Laos, and Cambodia . . . became abundantly clear on 30 March 1972. On that day, North Vietnam turned the low key "winding down" conflict into a brand new war with a massive, three pronged attack supported by armor and artillery. The North Vietnamese Army swept down through the DMZ and into MR I, out of Laos into MR II, and from Cambodia into MR III to menace the capital city of Saigon itself.[8]

Although this was the most serious attack on South Vietnam since the massive attacks of Tet-68, there were major differences. This time the North Vietnamese struck with twelve uniformed divisions in a conventional assault more reminiscent of Korea or World War II than of the long guerrilla war of Southeast Asia. U.S. and Vietnamese commanders

[6] Beecher, "Any Enemy Offensive," p. 14.

[7] *Ibid.*, p. 15.

[8] "Linebacker: Overview of the First 120 Days," *Contemporary Historical Examination of Current Operations* (CHECO Report), Headquarters, Pacific Air Forces, Honolulu, Hawaii, September 27, 1973, unpublished Government Document, p. 8.

were not surprised by the NVA use of artillery and tanks but were surprised by the conventional frontal assault across the DMZ into MR I.
The size and conventional character of the NVA forces that attacked
Kontum and Pleiku in the Central Highlands and at An Loc in MR III
were also a surprise. This was not a guerrilla action at all: the North
Vietnamese were conducting main-force operations with conventionally
armed divisions.

The stakes and the risks were high. In Paris, Mrs. Nguyen Thi Binh,
chief Viet Cong representative at the Paris peace talks, stated the Communists' goal:

> Our aim is to liberate all South Vietnam and to establish a government
> of national concord with its seat at Saigon.[9]

It was clear that a decisive defeat of the South Vietnamese would seriously weaken the Thieu Government in Saigon and might bring back
the instability that had so often plagued the Saigon Government
since 1955.

Clearly the North Vietnamese still had hopes that they could conquer and rule all of Indochina, no matter what the cost. But what were
the immediate objectives of this invasion? At a minimum they hoped to
discredit the U.S. Vietnamization program by defeating the ARVN in
a military showdown. They also wanted to reignite the antiwar elements
in the United States, hoping to embarrass the Americans as they had
in 1968.

In any event, General Vo Nguyen Giap, the Defense Minister of
North Vietnam, chose to conduct "a large scale, conventional, mechan-
ized war—something U.S. airpower is very good at countering."[10] This
was the kind of break the United States had been looking for—a chance
to end the ugly stalemate. John L. Frisbee, editor of *Air Force Magazine,* feels that General Giap miscalculated and gives him "low grades

---

9 "Now: Make-or-Break Test in Vietnam," *U.S. News & World Report,* April 17, 1972,
p. 17.

10 John L. Frisbee, "The Air War in Vietnam," *Air Force Magazine,* LV, No. 9
(September 1972), 48.

for his reading of both allied capabilities and intentions." Further, Mr. Frisbee said:

> Either he misjudged the effectiveness of airpower against mechanized forces, or he thought that the U.S. would not reinforce allied airpower to counter the invasion. When he ordered the attack across the DMZ, he must have been convinced that President Nixon would not authorize bombing in the North, much less mining of the harbors.[11]

In 1975, General Vo Nguyen Giap attacked again, and in that instance the United States did not reinforce with air power. Indeed, the United States chose not to increase its aid to its beleaguered former ally, and as a result South Vietnam was defeated.

Captured enemy documents outlined the Communist plans for the 1972 campaign, plans which seemed to follow a set timetable. First there would be a major drive in Military Region I toward Quang Tri and Hué. This would cause Saigon to send reserves north to reinforce. Then the NVA planned to open a second front in Military Region III northwest of Saigon. This would draw reserves from the Mekong Delta, after which the Delta would be vulnerable to small-unit attacks. A third front was planned in the Central Highlands around Pleiku and Kontum during a later phase of the offensive.

The action began in the northern provinces when the NVA 304th and 308th divisions swept south toward Quang Tri. Initially, the plan went well as the Communist onslaught swept nearly all the forward fire-support bases within the first few days. The attacks were spearheaded by Soviet-built T-54 tanks and were accompanied by heavy-artillery fire. The NVA 304th Division came right down the coast along the Gulf of Tonkin while the 308th circled in from the west. The attack started

---

[11] Frisbee, "Air War in Vietnam," p. 51.

under heavy monsoon cloud cover and for the first four days advanced without major air attacks against it. After the weather broke, the North Vietnamese were exposed and it was obvious that they were using different tactics in this offensive. An F-4 Phantom pilot, returning from a mission, was quoted by *Time*:

> It was unbelievable . . . I've never seen anything like it—columns of tanks, columns of trucks, even men marching along the road.[12]

This was the enemy that the South Vietnamese Army had to face. The Third ARVN Division met the 304th and the 308th NVA in Quang Tri Province and did not do well during the initial onslaught. The Third was a newly formed division with little combat experience and that spelled trouble. They fell back in a disorderly retreat and quickly gave up ten miles of territory. Because of the bad weather, they did not get much help during the first four days. Only the Vietnamese Air Force (VNAF) with its A-1s and A-37s were able to work under the 500-foot overcast. These small attack aircraft did well in helping to contain the initial attack. After being reinforced and regrouped, the ARVN stiffened and slowly gave ground over the next two weeks until the city of Quang Tri fell in late April 1972. In all they had been forced back eighteen miles in about three weeks and were holding the line at that point.

A second front was opened northwest of Saigon by the NVA Fifth, Seventh, and Ninth divisions. They had orders to move east out of Cambodia into the Tay Ninh–Binh Long area. On April 7, the small border town of Loc Ninh fell. Elements of four NVA and Viet Cong divisions were soon advancing along Highway 13 toward the provincial capital of An Loc. The Fifth ARVN Division withdrew down Highway 13 before superior forces. Eventually they were surrounded in the provincial capital. An Loc was under intense artillery and rocket bombardment and was totally dependent upon aircraft for supplies; the siege lasted eighty days.

In the center of Vietnam, in Military Region II, the North Vietnamese had overwhelmed Dak To and captured the airfield, had cut

12 "Vietnamization: A Policy under the Gun," *Time*, April 17, 1972, p. 39.

Route 19 from Pleiku to the sea and Route 14 between Pleiku and Kontum. The city of Kontum became a major target, but the ARVN held, aided by VNAF and American air power.

The North Vietnamese deployed three different Soviet tanks, heavy field artillery, truck-mounted rocket batteries, and Soviet-built antitank missiles. Ten antiaircraft regiments were estimated to have over four hundred AAA weapons. Surface-to-air missiles (SAMs) were introduced into South Vietnam for the first time. The SA-2 Guideline was moved into northern Military Region I, while the SA-7 Strella (a hand-held, infrared heat-seeking SAM) was widely distributed throughout South Vietnam. The emphasis was on heavy weapons in this attack. Tanks, artillery, heavy-caliber AAA, SAMs, radar fire control—these weapons established the conventional character of the North Vietnamese attack.

U.S. REACTION

President Nixon was committed to the withdrawal of U.S. ground forces from Vietnam and, indeed, after the Easter invasion the reduction of U.S. forces continued toward the May 1 goal of 69,000 men.[13] When the attacks came on March 30, President Nixon had only one U.S. military asset left—U.S. air power. But even air power had been reduced considerably since the bombing halt of November 1968, and Vietnamization had shifted the burden of the war more and more to the Vietnamese.

From a peak of forty-one squadrons in 1968 the USAF had been reduced to fifteen tactical air squadrons in March 1972. The U.S. Navy had three aircraft carriers on station off Vietnam in 1968; by 1972 this had been reduced to two. USAF fighter sorties had dropped by two thirds during the period, and B-52 sorties had been cut from 1,700 per month in 1968 to 1,400 in early 1972.[14]

One of the first steps taken by President Nixon to counter the Communist invasion was to order a major buildup of air power in the region.

[13] Robert B. Semple, Jr., "U.S. Spokesmen Stress Nixon Hasn't Decided about Withdrawals after May 1," *The New York Times,* April 13, 1972, p. 16.

[14] Major General Robert N. Ginsburgh, "North Vietnam—Air Power," *Vital Speeches of the Day,* XXXVIII, No. 23 (September 15, 1972), p. 733.

In response, the U.S. Air Force and the U.S. Navy redeployed fighter squadrons, B-52s, and attack carriers to the Southeast Asia theater. The U.S. Air Force's Tactical Air Command (TAC) deployed the equivalent of 15 fighter squadrons and 7,000 people as part of the buildup. The U.S. Navy rushed the USS *Kittyhawk* from the Philippines back to the Gulf of Tonkin to join the *Hancock* and the *Coral Sea*. Two other attack carriers steamed from Japan and the United States to join the fray.

U.S. air power blunted the NVA offensive, inflicting heavy losses on the enemy. Large numbers of tanks, trucks, and other vehicles were destroyed or disabled. The ARVN Fifth Division was supported almost entirely by air power during the eighty-day siege at An Loc in MR III. B-52s flew 250 missions, tactical fighters flew 3,500 sorties in close support, and over 600 C-130 airlift sorties delivered food and supplies.[15] In the face of intense ground fire, the C-130s made use of new radar air-drop tactics that allowed parachute drops of supplies from the relatively safe altitude of 10,000 feet.[16] The ARVN fought well after a shaky start in the early fighting, and the VNAF was given high marks for its performance. General Lucius D. Clay, Jr., commander of the Pacific Air Forces, called the VNAF performance "tremendous—the brightest spot of the whole Vietnamization program." The ARVN defenders at An Loc were cited by Major General James F. Hollingsworth, U.S. Army, who said he had "seen nothing in his thirty-four years as a soldier to surpass the determination of ARVN troops at An Loc."[17]

When the massive invasion began, it was apparent that the North Vietnamese were challenging the United States in a very specific way. The challenge required the United States to re-evaluate its position and decide on an appropriate response.

The Vietnam peace talks had been in session since early 1969. They were being conducted on two levels, a public plenary forum in Paris on one level and the secret negotiations conducted by Dr. Henry

[15] Ginsburgh, "North Vietnam—Air Power," p. 732.

[16] John L. Frisbee, "Airdrop at An Loc," *Air Force Magazine*, LV, No. 11 (November 1972), 40, 41.

[17] Frisbee, "The Air War in Vietnam," p. 59.

Kissinger on a second level. Beginning in August 1969, there had been twelve secret sessions between Dr. Kissinger and the North Vietnamese representatives Le Duc Tho and Xuan Thuy.[18]

At the time of the Easter invasion, Dr. Kissinger reported that the secret talks had been suspended for over six months, with the North Vietnamese unwilling to set a date for further meetings.[19] In the face of this intransigence and a major invasion across international borders, the President and the National Security Council decided on a new course of action.

A CHANGE IN STRATEGY

The first U.S. response had been a major buildup of U.S. air power. The second step, taken in mid-April, was the resumption of the bombing of North Vietnam, including some B-52 strikes in the Hanoi-Haiphong area. And third, on May 8, 1972, President Nixon announced an interdiction campaign against North Vietnam which included the mining of major ports and an intensive bombing campaign against the land lines of communication.

In his address to the nation on May 8, 1972, President Nixon explained the choices open to the United States:

> We now have a clear, hard choice among three courses of action: immediate withdrawal of all American forces, continued attempts at negotiation, or decisive military action to end the war.[20]

The issues were clear: concern for the remaining American troops in Vietnam, concern for America's commitments to its allies, and concern for American credibility. The President and his advisers

[18] Richard M. Nixon, "A Plan for Peace in Vietnam," *Weekly Compilation of Presidential Documents*, VIII, No. 5 (January 31, 1972), 121.

[19] Richard M. Nixon, "The Situation in Southeast Asia," the President's address to the nation on May 8, 1972, *Weekly Compilation of Presidential Documents*, VIII, No. 20 (May 15, 1972), 843.

[20] *Ibid.*, p. 839.

chose to meet strength with strength; the answer to the North Vietnamese invasion would be delivered with military power, and the
American component would be made up largely of air and naval
forces.

In direct reference to the decisions of May 8, Dr. Kissinger made the
following observation:

> What we are trying to prevent by this decision is an endless continuation
> of this process by which one attack after another takes place over a period
> of months without serious negotiations, and without any prospect for a
> settlement.[21]

The principal political objective was to convince the North Vietnamese that the United States was not going to withdraw unilaterally
and abandon its ally in the South. Neither was the United States going
to continue pointless negotiations that were leading nowhere.

The 1972 strategy took advantage of the increased strength of the
South Vietnamese forces and the increasing vulnerability of the North
Vietnamese forces. While continuing to deny sanctuary to the NVA, we
mounted an interdiction campaign against North Vietnam that had
three military objectives:

1. To reduce the flow of supplies into North Vietnam from external sources. This was accomplished by mining the harbors and interdicting the railroads and highways from China.

2. To destroy the existing stockpiles of supplies already in North
Vietnam. This was accomplished by a heavy bombing campaign.

3. To reduce the flow of supplies from North Vietnam to the units
in the South. This was done through a stepped-up interdiction campaign on the lines of communication to the South.[22]

As President Nixon put it on May 8, 1972, in his national address:

> I have concluded that Hanoi must be denied the weapons and supplies
> it needs to continue the aggression. . . . All entrances to North Viet-

21 Nixon, "The Situation in Southeast Asia," p. 845.

22 Lieutenant General George J. Eade, "The Effectiveness of Airpower in the North,"
briefing for reporters at a Pentagon press conference on June 8, 1972, pp. 1–5.

namese ports will be mined to prevent access to these ports and North Vietnamese naval operations from these ports. United States forces have been directed . . . to interdict the delivery of any supplies. Rail and all other communications will be cut off to the maximum extent possible. Air and naval strikes against military targets in North Vietnam will continue.[23]

In addition to adopting a more comprehensive strategy, there were important changes made in the operational management of the forces and in the rules of engagement. In the Rolling Thunder campaigns of 1965–68, many of the day-to-day tactical decisions were being made by civilians in Washington. Under the new management concept, U.S. senior commanders in the field were delegated the authority to make the important day-to-day decisions. The result was the restoration of tactical flexibility, an important ingredient in a more effective policy. The Joint Chiefs of Staff and civilian officials in Washington approved and validated the master target list—then the field commanders designed and executed their attack plans according to the latest intelligence, operational, and weather factors pertinent at the time.[24]

During Rolling Thunder operations, there had been large strike-free zones. These areas covered hundreds of square miles around both Hanoi and Haiphong and thousands of square miles in the buffer zone along the border between North Vietnam and China. There were many key military, industrial, and transportation targets that were immune to attack. The North Vietnamese soon learned to use the strike-free zones as sanctuaries against the air strikes. They also concentrated their air defenses in the areas that were open to attack.

The code name for the 1972 campaign was Linebacker. Under the Linebacker rules of engagement, missions into the strike-free zones would be permitted. Firstly, there was the realization that strikes in these areas were necessary if the operation was to be successful. Secondly, a new generation of precision-guided munitions, so-called "smart bombs," made it easier to permit strikes in highly populated or politically sen-

---

[23] Nixon, "The Situation in Southeast Asia," pp. 840–41.

[24] Frisbee, "The Air War in Vietnam," pp. 53–54.

sitive areas. The guided bombs had many advantages but one of the most important was that collateral damage could be controlled with a high degree of confidence.

The newly adopted operational management concept retained basic policy decisions at the highest levels of government but decentralized operational decisions to the field commanders. This practice worked well in Vietnam just as it had in many sectors of American industry. The tactical flexibility plus the more realistic rules of engagement resulted in a campaign that featured systematic and comprehensive attacks on target systems (petroleum, rails, electric power, etc.) that had not been possible before.

NEGOTIATIONS RESUME

There were three negotiating sessions, one private and two plenary, soon after the Easter-weekend invasion. Dr. Kissinger made these comments on the April meetings:

> We were confronted by the reading to us of the published Communist statement. It had taken us six months to set up the meeting and innumerable exchanges and when we got there, what we heard could have been clipped from a newspaper and sent us in the mail.[25]

Linebacker operations continued all summer amidst a storm of controversy over civilian casualties, bombing of the dikes, collateral damage, the waste of war, the futility of U.S. involvement, and the question of unilateral withdrawal. Meanwhile, substantive talks were resumed on July 19, 1972.

On October 8, 1972, Radio Hanoi announced a major breakthrough in the negotiations. Dr. Kissinger explained that Hanoi had dropped several of its demands (among them the demand for a coalition government) and from that time on was behaving "with good will and with great seriousness."[26]

[25] Henry A. Kissinger, "Vietnam Peace Negotiations," news conference on October 26, 1972, *Weekly Compilation of Presidential Documents*, VIII, No. 44 (October 30, 1972), 1565.

[26] *Ibid.*, pp. 1565, 1566.

The new strategy was working. The mining operations by the U.S. Navy had closed off the major ports of North Vietnam to the merchant ships that delivered the war matériel. In 1971, it was estimated that North Vietnam imported over two million tons of war matériel.[27] By the end of May 1972, imports were down to a trickle. The U.S. blockade had sealed off the ports of North Vietnam.

The second step in sealing off the flow of war matériel to North Vietnam required that the main rail lines from China to Hanoi be severed. The remainder of the rail system would also come under attack. This included the line that connected Hanoi and the port of Haiphong and the major lines that parallel Highway 1 from Hanoi to the DMZ.[28] Both the northeast and the northwest rail lines from Hanoi to China were cut within a few days. Rail traffic on these lines was virtually stopped. There were some fifteen bridges out on each railroad most of the time, and as fast as the North Vietnamese crews repaired them they were knocked down again.[29]

One of the principal reasons for the success of Linebacker I operations was the effectiveness of the precision-guided bombs. These weapons, using laser or electro-optical guidance systems, improved accuracies by several orders of magnitude over the old free-fall bombs. With the guided bombs, the airmen could consistently place a 2,000- or 3,000-pound bomb within ten to fifteen feet of the target. The new capability was dramatized on May 13, 1972, when one flight of four USAF F-4 fighters brought down the infamous Thanh Hoa bridge. This bridge had first come under attack on April 3, 1965, had survived the attacks of hundreds of aircraft, and had cost the United States dearly in terms of downed aircraft and lost airmen.

STALEMATE LEADS TO RENEWED BOMBING

On October 26, 1972, Dr. Kissinger made his famous statement that "we believe that peace is at hand." In spite of this optimism, an agree-

[27] Eade, "The Effectiveness of Airpower in the North," p. 1.
[28] *Ibid.*, p. 6.
[29] CHECO Report, p. 25.

ment was not signed. The North Vietnamese may have felt they could get a better deal after the November election. Negotiations were resumed on November 20, 1972, but by December 12, Dr. Kissinger reported that the North Vietnamese were not negotiating in good faith —that they were trying to make changes in already agreed-upon positions. He indicated that the United States was willing to resume talks at any time, but only "in an atmosphere that is worthy of the seriousness of the endeavor."[30]

Six days later President Nixon ordered the resumption of air operations against North Vietnam and explained his reasons as follows:

> ... On December 18, 1972, when our hopes for peace were so high, and when the North Vietnamese stonewalled us at the conference table—I found it necessary to order more air strikes on military targets in North Vietnam in order to break the deadlock.[31]

From December 18 through December 29, the United States "executed a contingency plan which called for all-weather, around-the-clock operations and continuous attacks on North Vietnam." The North Vietnamese air-defense system reacted by firing well over 1,000 surface-to-air missiles at the B-52s and fighters in the eleven-day period, compared to 2,500 firings in the previous seven and a half months.[32] U.S. losses were high in the first few days, but the defenses were quickly defeated. In the overall analysis the United States lost 26 aircraft in approximately 1,630 sorties for an average loss rate of 1.6 percent.

The effect of the bombing campaign on the North Vietnamese target system was profound. The air-defense system had been overwhelmed

---

[30] Henry A. Kissinger, "Vietnam Peace Negotiations," news conference on December 16, 1972, *Weekly Compilation of Presidential Documents*, VIII, No. 51 (December 18, 1972), 1464–68.

[31] Richard M. Nixon, radio address to the nation on March 30, 1973, quoted in *The Air Force Policy Letter for Commanders*, Office of the Secretary of the Air Force, Washington, D.C., April 15, 1973.

[32] Admiral Thomas H. Moorer, "Bombing of North Vietnam," testimony before the Subcommittee on Department of Defense Appropriations, House of Representatives, 93rd Congress, 1st Session, January 9, 1973, p. 11.

and had been unable to affect the outcome of the operation. The rail-road system had been brought to a virtual halt as bridges, marshaling yards, rolling stock, locomotives, and storage warehouses were destroyed or damaged. Electric-power facilities were heavily damaged; warehous-ing and supply depots had been extensively damaged. Airfields, SAM sites, military complexes, naval bases, ports, shipyards, and communica-tion centers were all subjected to heavy damage or destruction.[33]

It is interesting to note that guided munitions were not used exten-sively during the eleven-day raids because of poor weather conditions. The bulk of the ordnance in this operation was of the "old-fashioned" free-falling type. The accuracies achieved and the low collateral damage speak well for the proficiency of our present force, especially the all-weather B-52s, F-111s, and A-6s. During the spring and summer of 1972, the guided bombs had done a devastating job against a whole series of difficult targets, and when this was topped off by the intensive concen-trated attacks in December, even with non-precision bombs, the cumu-lative effect was telling.

In the face of the unprecedented attacks, the North Vietnamese did not react with their normal resiliency. Usually the repair and restora-tion efforts were organized quickly and repairs were underway within a short time after the attacks. This time, there were signs that the bomb-ing was wearing them down. The damage was more extensive than it had ever been and was concentrated in and around their major popula-tion and industrial centers. The matériel losses and the psychological pressure had been accumulating since May 1972. It was a heavy burden for the people and the Hanoi regime. There were definite signs after the eleven-day campaign that North Vietnam had had enough.

Contrary to the expectations of many critics, the heavy bombing re-sulted in relatively few civilian casualties. The targets were all military and industrial, the bombing was accurate, and the North Vietnamese were known to have a good civil-defense effort. Even though the bulk of the bombing took place near the heavily populated areas of Hanoi and Haiphong, the North Vietnamese themselves put the total killed at be-

[33] Moorer, "Bombing of North Vietnam," pp. 5-14.

tween 1,300 and 1,600 for the whole eleven-day period. *The Economist* tried to put the casualty figures into perspective:

> For between a thousand and two thousand people to die in great numbing horror, is not something that can be shunted out of the mind with the argument that worse things happen in war. But it is worth remembering that the German Air Force killed almost as many in a single night in what now seems to be the relatively mild bombing of Britain in 1940 and 1941.[34]

It is also worth noting that the total killed was smaller than the number of civilians massacred by the North Vietnamese in the city of Hué, South Vietnam, during the Tet-68 offensive.

On December 30, the White House announced that negotiations would resume on January 2, when experts would begin a round of technical talks in Paris. Dr. Kissinger and special adviser Le Duc Tho were set to meet again on January 8. It was also announced that the President had ordered a halt to all bombing north of the 20th Parallel for "as long as serious negotiations are underway."[35]

In 1969, Dr. Kissinger had characterized the American dilemma in Vietnam as one where "military success . . . could not be translated into permanent political advantage." In 1972, most observers agreed that the Linebacker campaigns had been a military success. On January 24, 1973, Dr. Kissinger announced a concomitant political success: an agreement had been concluded. The U.S. military involvement was near an end. During a White House news conference, reporters asked about the correlation between the bombing and the settlement. Dr. Kissinger was rather reticent about a direct connection, not wishing to speculate on the motives of the North Vietnamese. He did point out that the talks had been deadlocked in mid-December but that there had been a "rapid movement" when the negotiations resumed in January.[36]

---

[34] "The Use of Air Power," *The Economist* (London), January 13, 1973, p. 15.

[35] *Weekly Compilation of Presidential Documents,* VIII, No. 53 (January 1, 1973), 1809.

[36] Henry A. Kissinger, news conference on January 24, 1973, *The State Department Bulletin,* LXVIII, No. 1755 (February 12, 1973), 166.

Others were not so reticent; indeed, many saw a direct connection between the military events of 1972 and the negotiated settlement of 1973. As we saw in Chapter 6, Sir Robert Thompson was convinced that we had the war "won" at that point and should have pressed for a more satisfactory settlement.

The January 1973 agreement was enough to get the United States out of the war and bring the POWs home, but was not enough to ensure a lasting peace. The Paris agreement allowed the North Vietnamese to retain control of territory that they occupied following the invasion. For two years, the South Vietnamese held on with truce violations piling up by the hundreds. In 1975, with U.S. support dwindling rapidly, Hanoi launched another spring offensive. After the fall of Ban Me Thuot, there were a series of serious South Vietnamese mistakes as Thieu decided to abandon the Central Highlands and later the imperial city of Hué. Under the shadow of these mistakes and with the uncertainty of U.S. support, the 1975 spring offensive had a very different and unhappy ending.

Chapter 10

Tactics and Technology

In earlier chapters, it has been noted that tactically the American forces did very well, that behind the failure of force to achieve a solution lay faulty strategy rather than tactical weaknesses. That does not mean that there were no problems at the tactical level. There were problems aplenty, as is usual in any war, but there remains the nagging question of why a tactically proficient and technologically superior force could not bring the benefits promised. Did the Americans fall down on the tactical level? Did our technology fail?

Stephen Young:

Is it not fair to state that, even as late as 1968 and 1969, our approach was very much focused on nuts and bolts? In Robert Komer's phrase, were we not just looking for a "quick fix"—a solution today for yesterday's problem? We were not primarily concerned with the kinds of broad strategic conceptions or objectives that we have discussed here. We were not looking ahead to isolate the larger dynamics at work by which we could guide the course of future events more in our direction. Our fixation was with tactics, with techniques—the old American instinct for building the better mousetrap.

Colonel Ray Franklin:

An interesting aspect having to do with the ground forces and their probable commitments to battlefields in the future concerns the terrain associated with real world trouble spots. We found that in several stages in the Tet offensive we took people who were trained to fight in the field and in the jungle, and we went into cities with them. As a matter of fact, we committed three Marine battalions to Hué. One Marine battalion commander explained to me how he got to be an instant expert on city fighting: he learned about it on his way from the Phu Bai compound into Hué with his battalion. He had the doctrine document under his jeep seat when he got there. He was the duty expert on how to fight in cities. His battalion had never been trained to fight in cities. As a matter of fact, we have very limited training programs in city fighting. In the thirty years since we fought across Europe and up the Italian boot, through a lot of cities, the institutional memory has disappeared. The way to do it and the gear to fight with has more or less disappeared also. For instance, the city is an environment that separates the trooper from his supporting arms. How do you use close air support when the bad guys are only fifty feet away, across the street? How do you use artillery? How do you use "smart bombs"? How do you use all the things we have been investing all our money in for thirty years? We have been moving combat power back about ten kilometers into such supporting arms as artillery, helicopter gunships, and the like. The infantry does most of the dying and almost none of the killing any more. You can look at small-arms expenditures, which went from 20,000 rounds in World War II per enemy KIA (killed in action) to over 100,000 rounds per KIA in Vietnam. We give a nineteen-year-old high school kid a little squirt gun that has a selector on the side, and when he pulls the trigger it goes "phtt" and he doesn't kill anybody. Put him in town, and all of a sudden he is in serious trouble. He can't get on the radio and call for close air. He can't get on the radio and call for supporting arms. He can't get on the radio and call for all this help. It can't be used. It's physically and often politically constrained.

I was flying in and out of Hué all during Tet hauling in the bandages and bullets and moving the wounded out. In the northern end of town, where the Vietnamese and the Army were fighting, there were A-1s and all sorts of air support, but we were restricted from using it because we were near the temple. So there was very little supporting-arms fire at all.

The Marine battalions were fighting with what they could carry on their backs. So a very important lesson here is that we should look at organic weaponry for the small unit, and training, and doctrine, and tactics.

There is another lesson we should learn for the future. If trouble is going to happen in a Third World country, it is going to happen in the capital city. If the government changes hands, it doesn't change hands in the bushes. It happened in Santiago. It happened in Bangladesh—actually, there were a lot of troopers still available to fight in there, but when the capital fell, everybody stopped.

Our current doctrine says, "Stay out of town." It's a good doctrine, with two possible exceptions: You've got to find an enemy that will agree to go out in the open and slug it out, or you may want to look at the advantages the city offers the defender, say, in Western Europe. As somebody said today, "Pick your enemy." If I were a Soviet planner, I would take a look at what the American Army does best, and I would hardly face them in the open fields on a nice clear day. I'd pick the most hideous weather I could find in the world, and I'd probably go right down the main street of the biggest city I could find because we don't do either one very well. We don't practice in cities. We are poorly equipped.

I think that the wave of the future is going to be in small, mobile, hostile units, especially in the Third World. We are going to have to learn to fight in the built-up areas. We are going to fight with what we carry on our backs. Right now we are spending all our time and all our attention on supporting arms.

An example of our emphasis on built-up area warfare and weapons comes from the Army Command and Staff College, where two years ago they had no instructional hours of urban warfare, and last year they went to two hours, and this year they are going to ten. That's a quantum jump. The Russians, on the other hand, spend roughly 22 percent of their time in urban, fortified, and barrier (forest) warfare and how to fight it. They seem to have equipped their forces to do this job very well, too. The AK-47 is a crummy rifle at 300 meters, but at 100 meters, which is the assault distance, it is a very good gun. They have made some interesting performance/reliability trade-offs—you throw the AK-47 in the mud, pick it up, crank one round through it, and it shoots. You throw the M-16 in the mud, crank one round through it, and you have to stop and clean it. They have gone for the simple, idiot-proof weapons that are very safe but very effective in close combat.

Mr. Young:

When I was working with the Popular Forces (PF) in the Delta, what they wanted was what the Viet Cong had, and not what we were giving them. They felt more secure with the AK-47 and the B-40; both were idiot-proof and punchy assault weapons. My impression was that the Communists had come up with more effective weapons for small units in combat than we had.

Professor Francis West:

Let's not give too much credit to the AK-47. Maybe some PFs preferred it to the M-16, but really, on balance, the AK-47 is only marginally better than the M-16. There is no big difference now in terms of the squad-level infantry weapons except that we have the M-79 grenade launcher and small, good grenades. Perhaps we are too technologically advanced. And I think that General Abrams was very sensitive to the fact that we did get oversophisticated in Vietnam.

There are a couple of other lessons to be learned, though. Tactically or strategically, most military commanders vehemently denounce gradualism. The tactic of dribbling slowly in is opposed almost by every senior military man today. I don't quite know what that means, however, in terms of how we would actually employ our forces in a crisis.

The other thing, of course, is what General George Keegan referred to—the issue of control. Who's in charge here? General Keegan indicated that there was a problem with the civilians at the top. Of course, if you are a battalion commander, you have the same problems with what we called the "squad leaders in the sky"—you know, the three-star general who wants to deploy your fire teams. My hypothesis is, although everybody down the line dislikes it, that that's a function of technology, and we can expect more crisis management from the top. It really started in 1962 with President Kennedy trying to tell the Navy exactly where he wanted the destroyer to make the intercept on the ships allegedly carrying missiles. In terms of top control, although it is disliked, it is going to remain with us. As technology gets better, and you are able to communicate, if you are in charge you are going to be in charge in practice.

There are two other things: Firstly, the target acquisition we talked about in Vietnam was a function of our desire to fight the war according to certain rules, as Robert Komer put it. It was not that we could not see the enemy, however. My unit, for instance, saw 26,000 North Vietnamese in one year—alive, walking around. The problem was, of course, getting them to stand still the way we wanted them to stand still, long enough to knock them off with the weapons systems we had in hand, with the size of unit we wanted to use. If you wanted, at any particular time, to run a higher risk, put out a smaller unit in the jungle to "wander around for a while," the unit probably was going to make contact. The point was that we wanted to do it our way, with the size of unit that we wanted, and then we had a target acquisition problem.

Secondly, there is a high degree of dissatisfaction on the part of the attack pilots, both in the Air Force and in the Navy, because of the way they were employed in the Vietnam War. They have become almost cynical because of years of going after a small wooden bridge with a high risk of dying, and they recognized that there seemed to be little correlation between that and the war-fighting output. This relates to what General Keegan was saying about the proper employment of air power. I concur that it was Linebacker II and the B-52s that together were the straws that broke the back of the North Vietnamese. But, lurking under that phrase "proper employment," is a question—an ethical question—does that mean going back to bombing the cities, to the terror bombing of World War II?

What I had in mind went a little deeper than that. The United States had a nuclear policy which proclaimed that the way you deter a nuclear war is by saying that if a nuclear war comes we will kill the women and children on the other side. That is a moral issue for the political leadership as well as for the military.

Ambassador Robert Komer:

I haven't thought this through, but I suspect that, on balance, technology has hurt us more than it helped us in Vietnam, because it confirmed us in trying to find better ways to fight the war *our* way rather than the

Vietnamese way. If, instead of the literally billions we spent on new technology, we had listened to the advice of people like Ambassador Lodge, Sir Robert Thompson, Donald Marshall, Edward Lansdale, Thomas Thayer, Francis West—non-technologists all—I think we would have done much better tactically in Vietnam.

Sir Robert Thompson:

I want to address myself to that point. The major criticism I had tactically in Vietnam was that the one element in which you were never mobile was on your feet. You got landed from helicopters and the battle took place, but when the battle was over and you had won the battle, you even went out by helicopter. No one ever walked out. Now, the enemy, who was mobile on his feet, could actually decide whether he was going to have a battle with you in the first place, and he could break it off whenever he wanted to. But it is more than that, because this very definitely applies even in the situation where you had North Vietnamese coming down the trails in Laos and infiltrating into South Vietnam. That was his vulnerable area—the trails he had to use—and the incredible thing that I have found about Communists is that they always use the same trails and they go on using them.

One of the reasons they go on using them is that no one ever interrupts them. The odd bomb may hit the trail, but what does an odd bomb do to a trail? Nothing. The one technique that seems to me to have been completely lost, quite apart from urban warfare, is what I call the "long-range penetration technique" carried out by small parties who are capable of going out and living and moving, for a month or more if necessary.

The mistake, it seems to me, when you talk about mobility on your feet in these circumstances, is the mistake in the objective. People think they are going out to have a main-force battle with what they run into. That is not the point. The point is that the enemy has this web of trails. They are absolutely vital to him to carry on the war. Your objective is to deny him freedom of movement on those trails, not to have main-force battles—to look for main forces and just have main-force battles when you are on your feet. The classic example of this—and the reason why northern Binh Dinh could never be pacified—is that the North Vietnamese had a free run from southern Laos right through Kontum to northern Binh Dinh. No one, at any time, ever interrupted it. You can only interrupt it with small forces like this. When you think of the firepower that is available to the small unit—a dozen men or so—it only requires five seconds' fire—on the first thing that comes around the corner and then you get the hell out. You are not waiting there to have a main-force battle. You don't even know whether there is a regiment behind what comes around the corner, but it is very probably three hundred people with bicycles carrying rice and mortar ammunition and so on. If they start having to escort groups like that coming through the mountains, then they have to pull main forces off to do it.

Being ex-Air Force, I can say that the one person who would really understand this is not the Army general, it is the Navy admiral. This is very much like the sea. It is like submarines and convoy systems and so on. What we never had in this war were submarines on the ground, and submarines on the ground would really have tied the enemy up. It is these twelve-man squads capable of moving in those mountain ranges that would have performed like submarines.

Professor Francis West:
I worked with Marine reconnaissance and we used to do precisely that. I worked outside Khe Sanh in five- to ten-man units, the basic unit. We could see thousands of them—but our indirect fire systems were not good enough to hurt them. If we had to use artillery, the probability was very high that we were going to miss the North Vietnamese, who moved rapidly in single file.

Sir Robert Thompson:
Coming back to objectives—that was the American objective: to get kills on main forces. My objective is to tie up their logistics.

General George Keegan:
I would like to endorse Sir Robert's statement. In World War II a few battalions of irregulars tied down four divisions of Japanese throughout the Burma campaign.

At one time General Westmoreland asked for a plan to cut the Ho

Chi Minh Trail by a ground incursion into the Laos panhandle. It took six months to develop the plan. About four army divisions, ninety miles of asphalt road, four new airfields were required. My comment on this great piece of staff work was: "I would trade all of that for a dozen Ranger battalions." We have forgotten or lost a great combat art.

Professor West:

What they did to us at the DMZ is the classic counter-example to what General Keegan was suggesting. We began to send patrols out. Every patrol was making contact. So Generals Walt and Nickerson said, "Keep reinforcing it. Keep reinforcing it." But then, what the enemy did was to say, "All right. We are going to start to escort them." So they brought in their "anti-submarine escorts"—a very apt analogy. They began to bring in their teams, who had only one rule and that was: the minute we fire they get us to forget the cost and get us. Then we had to send a company. And that was not enough. They sent in a battalion and you know the history—it started with Hill 881 and then it escalated.

They were well aware of this and we got terrific kills against them, but every time we applied pressure, they applied pressure. It became a cat-and-mouse game out there, but it would get too big for a small unit to handle after a while—good though we thought we were!

Sir Robert Thompson:

I am talking about the tens of thousands of square miles of the Annamite chain. Anyone could walk into it and through it. I guarantee you that I had no problem whatever walking in and walking out the whole way across northern Burma in World War II; crossing the Chindwin River, crossing the Irrawaddy, and walking back again, with four or five Japanese divisions around us. There is no way they can stop you unless they play the very dirty game—if they sit on the trails and sit there for a very long time in the hope that you will happen to walk along that trail. Then they have got you, because you are moving and they are sitting. This is what you should have been doing to them. There is too much thought in this patrol business that a patrol is judged by the distance it covers, to a certain extent. You know, "We did twenty miles out there today." That is not my idea of what the patrol should be doing. You know the enemy are moving in that area. You get into that area—it is only a mile or two away. The point is that you should get in there in such a way that they will know you are there but they won't know exactly where you are. Then you have got them. You are sitting, and as long as they do not know exactly where you are, you are the one who is going to fire the first shot, and it is the first shot in those situations that counts.

Dr. Robert Sansom:

What Sir Robert was trying to raise was the objective of logistic inhibition, and Robert Komer, I think, the objective of establishing territorial control. I think that the longer you had the wrong objectives, the more you facilitated accepting the type of tactics that you are talking about. I would amend what Robert Komer said concerning the evils of technology and what someone else mentioned concerning the problem of too many resources: the problem was not technology but having excessive resources, which meant that you always found them on top of you, prescribing your tactics.

Jerrold Milsted:

With respect to Mr. Komer's comments on the adverse effects of the U.S. military's emphasis on technology, we should understand that, because we are preparing in the "worst case" to fight a technically sophisticated enemy, the requirements of the service force planning establishments demand a strong technological emphasis. In Vietnam, that planning was followed in actuality by a tremendous supply and service dimension which brought a grand-scale conventional-unit logistical base system into the combat zone along with operational elements. This "rear echelon" set up a standard of living for itself that could not be easily emulated, although it was certainly tried in some cases by the combat forces in the field. All of this tended to provide for a system of rewards and expectations in such a way that tactical professionalism was, I think, seriously degraded by virtue of the fact that the material and psychic rewards went to those who could employ or support the high technology systems rather than to those who could employ only basic combat tactics. The latter, of course, would be the individual soldier, the tactical adviser, the combat aviator, or what have you.

As a result of such emphasis on and distribution of satisfactions, basic tactics, I think, suffered. We apparently failed to learn in the Vietnamese environment some of the things that we were there long enough to learn about—for example, certain aspects of basic tactics peculiar to the local environment, particularly with regard to immediate-action drills, some aspects of fire and maneuver in the attack, and patrolling at the squad and platoon level on a foot-mobile basis. We also failed to learn from lessons of other people and from ourselves at earlier times, for example from Gurkha units before and during World War II.

One worries about any effort to put the painful experience of Vietnam behind us. Junior combat leaders who are coming along now, who were not in Vietnam, could well profit from what could be taught by those who were observant participants but who are now also being conditioned to forget it all to a certain extent. I think that self-examination in this area would now be very worthwhile and that a continuing effort is needed to get down to learning and reinforcing the appreciation of basic squad- and platoon-level tactics. By all means apply tactical technology where it is available and appropriate, such as in communications, night-vision devices, unattended ground sensors, and so on. The point is not to discount or discard technology but to get back first to the basic human performance criteria in tactics and the rewards and sanctions which support them.

Chapter 11

Problems of Force Management

National strategy in war or peace requires a coordination of the agencies that execute that strategy. Bureaucratic rivalry imperils national strategy, and the role of each executive agency must be kept in proportion to the objectives and in tune with the political situation which obtains. This is often said, but is less frequently dealt with in actual practice. In managing the military portion of this effort, what is the proper role of each of the military services and each of the joint military commands involved? What is the role of the services in determining how the war will be conducted? How is leadership to be developed in the field? And how, finally, does the civilian leadership in Washington evaluate the performance of its military leaders in the field?

The competing roles of groups fulfilling overlapping functions in the overall strategy was always a troublesome matter in our deliberations. Participants were attempting to focus on overall politico-military objectives, but it was difficult to keep "role" out. Occasionally there was astonishment at the roles some groups had played—as when Barry Zorthian registered his, on learning that eight French generals, reportedly, were brought into Vietnam by the Air Force, to advise on the siege of Khe Sanh without the knowledge of the American Ambassador: "It may have been a perfectly proper move and a necessary one, but the potential harm of such a move should certainly have been raised in advance." General Keegan, head of Air Force Intelligence, at a different juncture, made an articulate argument for restoring to the Air Force many functions that had been stripped from it over the years.

General George Keegan:
When the Vietnamese War started, the process had reached a point where the tools with which the Air Force could determine what impact it was having on the enemy's will, on the enemy's economy, on the enemy's ability to prosecute war, had been removed and divided among the new bureaucracies in Washington. The CIA became almost exclusively the final arbiter and judge of the impact of air power on the enemy in North Vietnam. The Joint Chiefs of Staff, with their supporting structure, exercised the targeting prerogatives only insofar as it constituted recommendations to higher authority. The process became very divisive. When people in my position finally got the blueprint of objectives, it was the work of the people who knew the very least about the conduct of air war, who knew virtually nothing about the limitations of air war, and knew virtually nothing about the operational restrictions—problems of munitions, finding targets, accuracy, mapping. At no time in the war, until the last campaign, directed by Mr. Nixon over the objection of virtually every adviser in the U.S. Government, including the military, was air power ever used appropriately. It was always used in such a form that the enemy was allowed to recover from virtually all of the physical effects of the pounding he was getting.

Why is it impossible in the United States, within the military, first of all, within the Air Force, within the Joint Chiefs, within the National Security Council, to use this very costly, but very effective tool—air power? Why is it impossible to arrive at a proper mix of political control and direction that permits its optimal use for optimal impact as early as possible, at least cost to the economy? I know of no time, save those eleven days, when air power was used properly for limited purposes for results that could achieve a settlement.

As I look back, from the ground support in Vietnam, the targeting in Cambodia, the nearly impossible conditions of operation in Laos, and the still more difficult conditions of operation in North Vietnam, my conclusion is that we used this tool very badly. As a consequence of that misuse, we probably will be precluded from using that tool effectively in the defense of the free world in the next two or three decades, and for me, effective use is non-use. If you are capable of using it properly, and clearly state and define how you will use it, then you succeed, and reach your nirvana, which is a higher assurance that you will not have to use this very costly resource. From that point of view, I have to judge the overall use of air power in Southeast Asia as a minus, except for Mr. Nixon's decision, born of political desperation, in the last eleven days.

A key question in a war fought so far from home, with political power remaining in Washington, but essential components of the direction of the war coming from CINCPAC in Honolulu and of course MACV in Saigon, is: Who will bring together the various strands of the war and provide coherence and direction? Our discussion began with personalities, but spread much further. General Lansdale argued that, on the whole problem of strategy in Vietnam, on "how we got there, and what we were planning to do," Robert McNamara was the person. For years, it was looked upon as "McNamara's war" in the White House and on the Hill. He made a considerable impact on Vietnamese and American leaders in Vietnam during his frequent visits there. Ambassador Lodge responded to that point, and the discussion is followed by remarks of Colonel Donald Marshall, who was on General Abrams' staff; and of Dr. Robert Sansom, who was an action officer for Vietnam on the National Security Council at the pertinent time.

Ambassador Henry Cabot Lodge:
There is no question. McNamara was the governing figure in the U.S. Government on this subject, and in my opinion he did very fine work. If he had a fault, it was that he felt he could quantify certain things you cannot quantify. When I first talked to him about this in 1963, he didn't seem to me to have understood the political and psychological factors in

Vietnam as well as he understood how many yards of barbed wire he had under order from New Zealand. When he met people who could advise him and inform him about the political and psychological factors, he certainly absorbed that. I think that he was a very extraordinary man.
Ambassador Robert Komer:
The only person who really tried hard to get unity of command was Mr. McNamara. While he failed, it was one of his strong suits. It was Sir Robert Thompson who kept pointing out, to McNamara and others, the Malayan example: someone had to be in charge. General Maxwell Taylor came out in 1964 with a very unusual letter from the President of the United States. I have always credited Robert McNamara as the inspirer of this letter. It said to Taylor: You are in complete charge of the whole affair—military, economic, political. You may set up whatever machinery you deem appropriate to this end. A military man, the Chairman of the Joint Chiefs of Staff, was being sent out to be Proconsul in the manner of Templer in Malaya. I was struck by Taylor's response in his book: the first thing he did was to go around and see the Joint Chiefs, CINCPAC and then General Westmoreland, to assure all of them that he was not going to interpret this mandate in a way which could really make him Proconsul. That was the end of the one time the Secretary of Defense managed to push unity of command to the point of a Presidential decision. I know that because later I suggested it twice, and McNamara told me to lay off, in no uncertain terms! He said, "I tried this and it can't be done."
Ambassador Lodge:
I think the arrangement we had was a perfectly good arrangement. Any ambassador would be out of his mind to try to direct the combat operations, for instance. On the other hand, if the Army wants to spend a number of piastres which are going to upset the South Vietnamese economy completely, if they are going to bring in contractors who are going to roughhouse and create untold ill will for us—at that point, the Ambassador has a right to say, "No." It depends on what the issue is.
Colonel Donald Marshall:
This is a problem that, needless to say, has been studied *ad nauseum*. General Taylor was being quite sensible, in that that letter does you

no good if you do not have the tools with which to exercise that command. The tie between Washington and the field, after all, was not cut at the time that the letter was issued.

Ambassador Komer:

McNamara understood that. I suspect that the letter was drafted in his office. It said to Taylor: You may set up whatever machinery you deem appropriate to this end. If I ever had a mandate like that, the machinery would have been set up.

Colonel Marshall:

But it can't be set up in Washington. That is the problem—you have got to tie in those two together before you can exercise it. You also have to tie it with CINCPAC, and with the Joint Chiefs, because it does no good to be Proconsul only within the borders of Vietnam, unless you relate to your other countries in the area and your field forces in the area.

Ambassador Komer:

We have to guard against simplistic concepts, but no one has argued that unity of command alone could do it, any more than General Keegan was arguing that air power could do it alone, all by itself. They were part of a much more complex thing. What impressed me about unity of command was that here we are arguing about policy, even about policy and strategy. My thought on unity of command was that the failure to have this unity of command meant that we were actually fighting several *separate* wars rather than one war.

Dr. Robert Sansom:

No one was comfortable enough with the facts and the intelligence to say, "I am going to fight this war and not that one."

Ambassador Komer:

Some of us were, and if we had unity of command we would have done it.

Dr. Sansom:

Unity of command to you means unity under you.

Ambassador Komer:

All right. Or under Ambassador Lodge. I remember when I first got involved in Vietnam, he was saying that the infrastructure is the heart of the matter, and we have got to get after their political-military control structure. If he had had command over the Vietnamese, if there had been unity of command over the Vietnamese *and* all the American assets, I daresay we would have focused more on that. If you want to talk resource management, the problem is how to get the resources devoted to the most important, highest-priority things. We never had that. It is very interesting to me that Abrams fought one war, but the only way I ever got pacification off the ground was to have two wars! My war and General Westmoreland's war! The funny thing—the strange paradox— is that we got that by unifying the command under the military. We rendered unto Caesar the things that were Caesar's, and in return I was delegated full authority to make the pacification effort go. We managed to do it with the Vietnamese, too. So it's a funny thing. Unity of command can lead to flexibility of execution!

Barry Zorthian:

At what point was there unity of command in Vietnam? Having watched for a considerable period out there, at fairly close hand with three different ambassadors involved, I would suggest that the answer depends on the face of the war, *without* reflection on personalities, necessarily, although personalities obviously get involved. I would think that control of Vietnam, insofar as an ambassador's authority is involved, was strongest during Ambassador Lodge's first tour, and during General Taylor's tour. The reason for it, I think, was the nature of the war. Ambassador Lodge did come out with a charter, and certainly, for that period, as I could see, had good control. But it was obviously a much more integrated civilian/military task, and it was an insurgency without American main-force units.

Maxwell Taylor's control was also fairly complete—those four stars from his tour as Chairman of the Joint Chiefs of Staff did shine and he certainly did not hesitate at many times to tell General Westmoreland that he did not believe he needed "x"—whether it was troops or supplies. Later, even though the Ambassador still had theoretical control, once MACV had grown to 500,000 troops it was hard to control the disposition or use of those forces from the political position of Ambassador. In addition, the support line was confused. If there was unity in Saigon, behind Saigon there was confusion, simply because there was no integrity of command, no unity of command either at the theater level in

Honolulu or in Washington. If there was one overall commander, it was obviously the President, and perhaps there was too great an involvement by the President.

Authority flowing to Saigon from Washington could come from the Defense Department, it could even come from CIA, AID, or USIA, depending on the particular area involved, and consistent with its counterpart in the field. A unified structure would have to be established in Washington, as well as in Saigon, if the very valid principle of unity of command is to be observed.

Professor Ithiel de Sola Pool:
There has been little discussion of Lyndon Johnson. I can understand that. There was a time when Lyndon Johnson was being so scurrilously and unjustifiably abused that it made many of us lean over backward to defend him. I continue to defend him as a great man who sought to do his best for the country and whose purposes in Vietnam were right. However, in retrospect, with the benefit of hindsight, I think we have to say that he failed to do what had to be done and what all of the experts knew had to be done.

To fight the war as a political war, he had to draw together the limited human resources of political expertise on Vietnam that existed in 1965 and 1966 and put these people in charge of an appropriate political effort with the military resources firmly under their control. The President, but only the President, could have done anything as drastic as that.

By 1968 and 1969, Robert Komer, thanks to the President's backing, had built, in CORDS, a capable counterinsurgency organization working with local security forces. In the pacification studies group he created the necessary small cadre of young men being trained in the language and knowledgeable about what was going on in the country. A political war was finally fought, but too little and too late. It was an addendum to MACV's massive, conventional, and self-defeating campaign. Nonetheless, the CORDS effort to a large extent almost saved the day.

Clearly, by 1968, we had learned something, but one cannot really contend that there was no way for the President to have understood the problem in 1965. There was basic awareness of the problem of so-called "People's Liberation Wars" well before that in the Kennedy years. Everybody of stature in the government had been put through a seminar on counterinsurgency. Supposedly they all realized that that kind of war was going to be quite different and that we would have to operate it quite differently. The failure of the President to act accordingly, with the requisite decisiveness, must be scored as a human mistake.

Since the President was not ready to create a new structure that would incorporate those understandings and the people who had them, and make the structure dominant over the established bureaucracies, then when happened did, I agree, have the inevitability of tragedy. No Ambassador, no COMUSMACV, can be made to take the blame for that mistake; their actions were the predictable instrument of the error. The only man who could integrate the psychological and political dimensions of the whole effort in a novel way was the man in the White House. That is where the buck stops.

Ambassador Komer:

I think Professor Pool is right in pointing to the central role of Lyndon Johnson during the period of our great escalation. A lot has been written about what he was trying to do. I was perhaps as close to what he was trying to do, in Vietnam, as anybody but Walt Rostow or Robert Mc-Namara. I used to go to the Tuesday luncheons—the War Cabinet, so to speak—and the buck indeed stopped there. The President *has* to change the name of the game if it is going to be changed. Nobody else can really skew around the whole bureaucracy. In fact, Presidents can't do it very easily—a number of Secretaries of Defense have failed, too.

I will say in defense of Lyndon Johnson that he introduced more institutional innovations—he approved, he backed more institutional innovations—than any President before or since with respect to Vietnam. Two have already been mentioned here today. First, he did agree with McNamara and Sir Robert Thompson that we should have a Proconsul in Vietnam, and he did pick the man they thought could best make the military operate as though it were a political conflict—Maxwell Taylor. It did not work, but Johnson signed the letter, which is a very important thing. The instruction followed through with other ambassadors, but no ambassador had the military weight of Maxwell Taylor, who came directly from being Chairman of the Joint Chiefs. Secondly, it was Lyndon Johnson who, after the February 1966 conference in Honolulu, set up the machinery for the other war; first Porter in Saigon and then me in Washington. I went to Lyndon Johnson in 1967 and said, in effect, "We have got the Washington part of this problem licked, but that machine out there in Saigon isn't paying any attention at all!" So the problem is in the field, and not in Washington. The problem is with performance, not with politics.

He is the one who, despite almost everybody's opposition, put the fledgling pacification effort under COMUSMACV, which was the time it first took off, partly because the military had all the resources. My view was a very simple one: if you are ever going to get a program going, you are only going to be able to do it by stealing from the military. They have all the trucks, they have all the planes, they have all the people, they have all the money—and what they did not have locked up, they had a lien on. So in that sense, LBJ did not do enough of what was needed, but he did more than any other Chief Executive and under some rather difficult circumstances. In other words, I think that Kennedy could have done more earlier, except that the need was not quite as apparent.

Monitoring the War— Computers versus "Art Forms"

Thomas C. Thayer

One issue that stirred controversy at our conference was that over the proper use of statistics, computers—in short, systems analysis. One view was that the computers merely made the normal sort of measurement much more precise; the opposite was that what the computer could measure most easily became the objective by which performance was measured, and that war, as an art form, could not be practiced by those trained to do so. In a paper, Thomas Thayer made the basic case for quantification and the use of computers.

Thomas Thayer:
In a war without fronts, such as the war in Vietnam, and particularly in one as fragmented and atomized as it was (with its 44 provinces, 260 districts, 11,000 hamlets, 3500 VC/NVA actions per month, 35,000 tactical air sorties per month, etc., all playing a part) quantitative analysis is essential (but, by itself, not sufficient) to a full understanding of what was going on. In no other way is it possible to keep track of the slowly changing patterns and movements that were so characteristic of this war, and to relate them to the achievement of U.S. objectives.

The quantification of the war is often criticized as excessive and largely misleading—the body count is a favorite example. Quantification may have been overdone, but analysis of key issues certainly was not. There was lots of stress on things like the body count, and this stress created an incentive system all of its own. But there is a difference between quantification, according to old-style rules of thumb, and analysis. The problem was that quantification became a huge effort, but analysis remained a trivial one. This is unfortunate, perhaps even tragic, because those limited analytic efforts that were undertaken yielded much useful insight into the war and into the prospects for achieving U.S. objectives, given the way the war was being fought. Unfortunately, it all had little impact.

The ensuing discussion between General Keegan, the Air Force's Chief of Intelligence, and Mr. Thayer began when Professor Allan Goodman asked General Keegan what happened to the organizational capability assembled for the defense of Khe Sanh.

General Keegan:
It was probably disbanded for all the usual bureaucratic reasons. Some went back to General Abrams' war; some went back to Ambassador Sullivan's war, or back to the Marine war. Each little group went back

to its doctrinal perceptions, trying to respond to what the Pentagon was using as the measure of performance. Was it trucks killed, sorties flown, bombs dropped? It was whatever went into the computer in Assistant Secretary Alain Enthoven's Systems Analysis Office at the Pentagon that really dictated the war. What he never knew is that when Khe Sanh came, I took his computer and threw it out the door, and used our own. I put the data that was necessary into that computer to make decisions, to monitor where the targets were. Khe Sanh was the only instance in the war in South Vietnam where, by putting all the intelligence together, we located every company of every battalion of every division. When we went out on a strike mission, it was against a known enemy. We "bookkeeped," through monitoring the communications, what we were really doing.

Mr. Thayer:

General Keegan and I clearly agree on a number of issues, including the view that the air campaigns were probably a minus for the war (although we probably disagree as to the reasons). I listened to his account of Khe Sanh with admiration for the way he orchestrated resources and applied intelligence the way it needs to be used in this kind of war— "count the blades of grass," establish the patterns, find the units and then clobber them when you are ready. Also, he presented the only case I have heard about in which we took advantage of the French experience. He says the French were brilliantly articulate and extremely helpful. Why didn't we seek their assistance more?

However, I simply cannot accept General Keegan's assertion that it was "the computer in Enthoven's Systems Analysis Office that really dictated the war." It just is not true. Enthoven's staff had no major effect on strategy or tactics pursued in this war—and particularly not in the air war.

Enthoven's people did not even have their own computer. The systems that General Keegan criticizes were established by the Air Force and the Joint Staff—not Systems Analysis—and most of them were laid on, as requirements, before Enthoven's office even began to look at the air war. As far as I am aware, we never had any success in having any impact on either establishing or changing any system of reports from Vietnam. Our only recourse was to analyze the data that MACV sent to Washington, and that we did.

But our analysis of the war, including the air effort, amounted to only an unofficial, unsolicited, and small-scale effort consisting mainly of making a number of pilot studies on various aspects of the war and publishing the in-house, unofficial Southeast Asia Analysis Reports. With few exceptions, neither the Reports nor the studies had a significant impact on major decisions. Despite polite interest by the MACV staff, the conclusions were not acted on, in my view and that of Dr. Enthoven. The analytical approach never did take root in the Vietnam decision-making process, with the possible exception of Komer's pacification program.

We did not set up any scorecards, and, frankly, we saw little evidence that anyone was taking our analyses seriously, although the Chairman of the Joint Chiefs of Staff did go to the trouble of trying to limit circulation of our SEA Analysis Reports (at the behest of the Air Force). Other than that expression of annoyance, we saw little evidence of attempts to grapple seriously with the issues we raised.

So I must categorically deny that we set up scorecards or that Enthoven's computer dictated the war. It just isn't so.

General Edward Lansdale:

Not only the Air Force—it was the ground forces as well whose performance was monitored by computers. You *were* keeping a report card. All your combat commanders, of whatever service, were very much aware that they had a report card that led to their future—to their promotions, their dismissal, and so forth—in a set of numbers—enemy killed, body count, truck count, and so on. Whether you intended it or not, whether McNamara intended it or not, you, in effect, were determining their actions psychologically by saying, "This is the report card; this is the key factor."

Ambassador Komer:

I am eager to disagree. The problem was not with the econometricians and analysts. The problem, if any, was with the decision makers if they paid too much attention to this. At least for my part of the war, I was grateful to the analysts and to the econometricians, who did a rather better job of analysis back in Washington (possibly because they were farther away) than our own people in Saigon.

Lastly, the report cards may have been written in Washington, but the report cards that influenced officer promotion were written right there in Saigon, and they never paid attention, at least in MACV. I cannot speak for the Seventh Air Force. They paid no attention to what the systems analysts were saying about report cards on the war. They didn't even read them!

General Keegan:

I hope we never do it that way again. The result of that kind of emphasis, highlighting the data that you received from the theater, had all kinds of indirect influence that, in effect, ended up steering the war. In Saigon, 80 percent of my analysts, who should have been devoting their time to studying the enemy, his logistics, his patterns of operation, were generating data exclusively for the computers in Washington.

For example, we were watching the number of trucks killed because that is what McNamara wanted to watch; that was the standard by which we were judged. We could not get the command and the operational elements to pay attention to a more effective way of impeding the enemy's logistics, which was, in one case, to block his mountain passes. We tried it for four months, and not one truck in four months reached South Vietnam. We were forced to abandon that because Systems Analysis in the Pentagon said our truck-kill rate was going down!

I hope that we never again allow the computer analysts to quantify the least common denominator, and the least important, except insofar as it gives some relevant measure of cost of the war—I hope that we never repeat that. The conduct of war is an art form. It is not something that is quantifiable and I hope we never again revert to a practice which almost crippled us.

Mr. Thayer:

I remain astounded at the allegation that our analysis steered the war. If it had been, a lot of things—particularly the allocation of resources and the strategy—would have been quite a bit different.

As to General Keegan's specific statements, his analysts were not feeding our data systems, but rather those of the Air Force and the Joint Staff. Don't blame that on Enthoven's group. They simply took the trouble to analyze the data and publish the results for consideration and comment.

As to blocking the mountain passes, I am aware of no four-month period, except perhaps during the rainy season, in which air strikes blocked the mountain passes and no truck reached South Vietnam. If that had been achieved at the peak of the normal infiltration cycle or at any other time, there would have been no doubt that the choke-point strategy was the one to pursue. But the choke-point strategy did not work, because the VC/NVA constructed alternative routes faster than we could choke them off. Nor did the bombing in North Vietnam, before the trucks reached the passes, have a decisive effect.

If we ever have the misfortune to get mixed up in a war without fronts like this again, we had better not just quantify it—we had better analyze it for all we are worth. You can't fully understand—or explain— a war like this unless you do some analysis of the statistics it produces. The patterns and trends must be identified and followed closely, because the war is a series of thousands of small, scattered events and movement is so slow that it is easy to miss it without careful monitoring.

The quantification should not have crippled anyone—but the lack of systematic analysis and misunderstanding of the basic patterns and movements of the war surely had a seriously adverse effect on the U.S.— South Vietnamese war effort.

Stephen Young:

We had to send up to Ambassador Komer from the field all kinds of statistics. Was there no difference in the value of statistics in 1968 as opposed to 1967? In 1967, when there were no clearly defined performance goals and objectives, most of what was sent was nonsense. But in 1968 there were very specific report cards, cards which measured real and meaningful output of performance at the lowest levels. It seems to me the important point is not statistics but the nature of the report card

—what is being measured. When the decision makers don't set down the right kind of objectives, then they get into trouble.

Dr. Sansom:

The distinction being that in 1968 you were beginning to relate statistics to *objectives* as opposed merely to *activity rates*.

Professor Arthur Smithies:

May I make one brief remark—because I do happen to be an economist? If I can just take a very homely analogy with which I am familiar: In the university and in the school, we grade examinations. I am quite sure that this method of grading has some effect on the teaching!

Chapter 12

"Costing" the Vietnam War

Was the Vietnamese War worth fighting in terms of the various costs to us? Every one of our participants "costed" the war differently, agreeing only that the war was fought in a profligate manner. Paul Nitze noted that the essential issue on which he had disagreed with Mr. McNamara about the conduct of the war was over the latter's well-known view that "the United States could afford anything in the way of defense which was necessary, and particularly with respect to Vietnam." American dollars would be traded off against American lives. But this, Nitze noted, resulted "in a lack of discipline which became one of the most important factors in the war."

Paul Nitze:
It was very hard for a number of people to contend with the essential question of how to fight the war in support of the Vietnamese people and to destroy the enemy forces in a way that was not counterproductive. McNamara was deeply affected by reading the manuscript of a series of articles later published in *The New Yorker* and as a book— *The Village of Ben Suc.* The author, Jonathan Schell, came into McNamara's office and briefed him on what he had seen in Vietnam. He said that he had been asked by *The New Yorker* to write a series of articles on the subject. McNamara put him in the next office, gave him a secretary, and

said, "Write it. I want to read it." He read the draft before it was even submitted to *The New Yorker*. He was horrified by its stories of meaningless and random bombings by our air force, by the cynical attitude toward human life which, it purported, permeated our forces. He circulated the draft in the Pentagon and to the commanders in Vietnam and asked for comments on what was wrong with it. Obviously, there were things wrong with it; it wasn't wholly accurate. But still the essence of it appeared to be valid. I think this brought him to the realization that we had not been fighting the war correctly; we were using firepower too indiscriminately, with insufficient discipline and in a manner which was often counterproductive.

The spread in views can be seen in Dean Edmund Gullion's view, stated prior to South Vietnam's defeat, that the costs of the war, however great, had to be measured in terms of the cost to our alliance systems and to our security generally had we not attempted to help the Vietnamese. But in losing the war, as it turned out, we got the worst of both worlds, because of the war's "opportunity cost," a point made by Admiral Elmo R. Zumwalt, who was Commander of Naval Operations at the time he made a presentation to our colloquium at Fletcher.

Admiral Elmo R. Zumwalt:
It is almost impossible to estimate the military and the political damage that was done to this country as a result of the way in which the Vietnamese War was fought and as a result of the decision to go in en masse. Firstly, for nearly a decade this nation was spending in substance 20, 25, and 30 billion dollars per year, depending on the year, for bombs, bullets, aircraft, and excess personnel to bring off that operation, while the Soviet Union was spending that amount of money for the capital gain of a superior strategic system, which has made a significant difference in the power balance of the world, and for the capital gain of non-

strategic forces which have also made a major difference around the world.

Secondly, this country erred in its political judgment about the ability of the citizenry to stay the course. Under the circumstances in which we got into the war, domestic turmoil took place and a wave of antimilitarism grew which has accelerated at the rate at which we have fallen behind the Soviet Union. The antimilitarism has been reflected, through our democratically elected representatives, in a series of progressively decreasing defense budgets. During each year between 1968 and 1974, it was possible to say that that year's defense budget was the smallest fraction of the gross national product since 1950. Each year in that period, it was possible to say that that year's budget was the smallest fraction of the federal budget since 1950. During the period of time that these reductions took place, our expenditures for defense dropped from 53 or 54 percent to about 27 percent of the federal budget while our expenditures for human resources have gone exactly the reverse, from about 30 percent up to 45 percent. During this period, while we dropped from 3.5 million military personnel to about 2.1 million, the Soviet Union did exactly the reverse, from 2 million to 4 million. During this period, each year it was possible to say that the U.S. Navy had the smallest number of ships since 1939. That remains true this year, as it will next year. We will not begin to recover for several years. So we have paid a serious military price in terms of our capability to feel confident about our ability to deter the Soviet Union, and I charge this off directly to the trauma of Vietnam.

Nevertheless, I believe that we have proved another thing of importance in the political-military contest. That is, once we had, by my lights, erred in initiating the U.S. part of that war in the way in which we did, it was right not to "bug out" at the time when the pressure was on the Administration to do so. And had we done so abruptly, we would clearly have knowingly turned over an area to the North Vietnamese Communists—an area which, by my recorded argument in the early 1960s, was not vital to our basic national interests but an area which by that time had become so because we had linked our sacred national honor to it. To the allies around the world, it was a very significant thing, and had we chucked one ally down the drain the connotation of this around the world could have had significance even greater than the dramatic changes in the military balance that have been taking place. I think it is important that it became a staged withdrawal rather than a precipitous withdrawal.

General George Keegan:
First, I would judge that the Soviets' conclusion from the war in Southeast Asia, inescapably, is that it was the most successful Soviet-sponsored proxy war in history. We thought we had a deal in Paris and the Russians would collaborate, but they deliberately rescued the North Vietnamese in July 1972. It was they who broke the blockade and found the means, despite the closure of ports, to push the largest tonnage of supplies through mainland China in history. Instead of moving it down the rail lines, which were all disrupted, they moved it down roads and into the canals. (Our intelligence in the field was so poor that we found this out in Washington before they did.) This war did more to advance Soviet objectives, long since declared in their annual Party Congresses, than any previous event in the preceding fifty-nine years.

It demoralized the United States; it disrupted our defense programs; it retarded our research and development (R&D) and, more serious than that, it almost destroyed Government-sponsored R&D by the academic institutions of this country. That R&D has been the base of our combat capability in technology since time immemorial.

Secondly, I think that the experience confirmed to the Soviets the value of their recent entry into the politics of the Third World. We now have conclusive evidence that the Soviets very nearly committed seven divisions to the rescue of Damascus and Cairo. That's the beginning of a whole new offensive style for the Soviets—their naval technology is a part of it; their airlift technology is a part of it; and the redesign of their weapons and of their electronic warfare capability which is now going on are also part of it. They have now decided after three brutal wars that maybe the United States has something in the fighter-bomber. I think in the next ten years we are going to see Alfred Mahan plus, brought into a completely new dimension. The most important part of that dimension is the impulse that they have got out of their proxy support of North Vietnam.

With regard to technology on the Soviet side, we have but to look to the Middle East to see how well they have learned the lessons of Vietnam. They know the United States will not fight at night, so the air forces were totally equipped, and the riflemen, the assault riflemen, the artillerymen, the tankers, the armored personnel carrier drivers were all equipped with the most sophisticated array of night-vision devices that we have ever seen. They were equipped to fight chemical warfare on a scale and in a mass that we never saw in World War I. Every Arab GI, every tank, every APC was fully protected environmentally against chemicals, biologicals, and radiologicals, and had the antidotal equipment, sensors, Geiger counters, detectors—beyond anything we have ever dreamed of providing in the United States. That is what we are going to find in Europe and I suspect we are going to find it in the Third World.

Lastly, the greatest surprise of all in the Middle East, which I think derives directly from the Soviet experience in North and South Vietnam, is the massive use of communications intelligence, whereby they read our communications, as they did the Israelis', and used this to great advantage for the conduct of their own electronic warfare. On our side, I think the war served to confirm, by and large, the soundness of the Air Force's technology base, the continuing importance of investing in a large military-industrial R&D base that can fabricate gunships overnight, make "smart" weapons which we now call guided weapons, develop the laser, develop electro-optical means, out of which has come a revolution in weaponry now permitting one fighter, day or night, to do the work that a hundred did just a couple of years ago. I think the impact on the Soviets of that and the impact on the free world, the NATO air world particularly, on the defense of Europe, will probably be the next round in the arms race.

I think the Soviets learned as much as we did, and the evidence of it we found in the Middle East. I think the Middle East is a reflection of what we would find in the NATO–Warsaw Pact area. We have a lot of

homework to do. As someone said to Congress just a few months ago, speaking about the Middle East war: "We were not surprised. Nothing new occurred. No new strategic principles—but a massive new disequilibrium has been created by the Soviet investment in such mass, in such firepower, in the ability to operate at night, the ability to use chemicals . . ."
Professor Geoffrey Kemp:
There are two variables I would like to put forward that I think might explain the United States national response to the whole engagement in Vietnam. Firstly, the number of U.S. military casualties sustained in the military theater. Secondly, the economic cost of the U.S. role in Vietnam. If you look at the various responses of particular groups in the United States over the years, the mainstream of American public opinion becomes extremely sensitive to U.S. military casualties in Southeast Asia.

As a college teacher, I clearly noticed that as U.S. casualties began to fall, and the draft count began to fall, so student protest on the campuses began to fall. I do not say this in a cynical way. It is an understandable phenomenon, but I do think that there is a very strong correlation between the perceptions that people had of the war and the probabilities that they might be killed in Southeast Asia.
Sir Robert Thompson:
We all know the figures that were bandied around. It was costing you, by 1967, 1968, as much as 30 million dollars a day and so on. But compare that with your increase in gross national revenue at the time.

But I must be very blunt on the matter of casualties. Forty-seven thousand men—I won't say in ten years, but roughly in five or six years. We took 60,000 casualties in one day on the Somme, and 19,000 killed. If you put that figure up as a prohibition cost, there isn't a war-torn country, and I include Russia and Israel in that, which wouldn't say, "Well, what are you made of?" I am being callous here, but if you meant what you were doing, that would not be considered a high casualty rate at all. The short tours are also to blame. The risk of casualties declines steeply for a soldier in his second year in Vietnam.

It was also argued that it is not the number of casualties, but over what period of time. In the American Civil War casualty rates were fifty times greater. By the time the Vietnamese War was in its tenth year, the public-opinion effect of one casualty was that of a hundred.

Professor Earl Ravenal:
This is a somewhat awkward question, because I am very much impressed by Sir Robert Thompson's analysis of the military situation on the ground, and I would tend to agree with his assessment that in many respects the war was won in 1972. But the thing that troubles me is that his analysis would appear to be restricted to the context of the war itself—the situation on the ground. The real question is one for American policy, and there the question is not what could have been done, but whether those things were worth doing, whether they were worth our paying the price. In other words, it is not quite convincing that the war —the battle, the cause of the South Vietnamese—was worth pursuing. It might well have been—*for them.* Or that eventually they became more capable of carrying a certain burden and winning impressive victories. We run into a larger problem. This is not to transcend the restrictions of the debate and get into value questions. They are not value questions. They are empirical questions, and they are addressed to the point that the ultimate constraints on the amount of American effort that could be expended really had to do with certain internal conditions in the United States. We can deplore them and we can inveigh against them and we can regret them; but somehow the expenditure was impossible, even for the marginal bit of effort necessary to beat off an unjustified aggression not considered, in the "gut" instinct of the American people, to be worth it. That is what really forms the ultimate parameter on American effort. It is also the most convincing lesson of the Vietnamese War: that although military victory might be conceivable within perfectly reasonable amounts of effort, seen in objective terms, for some

uncanny reason the American people have determined that this effort is not worth making.

Sir Robert Thompson:

I can give you one easy, straight answer to that. Please read the final two chapters in my book *Peace Is Not at Hand.* The next-to-last chapter is called "Soft Options," and the last chapter is called "Strategic Surrender." That is where you have to start weighing the costs. I will say this on cost, that I do think the Vietnamese War could have been fought cheaper in all terms, particularly in casualties and in troop commitments.

If I may digress onto another theme of mine. The answer to protracted war is stable war. This is a perfectly simple theme in that the whole aim of protracted war is that if one side has costs which are indefinitely acceptable to it, and imposes on you costs which are not indefinitely acceptable to you, it does not matter what happens in the battles. If that situation is achieved, that side is winning. The answer through stable war is that you have, therefore, to get into a position where the costs on both sides are tolerable, in other words, that you can hold a standoff forever and that neither side can alter that standoff—a sort of *de facto* stalemate on the ground—without a massive expenditure, like, for example, the North Vietnamese invasion in 1972, which was a massive expenditure from their point of view, and, one might add, from the Russian point of view.

Professor Arthur Smithies:

The consumption of resources by Vietnam was far greater than its gross national product. I think one has to start from that fact, which was an inheritance of our presence there. There is no conceivable economic way in which that country could support an armed force of a million people out of its own resources. Yet our political imperatives (of 1973–74) seemed to demand that they must in a short period of time. I hope it is not as true as the gloomiest predictions say it is, but I have an uneasy feeling that that may be the case, particularly in light of Paul Nitze's really acute analysis, and General George Marshall's point of view about our ability to carry on a sustained operation.

That brings me to the perplexing question—the strategy about which I know little, and about which I will have to think a bit from the point of view of these economic problems. Last summer when I was talking about this to people, there were two schools of thought, representing the "main force" argument versus the "security of the citizen" argument. Some people said that the way to demobilize was to demobilize the ARVN and concentrate the resources on the police to provide local security for returning refugees. The reply to that argument was that if the GVN shifted its strategy in that direction, they would lay themselves open to a main-force offensive. The argument on the other side was that if they continued a main-force strategy, they would lose the countryside. It seems to me that this represents an absolutely appalling dilemma, and I do not think it could be seen as a question of black and white. You cannot have a local-security strategy and no main-force strategy. You cannot have a main-force strategy and no local-security strategy.

Colonel Donald Marshall:

I should point out that everything that has been said has, indeed, been addressed officially. There is in existence an agreed strategic plan to deal with these problems, to utilize Vietnamese capabilities and Vietnamese concepts. The difficulty is that this plan was not executed, in large measure because of our home objections. For example, specifically according to plan, the Vietnamese troops are getting into things which are not traditional in our armed forces, such as raising their own food, getting into business, and so forth. We immediately raised military objections on our side because this was diverting them from their primary responsibility.

As to the total economic resource cost, you lower that in several ways. One, you change the nature of your force structure. Two, you change the nature of your fighting. Three, you change the basis of your fighting —so that the people who are fighting know what they are doing. One could draw a direct line from costs of the war to the point Mr. Nitze made on the decision by Mr. McNamara as to how we were going to fight the war. That decision, that we were going to spend dollars and not lives, provided the example and the precept and the direct teaching to our Vietnamese ally.

Professor Smithies:

Within a limited period of years, a military strategy in Vietnam could be devised whereby the war could have been prosecuted within the constraints of Vietnam's own resources.

Colonel Marshall:

True, if you had had adequate use of the innate leadership, and if you had strong guidelines. Our difficulty was that we were unwilling to declare such; there are many people taking part in this conference who predicted the course of events, but those predictions were not utilized by the decision makers.

General Edward Lansdale:

Before the defeat, the only real political party in South Vietnam was the ARVN—the Army of the Republic of Vietnam. Thanks to the Paris Treaty, the enemy sat astride the communications or in the areas of the major economic resources of Vietnam. It was quite properly pointed out that it was a larger armed force than the country could afford to have, but without it was lost any chance at all of making use of the economic resources, which are primarily agricultural, with an enemy threatening it continuously. So at some point here, we Americans would have had to be realistic about appropriations in Congress and to continue them long enough to give the Vietnamese a chance to work themselves out of this dilemma.

The American Style of War Made It Costly

Thomas C. Thayer

Besides the tragic cost in lives, the Vietnamese war was enormously costly to the United States in resource terms, partly because we used firepower to save casualties. According to the official Department of

Defense estimates, the war had cost $112 billion through June 1974.[1] These are not even the full costs to the Department, but the incremental costs (i.e., the expenditures over and above what would have been spent on the forces in peacetime) .

Why was it so expensive? The answer lies in the way we chose to fight the war—American style, with our most expensive forces. Operating a South Vietnamese division costs about one twentieth as much as operating a U.S. division. An examination of how the money was spent in Fiscal Year 1969, the year of highest costs, shows why the war cost so much. The Department of Defense estimates that the war in FY 1969 cost $21.5 billion. U.S. military activities consumed more than 80 percent of the total, and South Vietnamese military activities accounted for most of the rest.

U.S. air operations, including combat and support activities, cost more than $9 billion in FY 1969, twice the amount spent on U.S. ground forces. In both cases, almost all of the resources were devoted to interdiction operations and to main-force actions designed to destroy VC/ NVA military forces.

Pacification and the territorial forces received only about 6 percent of total U.S. and GVN resources in FY 1969.[2] Efforts to keep the South Vietnamese economy from collapsing under the weight of the U.S. presence consumed an amount equal to only 3 percent of the total expenditures.[3]

The tremendous U.S. expenditures in the war not only unbalanced the South Vietnamese economy, but eventually helped lead to unprecedented inflation in the United States, thereby adding still another kind of cost that can be attributed to the war.

In terms of resources, then, it was a "U.S. war" in which the costs of U.S. forces were immensely higher than those of South Vietnamese

---

[1] $145 billion in 1974 dollars.

[2] $1.3 billion, half GVN and half U.S.

[3] The data do not indicate whether these funds are also included in the pacification costs.

forces.[4] As to type of war, it was, in resource allocation terms, first and foremost an air war, and second, a ground attrition campaign against VC/NVA regular units. Pacification was a very poor third.

It is difficult to break out the pacification expenditures from civil and military outlays (the latter included territorial security), but it is clear that even the greatly expanded pacification program of FY 1969 received only a small fraction of the US/GVN outlays, even though it was supposed to be a major dimension of the combined effort. For example, in FY 1969, artillery support alone cost about five times as much as all of the Vietnamese territorial forces.

In the words of one high-level participant: "If we had ever realized at all levels where the money really went in relation to what impact it had, it is at least questionable whether the United States would have fought the war the way it did."

[4] In terms of the most important costs, namely casualties, the one-year tour for all U.S. troops, and the practice of a six-month tour for U.S. battalion commanders, apparently had the effect of raising the toll of U.S. combat deaths. Twice as many troops died during the first six months of their tour as in the second half. After the first month, the number of deaths decline as the tour progresses, without exception. Thus, the longer one stayed alive after arriving in Vietnam, the better one's chances for survival, presumably as the result of a learning curve, which then had to be repeated for each new arrival. Longer tours might have cut the toll.

Chapter 13

Was There Another Way?

Robert Komer

Ambassador Robert Komer played a large role in our discussions, as he also had in the war. He made two presentations at Fletcher, parts of which we have used in this chapter. One theme emphasized in all of his contributions is that "an essentially political conflict cannot be effectively dealt with primarily by conventional military means. . . . Hanoi was far wiser than we in seeing the struggles as essentially a seamless web, a political, military, economic, ideological, and psychological conflict." He also kept asking "how so many with so much could achieve so little for so long against so few." Whether or not pacification was a viable alternative strategy, as Komer argues, there can be no doubt in hindsight that Hanoi couldn't ultimately win via insurgency but rather had to resort to conventional military offensives by NVA troops. In this sense pacification finally "worked," though it was not enough. His essay is followed by conference discussions and part of a paper by Thomas Thayer.

A complex of built-in constraints made it difficult for America to perform in any other manner than it did—except, of course, to disengage.

Yet almost from the outset many advocated in various ways and with varying degrees of energy and persuasiveness what amounted in broad outline to an alternative approach—what might be termed a "counter-insurgency" strategy. Its antecedents lay as much in Philippine experience against the Huks and British experience in the Malayan emergency as in the prior French experience in Vietnam (in hindsight we should have learned much more from these).

This alternative approach is hard to define, because it never emerged in any single comprehensive format; indeed it varied in content and emphasis from time to time. Nor, as we see from *The Pentagon Papers,* was there ever a clear-cut confrontation between this and other approaches, with the policy maker being forced to decide. Nonetheless, there is a more or less clearly unifying thread running through the views of many officials. In essence, it was a different way of thinking about the problem—of seeing it as primarily political rather than military, and thus of approaching it in other than conventional military terms. This school saw the allegiance and continued support of people as the objective to be gained, not the defeat of the enemy forces, and so argued that military goals must be subordinated to political. Also implicit in their views was the recognition that, as primarily a Vietnamese political phenomenon, insurgency could not be dealt with as effectively by Americans as by other Vietnamese.

Politically, this school stressed the need to build viable and responsive political institutions—local and national. It called for "winning hearts and minds" via this and such other means as land reform, rural development, or anticorruption measures. In security terms it placed more emphasis on "clear and hold" by police and paramilitary forces to provide sustained protection to the rural population than on "search and destroy" operations targeted on larger enemy units. It also stressed good political intelligence.

The Pentagon Papers and other sources show that all these things were called for as part of US/GVN counterstrategy from the early days. The record is full of perceptive insights, not just from outsiders but from within the Establishment itself. There was no dearth of advice on how to fight insurgency by these and other unconventional means. The chief actors were hardly unaware of this dimension.

But there proved to be an immense gap between "policy" and performance. Whatever the policy called for, all too little actually happened out at the cutting edge. While many initiatives, experiments, and even programs were undertaken at one time or another, none was on a scale or in a manner to have sufficient impact and all were overshadowed by the big-unit war. And while many called at various times for some form of unified management machinery to pull together the various U.S. efforts, or even integrate US/GVN responses, little was done along these lines except in one field and that very late in the day.

All this is demonstrated by the checkered history of the many abortive US/GVN attempts to devise programs specifically tailored to coping with rural insurgency. These attempts had many names; the one most widely used by the Vietnamese (and Americans) has been pacification, borrowed from the French but having unfortunate colonialist overtones. Civic Action, Agrovilles, the Strategic Hamlet program of 1961–63, the 1964–65 Hop Tac campaign around Saigon, and Revolutionary Development (RD) during 1965–67 were only the most prominent. But however grandly designed, in reality all were small-scale efforts compared to what was going into the conventional war. In general, the GVN and U.S. military regarded them as essentially civilian business, which meant that all suffered from lack of adequate local-security support. For these and other reasons mentioned earlier, pacification and other counterinsurgency programs remained a small tail to a large conventional military dog, at least till late in the day.

Their only truly comprehensive test came belatedly in the so-called "new model" pacification program, which began in mid-1967. It represented the first time the GVN and the United States began allotting sufficient personnel and resources on a sustained basis to competing directly with the VC for control and support of the rural population— via largely paramilitary and civil means. Moreover, it was almost wholly Vietnamese in execution, though heavily influenced and supported by the United States. Since its cumulative impact provides the best available basis for inference as to what an alternative strategy might have accomplished if it had been dominant from the outset, the rest of my remarks will be devoted to the 1967–71 pacification effort and its results.

THE NATURE OF THE "NEW MODEL" PACIFICATION PROGRAM

Conceptually, all Vietnam pacification efforts were designed essentially to serve two constructive aims: (1) sustained protection of the rural population from the insurgents, which also helped to deprive the insurgency of its rural popular base; and (2) generating rural support for the Saigon regime via programs meeting rural needs and cementing the rural areas politically and administratively to the center. A secondary purpose was to help neutralize the active insurgent forces and apparatus in the countryside. In essence, then, it was a civil as well as military process.

The 1967–71 program differed from its predecessors less in concept than in the comprehensive nature and massive scale of the effort undertaken. It must also be seen as a product of the circumstances and constraints existing at the time. It came late in the day, only after costly U.S. military intervention had averted final collapse of the coup-ridden GVN and created a favorable military environment in which the largely political competition for control and support of the key rural population could begin again.

But the previous deterioration of the chronically weak GVN administration and security apparatus in the countryside made pacification an uphill task from the start. The new program also entailed a painful buildup and deployment of resources, which took at least two years. All this necessitated a crash effort, as did the time constraints uppermost in U.S. policy makers' minds. Few expected that the U.S. public would sit still at this late date for a slow, methodical ten-year campaign.

Since most available resources were in Vietnamese and U.S. military hands by 1967, since pacification required first the restoration of security in the countryside, and since what little GVN administration that existed outside Saigon had become military-dominated, it was also logical for the new pacification program to be put under military auspices. On the U.S. side the result was a hybrid "Rube Goldberg" type of civil-military advisory organization called Civil Operations and Revolutionary Development Support (CORDS). Paradoxically, CORDS resulted in far greater civilian influence on the pacification process than had ever occurred before, since civilians occupied most top CORDS positions. It also represents perhaps the most successful example of close and effective US/GVN collaboration in an almost wholly "Vietnamized" program in our Vietnam experience.

Though "new model" pacification has been called an "American" program, it remained by design primarily Vietnamese throughout. The Vietnamese-to-U.S. adviser ratio, even at the peak of U.S. involvement, was over 100 to 1. Of course, this was possible (especially on the security side) only because during 1966–69 the U.S. military assumed the chief offensive role against the Viet Cong/North Vietnamese Army (VC/NVA) —except in IV Corps—thus permitting allocation of South Vietnamese military resources to providing local security in the countryside.

On the other hand, the very fact that pacification was a basically Vietnamese enterprise entailed another series of constraints. Those who criticize the pacifiers for adopting oversimplified quantitative approaches to a highly sensitive task fail to realize that the only way to achieve early countrywide impact was to design realistically around these constraints. Providing sustained rural security and other support for eventually over 10,000 hamlets in 250 districts of 44 provinces almost required simple, mass approaches. It was essential to avoid a major weakness of previous efforts, when the securing forces stayed only briefly and then moved on, after which the hamlets often retrogressed. The GVN could not afford politically to neglect part of the country and concentrate only on a few areas. Pacification, coming along so late in the day, also had to make do with some low-quality Vietnamese assets that no one else was really using. Nor could it entail programs beyond the limitied capabilities of such degraded Vietnamese administrative structure as was left by 1967.

PROVIDING TERRITORIAL SECURITY

Pragmatically, the multifaceted 1967–71 pacification program is perhaps best described in terms of its components. A notable feature was the stress on sustained territorial security (local clear and hold) as the indispensable first stage of pacification. Earlier pacification efforts had partly foundered on the lack of this. The military—regarding pacification as civilian-agency business—had never provided adequate security resources. This was recognized in the imaginative Revolutionary Development (RD) program of 1965–67. Its cutting edge, the 59-man, RD Cadre team, was designed as an armed paramilitary force to provide protection as well as developmental help to the hamlet. Also relevant was the allocation of 40 to 50 ARVN battalions to provide temporary security in selected RD campaign areas in the 1967 pacification plan.

But large-scale pacification required full-time sustained protection at the key village/hamlet level on a scale far beyond that which could be provided by these expedients. The pacification planners saw the long-neglected Regional Forces and Popular Forces (RF and PF) as the logical force-in-being on which to build. They were all locally recruited, and the bulk of them were volunteers (partly in order to avoid the draft). RF served only in their own provinces and PF in their own districts. The placing of the RF/PF advisory effort under CORDS, in conjunction with the Republic of Vietnam Armed Forces (RVNAF) reorganization of late 1967, marked the beginning of a truly integrated civil-military pacification program on a major scale. At long last, primary responsibility for local protection of the rural population devolved upon local forces recruited from this population itself.

The RF/PF were re-equipped and upgraded, their command clearly placed under province and district chiefs, and their numbers greatly increased. They expanded by more than 100,000 in 1968 alone, and by 1973 numbered some 540,000 men in over 1,600 RF companies and

7,000 PF platoons. The Tet shock of 1968 led to a revival of another local-security mechanism, the part-time People's Self-Defense Forces (PSDF). These grew to over 4 million, equipped with over 700,000 weapons. Though PSDF often engaged the enemy, their most useful role was probably less in local defense than as a means of engaging the population politically.

Two other pacification subprograms were designed to help cut into insurgent strength. A revitalized Chieu Hoi program aimed at inducing Viet Cong to rally to the GVN and then at employing them productively. Also part of the "new model" pacification was systematization of the feeble GVN effort to identify and round up the clandestine Viet Cong cadre composing the politico-military administrative, terror, propaganda, recruiting, and logistic apparatus. Since this was the organizational key to the insurgency, dismantling it was crucial to any countereffort—as the British found in Malaya.

The little understood Phung Hoang (Phoenix) effort did not involve building any major new program but rather was an attempt to pull together the feeble and uncoordinated efforts of all GVN agencies under standardized police-type procedures. Like all pacification programs, it was run by the GVN; U.S. support was confined chiefly to advisory support on improved identification, collation, and measurement techniques. Phoenix did not violate the Geneva Convention, which does not apply to legal measures taken by a government against its own citizens in revolt. Such measures as indefinite detention without trial have been employed by most governments confronting similar threats, as in our Civil War or the Malayan emergency. Nor was it a program of systematic political assassination; the vast majority recorded as killed were slain by GVN military forces in the course of military operations. These were not even targeted on individuals, who were only subsequently identified as VC infrastructure cadre.

The other major aspect of the "new model" pacification effort was the many civil programs aimed primarily at: (1) revival of a modestly functioning rural administration; (2) rural economic revival to provide pragmatic incentives to the farmer; and (3) establishment of other essential rural services, such as medical and educational facilities, refugee care, and a civil police presence. Many of these programs, inherited from the USAID mission, were integrated into a comprehensive pacification scheme by the GVN Central Pacification Council and CORDS.

In March 1970 the Thieu regime also promulgated what *The New York Times* called "probably the most imaginative and progressive non-Communist land reform of the twentieth century." In contrast to the 1956 land reform designed by Wolf Ladejinsky, but only partially carried out, Thieu pressed it on a far larger scale. In little over a year, over 900,000 acres were distributed free to some 300,000 families (if other continuing programs are added, well over a million acres). Thus by 1973, well over half the rural population had already benefited from land reform, with potentially great sociopolitical impact.

The purpose here is not to represent the 1967–71 pacification effort as an efficient, high-impact program; it made no such pretense. Like most things in Vietnam, it was cumbersome, wasteful, poorly executed, and only spottily effective in many respects. Nonetheless, GVN and U.S. efforts in 1967–71 did manage to convert some innovative but small-scale experiments into a coherent, integrated, civil-military program big enough and consistent enough to produce gradually a significant impact on Viet Cong prospects in the countryside. As one measure, total pacification funding by the United States and the GVN rose almost threefold from roughly $58 million in 1965 to over $1.5 billion in 1970 (dollar equivalents), including military outlays (the largest is RF/PF funding). By 1970 roughly half the direct cost of pacification was borne by the GVN. Whatever its faults, the 1967–71 program stands out as one of the few efforts undertaken by the GVN and the United States at least addressed to the key problems of dealing with rural-based insurgency. It was a unique wartime expedient, designed specifically to cope with revolutionary war as it had evolved by the late 1960s in Vietnam.

MEASURING PACIFICATION IMPACT

Aside from a handful of in-depth studies of local situations (of which few are based on recent evidence), the most extensive data on the effects (good or bad) of the major 1967–71 pacification effort lies in the statistical and other reports developed for management purposes by the pacifiers themselves. Despite their many limitations, they represent a unique attempt at systematic collection and evaluation of relevant data mostly from the village/hamlet level.

Keeping periodic track of the changing situation in 44 provinces and 250 districts, over 2,000 villages, and over 10,000 hamlets—not to mention all the small-scale pacification teams (RF companies and PF platoons, thinly spread National Police and ID teams, etc.) —required stress on simple quantitative techniques. Another principle adopted was to have all possible inputs made at the lowest feasible level (hamlet if possible) —and then not to permit them to be changed as they traveled up the line. Systems also had to be designed realistically for input by relatively unskilled and overburdened U.S. field advisers. They were designed as U.S. reporting systems precisely to avoid the kind of overly optimistic Vietnamese reporting which had characterized earlier efforts. For the same reasons, emphasis was placed on generating detailed factual reporting rather than subjective evaluations. While some fudging of figures to show progress inevitably occurred, particularly when Vietnamese sources were used, a much larger source of perturbation was probably the frequent shifts in U.S. advisers.

Pacification 1967–71 contributed materially to the cumulative attrition of most components of Viet Cong active strength. Local pacification security forces (principally RF/PF but also the National Police, RD Cadre, and PSDF) consistently inflicted more casualties on enemy forces—and took more in return—than the ARVN itself. Their activities, as well as their sheer growing presence at the local level, greatly inhibited Viet Cong recruiting, taxation, propaganda, logistics, and even terrorism.

The Chieú Hoi program facilitated the rallying of over 200,000 *hoi chanh* ralliers (about two thirds military) after it began in 1963. Over 172,000 of these came in after 1966. Though many were low-level people, and some no doubt rallied more than once, the cumulative total must have put at least a crimp in Viet Cong strength. The great bulk of these ralliers were from III and IV Corps, where the indigenous Viet Cong insurgency was largely centered.

Pacification programs, in conjunction with other factors, had a similar effect on the Viet Cong-controlled rural population base. It was officially admitted that at the end of 1964 only 40 percent of South Vietnam's population was under Government "control"—a sometime thing in those days—and over 20 percent under Viet Cong control. Even when the Hamlet Evaluation System (HES) was first instituted, in January 1967, only some 62 percent of a mere 16 million people were then rated as even "relatively secure," some 18.5 percent as contested, and still 19 percent as admittedly Viet Cong-controlled. Furthermore, a high percentage of this increase in "relatively secure" population in 1965–67 did not occur because of increased security in the countryside, but rather as a result of refugee movements and accelerated urbanization. In January 1967, only some 46 percent of the rural population was rated as relatively secure. Even at the end of 1967 less than 50 percent of the rural population was so rated, and this dropped further as a result of the 1968 Tet offensive. But the figures for the end of 1971 rate about 97 percent of South Vietnam's 17.9 million population as "relatively secure," and 3 percent as "contested," and only about 7,000 people as still under wholly VC control.

Whatever one's prejudices as to the precision of these figures, there is little doubt that GVN domination of the countryside expanded rapidly after late 1968 at the expense of the Viet Cong-controlled population base, with inevitable efforts on Viet Cong recruiting capabilities. Of course, GVN general mobilization in 1968, which led to the buildup of RVNAF and paramilitary forces to over 1.2 million men, also operated to sop up manpower which might otherwise be available to the Viet Cong.

THE EFFECT ON RURAL SECURITY

Both eyewitness reports and a mass of data attest that the physical security provided the bulk of the rural population, while still spotty in some cases, was expanded considerably after the 1965 low point. There was a direct correlation between increases in local GVN security forces and the resulting improvement in security indices. It can also be inferred from the decline in the overall incident rate. The number of battalion-sized attacks and even lesser incidents was down significantly from all terror, sabotage, etc., from 1968 to 1971. It is worth repeating, however, that the overall decline in the intensity of the war can be attributed to many other factors besides pacification.

Equally significant, the war became largely localized. The incident rate and HES statistics show clearly that both the military war and terrorism impacted mostly on a few key areas. Leaving aside the "big unit" war in the almost unpopulated jungle and mountain areas along the borders, insurgency-type activity in populated areas was largely concentrated in the three provinces of southern I Corps, Quang Nam, Quang Tin, and Quang Ngai; Binh Dinh, Phu Yen, Pleiku, and Kontum in northern II Corps; and three provinces in the Delta, Kien Hoa, Vinh Binh, and An Xuyen. In most populated areas of the other 34 provinces, even terrorism had radically declined—in many cases to sporadic harassment.

That over a million refugees appear to have returned to the countryside (with help from the GVN) was another indicator of improved rural security. The number on the rolls declined from over two million at the highest point to around 450,000 by 1971. While refugee statistics (especially earlier ones) are not wholly reliable, they are sufficiently so to establish this broad trend. Civilian casualties also declined greatly.

Lastly, pacification spurred what amounted to a GVN-sponsored rural revolution. Politically, socially, and economically, the traditional face of the countryside was transformed, not just by war but by radical land reform, economic revival, new transport networks, mass communications, revived local autonomy, and other GVN measures aimed at competing with the VC attempt at political revolution. Much evidence exists that even the farmers turned against the VC, though they remained wary of the GVN.

WOULD THE OTHER WAY HAVE WORKED?

The gathering weight of evidence indicates that the 1967–71 pacification program, with all its flaws and weaknesses, contributed greatly at least to short-run GVN ability to cope with rural insurgency. And this contribution was via a program that was "Vietnamized" from the outset. It showed what the Vietnamese could do when adequately supported. Yet direct U.S. dollar input to pacification in the peak year, 1970, only about $730 million out of the many billions still being spent, made pacification probably the most cost-effective major wartime program in Vietnam.

Nor did pacification programs generally entail the counterproductive side effects on rural attitudes characteristic of many aspects of the conventional military war. Indeed, many programs (refugee aid, village development, etc.) were designed partly to compensate for these.

Thus, to return to the larger question, do even the results of pacification 1967-71 permit concluding that a more pacification-oriented US/GVN approach during 1955–71 would have led to a different outcome? That it worked in Malaya does not provide sufficient basis for analogy to the far more complex Vietnam. Such an approach would have had its best chance in the 1950s and early 1960s, before rural insurgency escalated into quasi-conventional war. If the GVN and the United States had started out this way in 1955–60, instead of putting their chief emphasis on conventional forces, the Viet Cong might never have achieved the momentum they did. As one of the *Pentagon Papers* authors concluded, while "an effective counterinsurgent force" probably could not have deterred Hanoi's intervention, it "might well have prevented effective prosecution of the guerrilla alternative the Viet Cong and DRV did elect to follow."

But could the GVN and the United States have created an effective counterinsurgency capability at that time? Diem was notably resistant to this type of advice, though we did not try very hard. Nor did a viable politico-administrative framework exist. On the other hand, the later Thieu regime did prove able to carry out, with vigorous U.S. backing, a major pacification effort under the even more adverse conditions of a shooting war.

By 1964–65 pacification programs almost inevitably took a back seat to the growing "big unit" war. From then on a regular military shield for pacification became indispensable. But did not the military effort tend to become an end in itself, to the comparative neglect of pacification? Was the balance of our effort optimal? Not in 1964–67 at any rate, when there was a hiatus in large-scale pacification efforts. Yet it is also only fair to say that pacification finally had its inning under primarily military auspices. A truly substantial GVN program finally got underway in 1967–71. But it was never more than a modest complement to the conventional military effort, not the dominant strategic thrust.

So whether a pacification or counterinsurgency-oriented response would have provided a better strategic alternative must remain a historical "if." Naturally it looks much better in retrospect than how we responded instead. Yet what was belatedly accomplished in 1967–71, even allowing for many other contributory factors, suggests that such an alternative approach might have led to a more satisfactory outcome. At the least, it would probably have resulted in less militarization and Americanization of the conflict. The enormous toll in human life and waste of resources—plus the tragic side effects—might have been far less. And isn't it the very contrast between these horrendous costs and the ambiguous results achieved that helped feed that U.S. disillusionment which foreshortened the long-haul low-cost effort to which we finally retreated?

Sir Robert Thompson:

If one tries to talk about speed in pacification, it must be remembered that it will take as long to get back to the preferred *status quo ante* as it took the other side to get to the new position. If one thinks in terms of 1959 to 1966-67, the pacification was bound to be very, very slow. But the pace was altered by the fact that the enemy lost the forces in Tet which would have defended their own rear bases against the pacification program. The success of the program, which really started in late 1968, was staggering. In normal circumstances I would not have regarded it as possible, no matter what amount of effort was applied. One has to bear in mind one thing about pacification. Pacification against an enemy going up is a very different thing from pacification against an enemy going down, particularly when people become conscious of this.

But to go back to the earlier period: given the aims, objectives, tactics, and programs employed prior to the American intervention in 1965, could the insurgency then have been defeated? I do not know the answer, but my guess is no, for the simple reason that the North Vietnamese would have come in. They ran out of their 80,000 southerners that they had taken round about 1963, and the North Vietnamese Army actually started moving into the South early in 1964. The first regiment came in October 1964. That decision must have been taken much earlier, and I strongly suspect that if the program had been going, and if we had not had all the troubles with President Diem in the summer of 1963, if things, in other words, had looked good, then North Vietnam would have interfered.

In an earlier chapter General Edward Lansdale wrote of the cultural and political gaps of perception between Americans and Vietnamese. Stephen Young, who worked for AID in CORDS, reminded us in our deliberations that politics was always at the bottom of American–South Vietnamese problems.

Stephen Young:
My role in Vietnam was very much that of a lowly parish priest, but I would like to comment at this point on behalf of several distinguished cardinals. The central lesson which I draw from our military experience

in Vietnam is that Vietnam was politics, Vietnamese politics. The war was only an extension of politics in another form. How often we have expressed that sentiment, yet how rarely did we use it to determine policy and shape programs.

The political objective was always the American objective—the survival of a non-Communist South Vietnam with the same prospects for independence and national integrity that any people deserve. In 1965 Ambassador Lodge defined an American "victory" in those very terms. In July of that year, when Secretary McNamara recommended to President Johnson that the United State commit large forces to ground combat, he took that objective as "victory." Yet very shortly after the dispatch of our expeditionary corps, we found ourselves in a position where the tools we were using were not right for the job to be done. It was as if we were trying to build a house with a bulldozer and a wrecking crane.

My point can be simply made. There was a mismatch between the American thrust and Vietnamese need. As American military power and assistance increased from 1964 to 1968, the cohesion of South Vietnam and the ability of the South Vietnamese to fight the war decreased. But as American power withdrew from 1968 to 1972, the South Vietnamese capacity for resistance and struggle in their own right grew apace. The war was always their war; it could be no other war. Yet we never articulated our massive power and abundant resources into conjunction with Vietnamese politics. We never located their good leaders, we never sought to define what they were fighting for.

Secretary Nitze brought up the two points of the war's cost and the American public's will to support such a foreign conflict. Both those weak pillars to our war effort could have been replaced with solid political support and lower costs *if* we had directly supported the nationalists in South Vietnam. Had we supported the best Vietnamese leaders, had we kept the demands of their political culture in the fore, they would have done most of the fighting and borne most of the cost—as they were doing in 1974. Our cost would have been less, and public willingness to bear that cost greater. And given effective nationalist performance in Saigon, the agonizing question "What are we doing in Vietnam?" would have answered itself. Americans will support an embattled people—Churchill and the English in World War II, Israel against the Arabs—but Vietnam did not look like that kind of political being.

I lay primary blame on the Foreign Service and the Department of State. It was their job to come to terms with the political culture of Vietnam. They contented themselves with the official business of counterpart relations and after-the-fact analysis. Of course, American academics never took the time or trouble to come to grips with Vietnamese nationalism. But they have the luxury of an irresponsible existence. Unlike the Foreign Service, lives and fortunes do not turn on their mistakes.

I want to carry on a bit with a few war stories. They are the best way to convey what so many have missed for so long. My first story is about Colonel Nghia on the opening night of the Tet offensive in 1968. He was at home in Gia Dinh on the outskirts of Saigon when the massive attack broke loose during the night. As a tanker, Nghia had led the coup against Diem. Diem and Nhu were shot inside his APC. Nghia and his friends had then led all the coups of 1964 and 1965—to the distress of our government. But unlike the generals who held power, Nghia could inspire and lead his countrymen. On that night in 1968 he was only the G-3 of the Ninth Division, having only recently been reinstated in the Army after a year in jail for the coups. Thieu made sure Nghia was kept far from his tanks. But part of the Viet Cong plan was to take over the South Vietnamese tanks in the Phu Dong camp in Gia Dinh and use them in an attack on Tan Son Nhut airport. They broke into the camp with their drivers and gunners trained and ready but the tanks were gone. Fortunately, they were out on maneuver.

But the Viet Cong then got on the radio frequency of the Armored Command to send out false orders to the tank units. When the South Vietnamese JGS tried to get the tanks to speed to the defense of Tan Son Nhut, the unit commanders refused to move, unsure which order was the correct one. Nghia had a radio in his house and heard all this traffic. He knew that defense of the airport was critical to blunting the offensive. So he went on the air and said, "Comrades of the Armored Command, this is Nghia. Listen to me. Go immediately to the rescue of Tan Son Nhut." He was obeyed, and the airport (including General Westmoreland's headquarters) was saved. The name of a man who had no formal command could rally South Vietnamese soldiers.

My second story is from the 1972 Easter NVA offensive. After Quang Tri had been lost and the Third Division decimated, Hué was in a panic. The NVA was advancing, the people were fleeing. Airborne troopers were beating up Third Division soldiers, fires were breaking out near the marketplace. It looked as if central Vietnam was lost. At the last moment President Thieu sends up *one* man to save the situation and blunt the NVA thrust. In Vietnam the right man is all you ever need to get dramatic results. Thieu picked General Ngo Quang Truong. Truong had held out inside the imperial city of Hué for weeks during the 1968 offensive. His few troops were completely surrounded by the NVA but they held on. Now Truong had returned to Hué in equally desperate circumstances. He arrived at five in the afternoon, went on the radio at seven. He said, "Soldiers and citizens of Military Region I, this is General Truong. I have taken command. Tomorrow morning all deserters will report back to their units; all looting will cease forthwith."

The next morning the deserters reported back and the looting stopped. Then numerically inferior South Vietnamese units went on to recapture Quang Tri. Like Nghia, Truong had what it takes to lead, at least in 1972.

My next story is also from the 1972 offensive. An Loc: Battered and outnumbered South Vietnamese troops fought on and on until the better parts of two NVA divisions were shattered by American air power. Our air power did indeed finish off the enemy, but only ARVN tenacity gave our Air Force the opportunity to strike. If the ARVN had broken, there would have been no need for air power. An Loc held because the province chief, Colonel Nhut, rallied the defenders. In the first weeks of the offensive, Nhut pulled together RF, PF, police, self-defense militia —little guys here, little guys there—to shoot up and stop the first waves of North Vietnamese juggernauts. The American-trained Fifth Division and the American-trained and-pampered two-star commanding general were hopeless. They had American stuff but no Vietnamese soul. Nhut had soul but no stuff. Nhut won. It was the same with Truong and with Nghia.

One more story, which is the best. During the 1972 offensive the ARVN regiment in northern Binh Dinh Province abandoned ship and ran. The Third NVA Division then swept into Binh Dinh. But within several months, the Third NVA Division had been chewed to bits by the local provincial forces—RF and PF, the little guys to whom Westy would not give decent weapons until after Tet-68 when Komer asked him to. But in Binh Dinh the province chief, Colonel Chuc, turned local troops into a superior fighting force. He did it through leadership.

Right next to our airbase in Qui Nhon, the provincial capital of Binh Dinh, was a temple for a mystic cult of Len Dong, dedicated to the worship of Tran Hung Dao, the Vietnamese general who defeated the Mongols of Kublai Khan in the thirteenth century. Now Colonel Chuc went to the temple, entered a trance, and received a message from Tran Hung Dao. The great leader gave him a plan to defeat the northern invaders. Along with the plan went a magic sword. Thereafter, Colonel Chuc was always followed by a sergeant bearing an ancient sword on a velvet cushion. The local troops knew that the spirit of Tran Hung Dao had returned to lead them on to victory. They then accomplished what years of American advisers could not do. They beat the NVA.

Professor Allan Goodman:
One of the things that always struck me whenever I went to Vietnam was that people working there had a shadow army, a shadow cabinet, a shadow government, a shadow civil service—people who were not currently in favor, who had been kicked out, but who were always better than those who were in. The only person I ever saw really try to work, either to get the "outs" in or to deal in an effective way with a subject like corruption, which affected the leadership of both the Army and the Civil Service, was Robert Komer, with his seminars and various

novel approaches. My question is this: What do you do to get the "outs" in if you can't "take your marbles and go home"? If you can't shut off, really, any more of the commercial import programs? If you just simply can't say, "The U.S. mission is leaving"? What if your staff says, "This guy is really terrific and he really should be in command of the division"?
Ambassador Komer:
Without being too self-serving, let me say, on this question of leverage, that I started out looking at Vietnam as a problem in resource allocation, and ended up looking at Vietnam more as a problem in getting the right Vietnamese in the right jobs. To my mind, it was much less the issue of whether you want to build up the RVNAF quantitatively or give them more ammunition to shoot. It was much less a question of the size of the ARVN or the size of the Vietnamese Civil Service than of the qualities of leadership. I am fascinated that most of the people that Stephen Young mentioned, except for Truong, were then picked up in pacification—Colonel Chuc, Colonel Diep, etc. To me, you can have an ARVN half the size, if it were just twice as effective! In fact, I'd settle for 14 percent more effective. In a sense, I am agreeing with Sir Robert Thompson and General Keegan that we Americans had far too much of a quantitative, resource-oriented approach to Vietnam. The problem we never solved was how to get the right people in the right jobs doing the right thing at the right time.

Now, I will grant, as Robert Sansom says, if you do not know what the right things are, it is a little difficult, but what always impressed me about Vietnam was that we understood far better what needed to be done than we ever figured out how to do it. So, with the benefit of hindsight, whatever we did in the field was not half sufficient. Now, CORDS did go after the province and district chiefs and the officials. MACV had lists of incompetents—regimental, division, and corps commanders—but I cannot recall MACV getting anybody relieved for incompetence or cowardice or corruption or anything else, with one glittering exception. I remember General Abrams at one point talking about the commander of the Eighteenth ARVN Division, our great friend General Giai. "That man is not only the worst general in the

Vietnamese Army, he is the worst general in any army!" My question back was, "Why don't you go tell President Thieu and get him fired?" I saw Thieu the next day, so after going through the amenities I said, "Mr. President, let me tell you a story. At lunch with COMUSMACV and General Abrams yesterday, we were discussing the RVNAF leadership. Do you know that you have in your army the man whom General Abrams said was the worst general in any army?" He asked who and I told him General Giai. It may be only coincidence that Giai was replaced not too long thereafter.

Now, as to the question whether we ever threatened to turn off programs as leverage: indeed we did. In Ambassador Lodge's time, AID occasionally turned off province programs and it worked. They got two province chiefs relieved that way. My instinct was, if it worked then, we ought to replicate it on a much grander scale. We kept turning off support for police field-force companies too. You have to pick your program. When I suggested to Westmoreland and Abrams, "Look, the way to get rid of the commander of the Eighteenth ARVN Division is just to cut off all his support," Westmoreland's answer was—I thought a rather good one—"You cut off all support to the Eighteenth ARVN and the Viet Cong will know it as fast as General Giai. The next thing you know, here they come through Lam Dong!"

It is a complicated issue. One trouble is that our leverage declined as our commitment increased. Now Robert Sansom may remember that it was fashionable in Washington to say that, as we disengaged from Vietnam over the four years from 1969 through 1973 and our commitment went down, our leverage decreased. I felt the exact opposite at all times. When we Americans would do everything ourselves if the GVN would not do it, then they felt no real need to perform. When we started leaving, each remaining marginal increment of our assistance was more important than ever. But in hindsight we never used leverage to the extent we should have.

Ambassador Henry Cabot Lodge:
When we cut off the commercial import program, it did work. Unfortunately, Mr. Diem was assassinated a week later, but he had enough of a shock to talk to us about the things we wanted to talk about and

which he had absolutely refused to discuss up to that time. Indeed, when Diem finally caved in, I had just cabled Washington that we had failed.

The following section is taken from Thomas Thayer's paper "Performance in the Vietnam War: Five Key Issues."

On Pacification

Thomas C. Thayer

Security for the South Vietnamese population from Viet Cong and North Vietnamese harassment and exploitation has always been an essential part of pacification in South Vietnam and a key objective of the US/GVN war effort, although it was given much less emphasis than attrition. Population security is used here as the key criterion for evaluating pacification progress, although the pacification effort, despite its relatively meager resources, encompassed much more. Efforts to measure the level of security began at least as early as 1963, well before the commitment of U.S. ground combat forces in mid-1965, and continued throughout the war amidst publicity and controversy.

Early attempts to measure the security of the South Vietnamese population were oversimplified, of poor quality, and exaggerated the amount of security that actually existed in the countryside. For example, after the death of President Ngo Dinh Diem in November 1963, the number of "secure" hamlets in Long An Province was revised downward from over 200 to about 10.

The Joint GVN-US reporting system adopted in May 1964, and continued until June 1967 (when the U.S. Hamlet Evaluation System, HES, took over as the single, official system), attempted to portray military security, with little emphasis on administrative control and economic development. Reports on each hamlet in the GVN pacification plan were developed by the U.S. District Adviser and the Vietnamese

District Chief and sent separately to their respective headquarters at province and Saigon. The U.S. adviser was supposed to make an independent assessment, but this was often impossible because he seldom knew the history of his district very well and had to rely on Vietnamese interpreters to obtain information in the hamlets. Thus, the system is best described as a joint GVN/US one.

There is probably an optimistic bias in the 1964–67 statistics because the reporting tended to concentrate on changes resulting from ongoing work. As a result, backsliding in areas previously "pacified" probably didn't show up as well as progress in active areas.

A major new departure occurred in January 1967, when U.S. advisers began reporting their evaluations of hamlet status through the HES. Shortcomings in the previous GVN/US reporting of population and hamlet control in South Vietnam led the Secretary of Defense, in October 1966, to request a better system for measuring pacification progress, and the HES was the result.

The HES was designed to yield comprehensive, quantifiable data on the security and development of every hamlet in South Vietnam under some degree of GVN control and to identify hamlets under VC/NVA control. The system was completely automated for computer processing, and duplicates of the CORDS computer tapes were sent to Washington.

The system was a U.S. reporting system, although American advisers had to work closely with their Vietnamese counterparts in implementing parts of it. This turned out to be a critically important difference from the old GVN/US system, because it gave the U.S. adviser complete control of the final scores and enabled him to make an independent report on the pacification performance of his Vietnamese counterpart. Also, the new system represented the view from the cutting edge, since higher echelons were not allowed to change the ratings.

The top Vietnamese officials in Saigon came to rely on the HES as an independent report card on their provincial and district leaders, and this gave U.S. advisers in the field a good deal of leverage on the latter. While pacification always remained a Vietnamese program, in contrast to the military effort, it was graded by the Americans, and even the President and Prime Minister of South Vietnam acted on the reports.

The composite HES scores[1] were weighted more toward social and economic development than the criteria for the 1964–67 GVN/US reports and gave a better measure of permanent pacification progress, as opposed to increased military protection. The latter, of course, can be examined separately in the HES, as can many other questions.

The data from the GVN/US measurement system suggest an increase of 4.2 million people in the "secure" category between December 1964 and June 1967 (two and a half years) and a reduction of about 900,000 in the number of people under "VC/NVA control." In terms of percentages, the "secure" population increased from 42 percent to 64 percent of the total.

The gains would appear to be significant ones for the GVN, but the data suggest that much of the increase resulted from movement of people into GVN secure areas instead of expansion of territory (hamlets) protected by allied military forces.[2] Take the period from December 1965 to June 1967, for example, when secure population increased by 2 million. There were about 1.2 million officially recorded refugees during the period, which may account for 60 percent of the increase.[3] Natural population growth (at least 2.5 percent per year) would account for another .3 million (15 percent) of the increase.

Other factors could account for the remainder: extension of friendly protection; job seekers moving to the cities; "unofficial" refugees; and overoptimistic evaluation of programs. The hamlet data suggest that extension of allied protection is probably the main factor. About 500 hamlets were added to the secure category, and the average population per hamlet countrywide was about 1,000 at that time, so this would yield the 500,000 people needed to complete the 2 million gain.

[1] Each hamlet or population unit emerged with a composite score ranging from A–best through E–bad or as VC/NVA-controlled.

[2] For example, "secure" population increased by 700,000 between December 1966 and June 1967, but the number of "secure" hamlets showed little, if any, increase.

[3] Although up to half of them may have returned home after the winter–spring fighting subsided.

This is not to say that the gain occurred precisely this way, but simply to indicate the kinds of factors at work, which in turn suggest that the trend may be reasonably valid.

Intelligence reports and captured VC/NVA documents lend some credence to the trend in VC/NVA loss of control, but they also suggest that the Viet Cong control figures may be too low. For example, a captured document of early 1966 states that 5 million people lived in "liberated" (VC/NVA) areas and 9 million resided in Government-held areas. The GVN/US estimate for December 1965 shows 9 million in the "secure" category, but only 3.6 million in the Viet Cong-controlled category, a shortfall of 1.4 million.

The same captured document laments the loss of a million people from the countryside into Government-controlled urban areas as a result of the presence of U.S. troops. The GVN/US estimates show a loss of only 200,000 in Viet Cong control between June 1965 (arrival of U.S. combat troops) and December 1965. But the contested category dropped by 900,000 during the same period, and this may account for the rest of the "million" to which the document referred.

Another captured document, dated October 30, 1966, indicates that allied operations and programs produced "some relatively significant results" in the form of 400 additional GVN hamlets "built" and 400,000 people brought under GVN control. Other documents refer to loss of VC/NVA influence and control over the rural population and describe the declines in VC/NVA food production, tax revenues, and manpower as a result of shrinkage in their population base.

The trends shown in GVN/US reports are also consistent with results of the September 1967 Presidential election in South Vietnam. About 5.9 million voters were registered for that election, more than one half of the secure population of June 1967. This was a gain of 600,000 over the number of registered voters a year earlier. The GVN/US estimates show an increase in the secure population of 1.5 million over the comparable period (June 1966–June 1967), of whom approximately one half would be eligible to vote. Details are not available to verify that both gains occurred in the same population group, but the trends, at least, moved in the same direction.

In summary, then, the GVN/US figures, captured documents, and the voter registration statistics all suggest the same trends. While the evidence is by no means conclusive, it does suggest that the movement portrayed by the GVN/US reporting system is probably not too far wrong. The "secure" population is probably overstated somewhat, and VC/NVA control was almost certainly greater than the data show, but the fundamental trends appear to be reasonably sound.

Turning now to the HES, the major trends from that system suggest that:

1. A total of 8.2 million people were made "secure"[4] during the five years between December 1967 and December 1972. This raised the percentage in this category to 80 percent of the total population in South Vietnam.

2. The Tet offensive losses were recovered by the end of 1968. Indeed, largely because of the Accelerated Pacification Campaign, some 1 million people were added to the secure category by the end of that year.

3. The pacification effort really took off in 1969, when 4.3 million people were added to the secure category. The contested and VC/NVA-controlled populations fell below all previous levels.

4. The VC/NVA offensive in 1972 eroded the gains, but not in any major way for the country as a whole.

The table below shows what happens when a time series is constructed joining the GVN/US system and the HES system results. The linkage is crude and simply assumes that the HES A–B–C population is roughly equivalent to the GVN/US "secure" population, which was the case in January 1967, when both systems were operating side by side. The results are not precise, but they do suggest significant allied progress between December 1964 and December 1972.

The data indicate that the GVN gained some sort of influence or control over more than 11 million people. In percentage terms, the gain is from 42 percent of the total population in 1964 to 93 percent in 1972. The qualitative improvement does not show in the table, but from detailed HES data it can be determined that 15.4 million of the 1972 figure

---

4 The top two ratings in the HES, i.e., A- and B-rated population.

represents population in the A and B categories, versus only 7.2 million of the 1967 figure.

	The South Vietnamese Gain Influence or Control over 11 Million People		
	1964	1967	1972
"Secure" population* (in millions)	6.8	11.5	18.0
Percent of total	42%	67%	93%
Total population (in millions)	16.1	17.2	19.3

* "Secure" category from GVN/US system for 1964; A–B–C HES population (total scores) for 1967 and 1972.

A key question at this point is the validity of the HES results. It has already been suggested that the GNV/US system results were not too bad. How good, or bad, was the HES?

A number of formal studies were conducted to check the validity of the HES, particularly in its first stages from 1967 through 1969. From these studies, and working with the data from the system, the following consensus developed among those who analyzed the HES data over the years:

1. Changes in the HES security scores are sensitive enough to identify progress or regression in areas over time.

2. HES measurements are not precise enough to make point estimates—i.e., to measure precisely the position along a scale from "least secure" to "most secure." The precision, naturally, increases for higher levels of aggregation. At lower levels (village, district, province) it is generally agreed to be on the order of plus or minus one letter grade.

3. Comparisons between different geographic areas in South Vietnam at a single point in time may be of questionable validity, because of wide differences in the characteristics of various areas.

Considerable insight into the reliability and meaning of the HES trends can be gained from analyzing the details reported in the HES.

An example of one such analysis is presented below. It describes the development of an indicator of rural control and its trends.

Of course, the HES trends presented above included people living in cities in the secure population. They were reasonably secure to begin with and, with few exceptions, remained so throughout the period. The emphasis of the pacification effort was on the rural countryside, and the situation there is masked by the presence of the urban population in the estimates.[5] Moreover, the HES data shown so far includes many items besides security factors, because many of the HES questions relate to the socioeconomic and political situations. However, the HES trends for the rural population alone tend to follow the same lines.

To overcome these problems, an indicator of rural control was developed out of HES data. It uses ten carefully selected HES questions and begins with the assumption that a primary objective of both sides in the Vietnam War was to achieve *control* of the people and resources of the countryside. The rural control indicator assigns a hamlet to the side which has enough military and political strength to administer the hamlet effectively while preventing the other side from doing so. Doubtful cases are assigned to a "neither side controls" category.

The control indicator portrays a somewhat different rural picture than the HES total scores for the entire country:

1. In December 1969, the total HES scores suggest that 71 percent of the population is "secure." However, only 48 percent of the *rural* population is under South Vietnamese "control."[6] In 1972, the figures are 80 percent versus 63 percent.

2. The total HES scores indicate that pacification progress was slow in 1970 (gain of 4 percentage points) after large gains in 1969, but the rural control indicator suggests that pacification really began to take

---

[5] Although CORDS consistently abstracted rural data by itself from the HES as a management tool. One of the virtues of the HES is that it allows easy computer separation of such data elements.

[6] HES A–B security scores for rural population alone indicated that 55 percent of the rural population had A–B security ratings, versus a reading of 48 percent for rural control. The rural A–B ratings for the HES showed the same trends as the rural security indicator, but usually were 8 to 10 percentage points higher.

hold in the countryside during 1970 (gain of 19 percentage points) .

3. The impact of the 1972 offensive shows more clearly in the rural control indicator. GVN control slipped 8 percentage points[7] (versus 4 percent for total HES scores) , and VC/NVA control rose 3 percent (versus 0.2 percent) .

The astonishment was usually expressed in response to a casual comment from the new arrival that he had taken a jeep and driven from point A to point B by himself. The old-timer would sputter, "It used to take a battalion to travel on that road." Such exchanges were frequent.

In conclusion, it is apparent that pacification, as measured by the HES results and the other data presented here, took hold gradually and made great strides in 1969 and 1970. Most of those gains held through the intense fighting of 1972, although significant regressions were clearly evident in the areas of most intense combat.

Great progress was obviously made in gaining influence and control in the South Vietnamese countryside. Most of the credit for this probably belongs to the pacification program. It undoubtedly benefited from the big-unit war, which made it difficult for VC/NVA main forces to operate in the populated areas, but it seems clear that, without a pacification program, the gains would not have been anywhere near as great.[8]

The security improvement in the countryside permitted other important developments. Food production rose dramatically, reducing South Vietnam's reliance on rise imports and bringing new prosperity to the farmers. The improved security also permitted the massive 1970–73 land-reform effort, which distributed 2.5 million acres of land to 800,000 tenant-farmer families. As a result, the farm-tenancy rate dropped from 60 percent of all cropland down to 10 percent of it.

The results of the pacification program, which was Vietnamized

[7] By July 1972 it had dropped to 62 percent, or 15 percentage points below the previous December (1971) . The HES, as well as showing progress, rapidly showed the impact of VC/NVA offensives or other setbacks. Regressions showed up fairly clearly and were not masked to any significant extent.

[8] After years of criticism of the HES results, it is amusing to read (in 1974) accounts of the situation in South Vietnam which cite the strong GVN influence and control in the countryside.

from the beginning,[9] could have been the most important long-run development in South Vietnam to emerge from the war. At any rate, the results were achieved for less than 6 percent of the total resources expended in the war.

After all the calculations and assumptions made to construct the rural security indicator, it is ironic—and significant—to see that both ways of measuring pacification progress show the same result between 1969 and 1972. The HES total scores indicate that 2.9 million people were made secure during the period. The rural control indicator suggests that 2.8 million people were brought under control in the rural areas.

At the minimum, the data suggest that, after 1969, the pacification program was really reaching out into the countryside, in contrast to earlier years when much of the progress consisted of people moving from the countryside into the secure areas. The statistics also suggest that one can gain almost as much insight into the rural situation by using the HES A–B scores for the rural population only, as CORDS officials did.

Another way to add perspective to the HES results is to examine the security situation as reported independently of the HES. Casualty data, public-attitude surveys, and reports of the security conditions of roads and waterways furnish data for crude comparison.

Allied casualties and favorable HES results tend to move in opposite directions. During 1969 through 1971, allied casualties declined each year and HES security ratings rose. In 1972, casualties rose with the VC/NVA offensive and the HES showed a loss of security for the population. This is a crude comparison, but it does suggest that HES results moved with the tempo of the war. When things were going poorly for the allies, the HES showed it—and vice versa.

The public-attitude surveys suggest that, on average, hamlet residents felt less secure than the HES ratings showed. In one comparison,

[9] In 1970, for example, the CORDS advisory organization in MACV was authorized 7,627 personnel, or about 2 percent of the total U.S. personnel in South Vietnam at the time.

44 percent of the hamlet residents described their hamlets as less secure than the HES rating indicated; 54 percent of the respondents generally agreed with the HES description of their hamlet; and 2 percent said security was better.

An early study of HES validity, employing U.S. researchers in the field, found the same phenomenon. Hamlet residents were more conservative in their assessments than were the independent researchers. The latter imply that the results were as much in the eyes of hamlet residents as in the facts of the situation. Perhaps the attitude survey results have the same characteristic.

The data reporting the security status of essential roads and waterways support the HES population security trends in general. There are problems with the time series, but in December 1971, 80 percent of the essential roads and 75 percent of the essential waterways were considered safe.

In addition, polls in the summer of 1972 suggest that 75 percent of the rural population had no difficulty getting themselves or their produce to market. In this case, the polls are more optimistic than the HES data, which indicated that 70 percent of the rural population was free of VC/NVA taxation on produce moving to or from their hamlets.

Thus, the progress in making roads and waterways safe for travel was significant. All three sets of data support the assertion that conditions were reasonably good by the end of 1971, and they held fairly well in 1972.

Comments of U.S. advisers and other U.S. personnel returning to the United States in 1971 and 1972 consistently supported the notion that considerable progress had been made. Often, the returning person, whose experience in Vietnam was normally limited to one year, was unaware of the significance of his remarks, until another person, who had served in the same area a few years before, expressed astonishment at the conditions being described.

Chapter 14

Vietnamization and the Territorial Forces

A concern that often surfaced during our deliberations was: Who should have been fighting the war, the Americans or the Vietnamese? The United States increased its forces dramatically after 1965, so much so that the period and the buildup are characterized as the "Americanization" of the war. From a military standpoint the increase came as a result of the increased strength of Viet Cong and North Vietnamese brigade and division-sized forces; the South Vietnamese infrastructure was also in danger of a total collapse. The insurgency had reached (or was approaching) Mao's Stage III, in which guerrilla units would come together into main-force units and defeat the Government's conventional units in combat.

Americanization was regrettable for what it did psychologically to the South Vietnamese Armed Forces and Government. It was counterproductive. It robbed the South Vietnamese of a vital stake and a controlling interest in their own destiny. The buildup also diverted attention and resources away from the training of the South Vietnamese, especially the paramilitary territorial forces that were so critical to the pacification effort.

In this chapter a discussion of Vietnamization is followed by a paper on the Special Forces and one on the territorial forces.

Dean Edmund Gullion:
A question that has been a mystery to me since 1949, when I had my first contact with Vietnam, is why it took us until 1968 to build a Viet-

241

namese Army. I do know why the French did not do it. Firstly, because they did not want Vietnam to be that independent, and secondly, when they decided they did want an army, they began to be afraid that they would train young men in three months, who would then go over to the enemy. So they wanted to train officers at a year-long training school. Why did it take us really until 1968 to get into gear on this army?

General Edward Lansdale:
It did not take until 1968 to build a Vietnamese Army. The U.S.-trained Vietnamese Army was begun in 1955. Whatever it was, it was an army with which we could start to think about Vietnamization. At the beginning, we and the Vietnamese looked upon it as something of their own, with our role being that of training them to run it effectively. It was not called Vietnamization at the time. It was U.S. training and support, but it was a Vietnamese Army. The Vietnamese worked to defend their own country. They had a President. They had a chain of command. This is completely aside from the point of whether it was the right army, whether it was an effective one or not—it was their own. But I think one of the things that dragged us into Vietnam with our own forces was that it was not good enough.

Sir Robert Thompson:
True, only by 1973 did you get a really good army and there are two basic reasons for that. One, they had to do it, and they had to think it out—which they were doing. The ARVN survived on one fifth of the ammunition and one tenth of the gasoline that they would have had if they had a full American backup as they had in 1971. That comes through in the casualty figures; whereas the other side's casualty figures are about half of what they were in 1969, the ARVN casualty figures are six sevenths. They had to make up for that economy by manpower, and they also did it, of course, by a very considerable change of tactics.

There is a second reason that comes through here. Not really until the Tet offensive did the Vietnamese get a very clear view of who the enemy was. It was the North Vietnamese Army. In other words, you had a new motivation inside South Vietnam, particularly from 1972 onward. They had a clear enemy whose guts they hated, and you couldn't really say that about the earlier periods quite as clearly as that.

Dr. Robert Sansom:
Particularly in I Corps, after the Tet offensive, it became very clear who
the enemy was, and I think that was the key to everything. It has been
asked, "Why didn't we build up the ARVN faster? Why didn't we develop the territorial forces?" You have got to get back to the motivational question, which is one part leadership, in terms of which general
you put in, or which battalion commander. But there is a second part
of the motivation—prestige: why he might want to be in that force. You
can't build it just with resources, you have got to build it with motivation. One of my strong beliefs is that in the South, in the Delta, in III
and IV Corps, in the 1968–69 period, if economic circumstances had
changed, if the land-reform issue had gone ahead, then there would
have been time for the forces to reach some reasonable level. Then when
we told them to march out, there would be somebody to march out.
This has been part of the political problem on which I have no expertise, but you can't just say, "Why didn't we start building those forces
earlier?" They would not have come in. We needed troops and they
would not stay.

When did we decide that the Vietnamese Army was the army to
whom we had to turn responsibility over? We really did not face that
decision until 1968. In 1969 I was visiting MACV, trying to find out
how much of the staff echelon were working on tables of organization,
equipment, and the rest of it. I was amazed to find out how recently
it had begun, how little had gone into this sort of thing. There *was* a
Vietnamese Army from 1952 onward, of a sort, but it is curious, we had
never really thought of this, because we had done it so badly, I suppose,
in the 1960–65 period. Until 1968 it didn't occur to us to say, "Well,
this is the army that is going to have to bail us out of this damn thing
after all."

General George Keegan:
I would like to throw some light on this question. We were motivated
by three considerations. One of them applies equally to the ARVN and
to air power. We trained an army and we trained an air force. Wrong
equipment, wrong tactics, maybe, wrong doctrines, but we produced an
army. As to equipment, tactics, and doctrine, it was not until 1968 that

the Air Force began to think very consciously along the lines of General Abrams' realization: we are going to have to make this fellow self-sustained. But we were very late in providing them with a logistic base on which they could sustain themselves. That is even more complicated than slowly training airman. It involved a lot of discipline, supply, repair and matériel, and warehouses.

The last consideration is a political one. We were most anxious for the South Vietnamese not to go it alone. So they took what we gave them. It was not adequate to support them if they should face a real aggressor from the North who would throw in his air power and his mobile SAMs. I regretfully conclude that there was only one way to deal with such an eventuality: the United States Air Force would have had to get back into the act to help them defend themselves, because they were not equipped or trained. Having said that, if one needed an air force to provide ground support for the defense of Europe, I know of only one air force, excluding our own, superior to the Royal Air Force, and that would have been South Vietnam's. The Vietnamese make fine combat pilots.

Admiral Elmo R. Zumwalt:

On the more positive side, our Vietnamization effort also taught us something about the way in which to deal with our allies. There was a great deal of concern when we began the Vietnamization process that this could not take place in the brief time span that was left. It was done successfully because the American military man has learned his lesson. From that earlier era of the "Ugly American" he has learned how to communicate and how to deal with an ethnic and cultural group significantly different from our own. In the case of the U.S. Navy, in a period of three years we turned over a thousand boats, forty repair bases, we trained the equivalent of a division of South Vietnamese in repair maintenance and supply support, and turned over the fighting of that war along the 1200-mile coast of the Delta region of South Vietnam. We did it on the most intimate possible basis, that is, an American and a Vietnamese sailor were brought aboard each craft and ship, and when that Vietnamese sailor qualified, the American sailor went home. It was done with grace and élan and in a way that left a good taste in the mouths of the Vietnamese. This has taught us much about how to deal better with our allies around the world in other circumstances. It has taught all the services a significant lesson.

The question of why the territorial forces had not been developed sooner was asked and answered by Robert Sansom, in terms of the lack of motivation among the South Vietnamese until after the 1968 Tet offensive. If there was a motivational problem among the ethnic Vietnamese, the CIA and the U.S. Army's Special Forces had found a considerable measure of fear and discontent among the minorities living in South Vietnam. These people became the target for an unconventional warfare operation aimed at rallying them to the Government's cause.

The 5th Special Forces Group had its headquarters at Nha Trang during most of the war. It had a countrywide mission cutting across the boundaries and command lines of the four military regions. The commander was a U.S. Army colonel, who reported directly to General Westmoreland and later General Abrams. They had begun operations in South Vietnam in the late 1950s and were well established by 1965 when the regulars arrived, and they were frequently at odds with the regulars because of differences in basic philosophy, doctrine, and tactics. These two very dissimilar organizations were superimposed upon the same terrain and populations; the result was an uneasy truce which ultimately led to the withdrawal of the Special Forces from Vietnam in 1971. Most of the Special Forces' activity had been conducted among the ethnic minorities in remote regions away from the major population centers along the coast. Their operations were in sharp contrast to the "search and destroy" tactics employed by the regular American units.

Colonel Robert Rheault became a Green Beret in 1960 and rose swiftly, to command the 5th Group in 1969. After only two months in his new post he was stripped of command and imprisoned. The case involved a Vietnamese double agent caught spying, whose services were terminated "with extreme prejudice," according to press accounts. But after much publicity and investigation, all charges and allegations against Colonel Rheault were dropped; he retired from the service shortly thereafter.

The Special Forces and the CIDG Program

Colonel Robert Rheault

The first Special Forces (SF) commitments in Vietnam came as early as 1957 and were very much in line with what they had been doing all over the free world—helping friendly nations train elite units.

The early Military Assistance Advisory Group (MAAG) in Vietnam was not concerned with insurgency or revolution and busied itself instead with building a conventional army to repel a Korean-style invasion from the North. The SF mission fell in line with this concept and helped create an offensive guerrilla-warfare capability, the Vietnamese Special Forces. Later teams took on the training of the Vietnamese Army Ranger units.

As time went on and the pattern of the war and the U.S. involvement changed, Special Forces in Vietnam were to find themselves in all kinds of roles and missions. Far eclipsing all of the other SF activity in both size and scope was the Civilian Irregular Defense Group (CIDG) program. In the conduct of this unique program over a period of some nine years, Special Forces became involved in every conceivable aspect of counterinsurgency: military, economic, psychological, and political. The CIDG program involved thousands of United States Special Forces soldiers, hundreds of thousands of Vietnamese civilians, millions of dollars, and hundreds of camps spread from the Demilitarized Zone to the Gulf of Siam. It is a story of teaching the Vietnamese how to shoot, build, farm, care for the sick, or run agent operations. It was working with the religious and ethnic minorities of Vietnam: the Montagnards, the Cambodians, the Hoa Hao, and the Cao Dai. The program was both praised and reviled by Americans and Vietnamese alike and was on the verge of being destroyed many times—not by the Viet Cong, but by its creators, the American command; and by early 1971 it had disappeared from the scene.

In the overall context of U.S. involvement in the Vietnam War, it was certainly a relatively small operation, at least small in size and in cost; but it had within it some germs of counterinsurgency sense. Perhaps it might help show, in its successes and failures, how and why we failed in Vietnam and maybe even how we might have succeeded.

The Civilian Irregular Defense Group program was a U.S. Army Special Forces operation from start to finish, but it is the Central Intelligence Agency and not the military that gets the credit, or the blame, for starting it. It was indeed the military who later converted it (or, as some feel, perverted it) and who finally killed it.

The idea for the CIDG program was born in 1961, at a time when the level of hostilities in Vietnam was still relatively low. The Viet Cong were concentrating their activities on the rural population, and armed clashes between Viet Cong guerrilla units and elements of the ARVN were rare and small. To those who understood revolution or insurgency and to those in the CIA who started the program, it was obvious that, as always, the greatest portion of the peasant population was committed ideologically to neither side and wished only to be left alone. It was equally obvious that effective propaganda, revolutionary organization, and terror tactics were bringing thousands of peasants under Viet Cong control. Many concepts were in the mill for grappling with this problem, but the CIA originators, mindful perhaps of failures in Laos with the flatland Lao and of success with the Meo, looked to the highlands of South Vietnam. There, in relative isolation, lived some 500,000 primitive tribesmen spread over nearly 75 percent of the country's land area, while the remaining 14 million Vietnamese lived mostly jammed into the fertile deltas and coastal lowlands. The highland tribes of Vietnam were of Malayo-Polynesian or Mon-Khmer ethnic stock who had been pushed back into the hills centuries ago by the more advanced Sino-Mongoloid populations that moved into the rice-rich deltas and lowlands. Throughout history they were looked down upon as *moi* (savages) by the flatland Vietnamese and treated as second-class human beings, to say nothing of second-class citizens. The French and later the Americans called them Montagnards (a French term meaning, simply, mountain men).

After the Geneva accords and the departure of the French, Vietnamese moves into the highlands caused real problems. First came the refugee settlements and the Diem Government, which took the best land, brought taxes, and outlawed the crossbow. Then came the Viet Cong seeking sources of food, recruits, labor, and intelligence. The Montagnards saw little that appealed to them in either group, avoided both when possible, and went along when they had to.

The CIA planners saw the threat and the opportunity to step into the role vacated by the French, but they may have overlooked an important difference. The French had been engaged in a mission of divide and conquer to preserve colonial rule in their own right. The United States was launched on a program to help South Vietnam unite and stabilize all of its diverse political, ethnic, and religious factions. Certainly the Montagnards failed to see the distinction and welcomed these new "round eyes" as protectors against the hated flatland Vietnamese.

The highland jungles in Vietnam could provide base areas and infiltration routes for the Viet Cong. The partially alienated Montagnard population in this same area was willingly or unwillingly providing scouts, porters, growers of food, and sometimes even recruits. If this population could be protected or, better yet, could protect themselves from exploitation, the Viet Cong would be deprived of much-needed support.

The program initially was defensive in nature. It was population denial, a real key to counterinsurgency success. It was felt, and with considerable justification, that Vietnamese-Montagnard alienation was too deep to contemplate an effective program in the highlands with Vietnamese leaders. It would have to be an American show, and the problems of integrating the program into the overall effort would be left for later. An initial area and tribal group was selected: the Rhade tribe, living mostly in Darlac Province in the Central Highlands. The

Rhade were one of the largest tribes and certainly the most advanced and intelligent. Views and proposals were hammered out in late 1961, and in January 1962 representatives of the Government of Vietnam (GVN), Rhade tribal leaders, and the United States "Combined Studies Group" (one of CIA's many euphemisms) met and agreed to certain principles. The Rhade would denounce the Viet Cong and support the GVN. The GVN agreed that the CIA would run the program and the Vietnamese civilian and military officials would keep hands off. The CIA agreed to run the program, to fund it, and to *coordinate* with the Vietnamese. The Americans and Vietnamese agreed to expand the program if it succeeded. As they had in Laos, the Agency called on Special Forces to provide the troops; and on the island of Okinawa, Captain Ron Shackelton, commander of Detachment A-113, was alerted for Vietnam.

The concept for the Village Defense Program (VDP) was quite simple. It was merely to arm and train enough of the Rhade so that they could protect themselves against the Viet Cong. The VDP did not involve moving people away from the Viet Cong or engaging in massive combat operations. Neither was necessary or desirable. The Special Forces team would establish itself in a centrally located village, prepare a simple defense, and recruit and train a small "strike force." This strike force would be the only full-time military force used and the only paid troops. They would provide soldiers to help a village under attack, to reinforce a threatened area, to patrol between villages, to gather intelligence, and to set ambushes. Next would begin the training of village defenders. These men would be taught only the basics of village defense and small-arms operation and would return to their home villages to live and work (fighting only when necessary). A simple radio would be provided to call for help from the operational base or neighboring village. As soon as a ring of villages had been prepared and defended, the perimeter would be pushed out further to embrace even more villages.

Captain Shackleton and his team established themselves at Buon Enao and immediately set to work. The reaction of the Rhade was positive and heart-warming and defended villages multiplied. The reaction of the Viet Cong was not long in coming either. The Viet Cong turned against undefended villages outside the security circle. Refugees fled to Buon Enao and at one time numbered several thousand. Not only were they cared for and given the means to build homes and raise crops, but they were retained in their original village organization and ultimately resettled as a group in their original area—this time with trained defenders. It was slow and painful, but it worked. By April 1962, 28 villages were in the program, 1,000 village defenders had been armed and trained, and a 300-man strike force was operational.

The Vietnamese never did like the program much, but its effectiveness could not be denied. The bypassed problems of Vietnamese-Montagnard enmity would emerge later, but not yet. Additional teams came in from Okinawa to continue and expand the concept. By the time Shackleton and his team had completed their six-month tour in August, the program was well underway with 129 Rhade hamlets protected by close to 10,000 village defenders.

Naturally, as time went on and the pace of the war quickened, the concept and its implementation changed. The initial idea had been essentially passive defense, but gradually the concept evolved into one in which the SF team moved into an area, built a type of "frontier fort," and recruited and trained three to five strike-force companies who defended the camp and patrolled and secured the surrounding area. The village-defender idea died out, and the program took on a more military and more offensive flavor.

As it spread to other areas, the program began to be bastardized. Military authorities wanted a camp in a certain area for military reasons with no regard to the political or demographic facts of life. SF teams started to lift companies of trained "strikers" from one place to another to accomplish the *military* mission.

The concept, however, was basically sound; it was based on an understanding of revolution and the importance of the people; and most of all it was carried out by Americans who understood and believed in what they were doing, and who had the patience, imagination, and dedication to see it through. The whole concept of the operation had always been, from the earliest guerrilla days, to get the indigenous people to do the job. It was only natural that this doctrine was carried on into the noncombat effort as well. A range of programs was conducted under the heading of civil affairs and psychological operations. These programs included construction of dependent housing, presentation of entertainment by culture and drama teams, medical patrols, newspapers published in the Montagnard dialect, inoculation against disease, bridge building, rehabilitation of village marketplaces, training for nurse's aides, dissemination of leaflets, and even the aerial movement of two trained elephants.

Success led to expansion, and the CIDG program pushed out in many directions. If the concept could work with Montagnards, why not with other population groups? Rapidly the CIDG program grew from mere population denial in the highlands to a countrywide extension of the strategic hamlet program, an effort to push the Government presence out beyond the limits of other agencies. By 1963 there were 30 camps; by 1964, at least 40, with some in all of the four corps tactical zones. CIDG strike-force strength was up to 20,000, and Ron Shackleton's seven-man team had grown to a provisional group of over 1,000. CIDG camps sprang up in the rubber plantations of III Corps, in the desolate Plain of Reeds, and along the canals and rice paddies of southernmost IV Corps.

By accident, or by design, SF found itself dealing with most of Vietnam's religious and ethnic minorities. These groups were alienated from the Vietnamese majority and its government and represented an untapped manpower resource. Further, the Special Forces preferred to set up in the remote regions and in the border areas, where many of the minorities had settled. By 1967 the 5th Special Forces Corps (Airborne) numbered some 3,000 men. They were scattered from the huge, sprawling operational base at Nha Trang to the small back-country camps in over 80 different locales, and were "advising" or leading almost 60,000 native irregular troops.

The CIDG idea had been born in an era of little heavy combat, long before the injection of regular North Vietnamese Army units and U.S. infantry and air-mobile divisions. The camps had performed generally well, but had never been built, equipped, or armed to withstand a large-scale assault. Furthermore, most camps were by definition in remote areas and hard to bail out when trouble came. In the early days there was little chance of getting help from *any* source. Some camps were overrun but generally were able to hold out until help arrived. As the intensity of the war increased, however, and more and more North Vietnamese regulars entered the fighting, the camps became increasingly vulnerable.

In this environment, "hardening" the camp defenses would not be enough; relief forces were also needed. On the old theory that "if you want something done, you'd better do it yourself," Special Forces created its own mobile reaction forces, or "Mike Forces." These units could be used as mobile forces for any number of purposes: to reinforce a threatened camp, to patrol areas not covered by camp strike forces, to run special missions in remote areas, and to bail out camps in trouble. This was a further departure from the original CIDG concept in that these new units had no particular roots in the areas where they fought. In fact, by 1969, one would see examples such as Rhade Montagnards fighting on the Isle de Phu Quoc or in the swampy Rung Sat west of Saigon. But the tenor of the war was changing, and SF had to use the Mike Forces to protect their camps. The mobile reaction forces started in a very small way with one battalion in Da Nang in 1965, were built up rapidly during the next two years, and ultimately reached a strength of nearly 10,000 troops. Each of the four corps tactical zones of Vietnam had a Mike Force of one or more battalions. A fifth Mike Force was also formed at the Special Forces headquarters at Nha Trang for use countrywide.

All the ethnic groups, including some Vietnamese, were represented. There was a heavy percentage of Cambodians in III and IV Corps, while the Montagnards dominated the Mike Force in the Central Highlands and at Nha Trang.

The Mike Forces of 1969 were modern with their camouflage uniforms, jump wings, steel helmets, and up-to-date M16 automatic rifles. They were a far cry from the simple pajama-clad peasant village defender of 1962 who was armed with a World War I Springfield M-1903. But the enemy had changed as much or more. AK-47s, Soviet rockets, and Chinese heavy mortars had made it a "new ball game." Special Forces had adapted to the change by developing the Mikes; but they had not lost sight of the ball—the people. The essence of the program was still in the CIDG camps and with the population that these camps protected.

As mentioned earlier, it was the Central Intelligence Agency which conceived of the initial CIDG program, started it, and ran it during its early days. Fortunately for the continued success of the CIDG program, when the CIA departed they left their special funding and support system behind. It was a CIA support system that backed up the CIDG program even after the Agency had moved out of the operation. There was only one alternative to the CIA support and that was MAP, the Military Assistance Program. This program was designed to help advanced friendly nations build their armed forces to counter some future conventional threat. It was not designed to fund the support needed to fight an ongoing insurgency. Furthermore, MAP money and equipment passed to Vietnamese control upon arriving in-country. The money for the CIDG program, on the other hand, remained under U.S. Special Forces control right down to the A-team level, and that was important.

Without the special funding system of the CIA, there simply could not have been a CIDG program. Legislation prohibits the expenditure of MAP money to pay indigenous troops directly. Gold-flow restrictions forbid the purchases of large quantities of non-U.S. goods; but CIDG soldiers were paid, fed, clothed, equipped, housed, and even buried with inexpensive locally procured materials.

It is doubtful that the expenditures versus accomplishments of the Vietnam War can ever be adequately documented, for war is by nature an incredibly inefficient and wasteful business. It is too bad, because if it could be done there is little doubt that it would show that the United States got a better return on the CIDG dollar than it did on any other. It is the fond and perhaps vain hope too of the few men who know and understand the unique nature of the CIDG funding system that it might serve as a model for providing support to any future U.S.

operation struggling with the complex problems of counterinsurgency. In spite of the well-known and highly publicized withdrawal of American troops from Vietnam, it came as quite a surprise to many to read in the press in mid-1970 that the Special Forces were coming home. Most people, whether they were only generally aware of Special Forces activities or thoroughly knowledgeable, had assumed that the Forces, which had been among the "first in," would be very nearly the "last out."

The official explanation, that this was all merely a part of overall troop withdrawal and Vietnamization, certainly failed to stand up under even the most casual scrutiny. On the very face of it one wondered at the withdrawal of a unit made up of 3,000 highly trained and dedicated volunteers, while conventional units heavily larded with some 300,000 disgruntled draftees remained. One could not help but ask how much headquarters fat remained while good boondock muscle was excised? How many white-coated soldier waiters and bartenders in General Abrams' mess, PX managers, lieutenant colonels, staff officers, sedan drivers, and awards-and-decorations typists remained? And more to the point, why destroy a small, inexpensive, and immensely effective program which provided so much in the area of security and intelligence in the remote areas and among the minority groups?

There is no easy answer, but the decision invited speculation that emotion rather than logic may have governed; that after eighteen years of existence, Special Forces still aroused the old animosities; and worst of all, that after all these years in Vietnam, MACV still did not understand either the CIDG program or revolutionary war.

It may be too soon to attempt any objective assessment of the U.S. involvement in Vietnam, and it is equally difficult to say a final word with regard to the Special Forces' contribution. However, certain questions and conclusions seem to stand out.

One may well ask: Was the long-range objective of the Montagnard program sufficiently well defined and was it in the context of the United States' ultimate objectives in Vietnam? Did the Special Forces deny the Montagnard population to the Viet Cong at the cost of further exacerbating animosities and suspicion between the Vietnamese and the Montagnard? Could this have been avoided by a more sophisticated political approach?

Could Special Forces have avoided the "militarizing" of the CIDG program and the immobilizing influence of the fortified camps? Could Special Forces have been more effective operating in a smaller, quieter, and more flexible way, detached and divorced from the MACV military juggernaut, functioning perhaps under CIA?

On balance, the program *did* accomplish its original objective of denying large portions of the uncommitted population to the Viet Cong. Furthermore, it mobilized and involved thousands of the ethnic and religious minority groups in the struggle for the survival of the Republic of Vietnam. This is not to say that the root problems of disunity were erased; but at least these people participated in a Vietnamese national effort.

The CIDG program had its roots in the population of Vietnam and its camps in the remote areas and hinterlands. Thus it provided contact, protection, and a source of intelligence in many areas otherwise untouched by the Government of Vietnam.

Although technically commanded by Vietnamese, it was highly responsive to U.S. influence and control, yet did not require the high expenditure of dollars and U.S. lives that marked a pure U.S. unit.

Successful counterinsurgency (and there are some who argue that the two words are a contradiction) must be waged with great skill and infinite patience across a wide spectrum of activities that are largely political and only occasionally military. The United States might have fared better in Vietnam with a few less bombers and artillery pieces and a few more specialists prepared to deal with civilians and irregular problems.

The CIDG, under Special Forces command, was not really part of the pacification program run by the Government of South Vietnam. That may have been its Achilles' heel in the final analysis, as it became in-

*creasingly evident that an "American solution" to the insurgency prob-
lem was not the correct course of action. The CIDG program was
"people-oriented," however, and it did provide a large measure of local
security.*

*There were two other important classes of local or territorial forces
that must also be considered. These were the Regional Forces and the
Popular Forces, paramilitary units which were responsive to the South
Vietnamese governmental hierarchy. After the Special Forces went home
in 1971, the camps and forces of the CIDG program reverted to the
South Vietnamese Government and many were integrated into the Government's own territorial-force structure with a role in providing local
or territorial defense. Thomas Thayer discussed the role and the effectiveness of these forces.*

Territorial Forces

Thomas C. Thayer

The Regional Forces (RF) and the Popular Forces (PF) were the
main territorial troops operating for the GVN in the countryside, but
they received only a small share of the resources devoted to the war.
Both relied heavily (but not exclusively) on local recruiting and normally did not operate outside of their province or district, although
some RF troops fought outside of their provinces during the 1972
VC/NVA offensive, particularly in Military Region IV.

Between 1966 and 1972, the RF/PF forces grew by 73 percent. The
increase was fairly uniform among the four Military Regions (MRs),
whose gains ranged from 61 percent to 80 percent. The distribution of
forces therefore changed very little, as the entire force structure grew
from 300,000 troops in 1966 to more than 500,000, in 1972.

RFs, operated in 100-man companies, doubled between January
1968 and December 1972, from 900 to 1,800. Some of the companies

were organized into RF battalions, but the company remained the basic operating unit.

The buildup of Regional Forces shows up primarily as additional units assigned to hamlet and village security until December 1969, although companies on offensive missions increased sharply too. After 1969, as the need to use RF/PF for hamlet-village security missions declined, they shifted to local offensive operations. In December 1969, 43 percent of the companies were on hamlet-village security missions. This dropped to 24 percent two-and-one-half years later, as the percentage of units on active missions increased from 27 to 50 percent.

The RF patterns in the four Military Regions are similar to the countrywide pattern. The data show a pervasive buildup of security forces which then shift to more active operations as security in the rural areas improves. The period starts with 750 RF companies on security missions versus 140 on active missions, and ends with more than 800 companies assigned to active missions.

The Popular Force platoons, 30-man units who operated in a specific village or hamlet, doubled between January 1968 and December 1971, and then decreased by 600 platoons, for a net growth of 80 percent. The number of PF platoons went from approximately 4,200 to more than 8,000 and then dropped to about 7,500, for a net gain of more than 3,000 platoons.

As expected, the PF buildup focused on security missions, although the platoons on active missions increased too. Platoons on hamlet-village security missions accounted for 72 percent of the platoons. By June 1972, this had declined to 60 percent. In the same period, platoons on active missions increased from 7 percent to 18 percent.

As with the Regional Forces, the Military Regions reflect the countrywide pattern in varying degrees, indicating similar movement throughout South Vietnam.

The RF/PF buildups and their gradual shift to more active missions accord well with the HES (Hamlet Evaluation System) results, which show the National Police and the People's Self-Defense Forces taking more of the responsibility for hamlet security as time passes.

The HES data also reflect the sharp decrease in RF responsibility for hamlet security, and the much slower decline in the PF role. The RF/PF took the brunt of the war, more than any other South Vietnamese armed force. They had a higher proportion of combat deaths than the regulars, and were the prime targets of VC/NVA attacks until 1972. The RF/PF share of combat deaths was higher than their share of the RVNAF force. In 1971, for example, the RF/PF accounted for 50 percent of the force, but 60 percent of the combat deaths, and this figure may be conservative. The intensity figures—combat deaths per 1,000 personnel strength—show the same relationship. In every year except 1968, the chances of getting killed in the RF/PF are higher than in the regular forces. Moreover, the gap between the RF/PF and the regulars widens each year from 1969 through 1971. Relative to the regular forces, service in the RF/PF got more dangerous each year.

One reason for the widening gap between the regular and the territorial forces is that the territorial forces accounted for an increasing proportion of the RVNAF killed in VC/NVA attacks. They suffered 55 percent to 66 percent of all RVNAF deaths from such causes in every year except 1972.

The other side of the coin is: How well did the RF/PF inflict casualties on the VC/NVA forces? The data suggest that the RF/PF accounted for about 30 percent of the VC/NVA combat deaths inflicted by RVNAF forces, and this figure, too, may be conservative. In any case, it is clear that the territorial forces inflicted a lower percentage of VC/NVA casualties than they took (33 percent inflicted versus 60 percent taken in 1971).

Several factors help to explain the discrepancy. First, the territorial forces operated in the rural areas, where the VC/NVA found them more readily available, softer targets than the regular forces. The RF/PF bore the brunt of VC/NVA offensive actions, and the VC/NVA enjoyed exceptionally favorable kill ratios in such actions. At one point, actions initiated by the VC/NVA inflicted 28 percent of the total allied combat deaths, while costing them only 5 percent of theirs. The RF/PF suffered accordingly.

Second, RF/PF fights with the VC/NVA tended to occur at night, often unexpectedly, and far from combat support. Data from Military Region III for October 1966–March 1967 suggest that, when attacked, RF/PF troops received outside support only 45 percent of the time, and ground reinforcements arrived only 11 percent of the time. The other side of the picture is even worse. When their offensive operations contacted the VC/NVA, the territorials received outside help in only 17 percent of the MR III actions, and ground reinforcements in only 3 percent of them.

With Vietnamization, the situation undoubtedly improved, but even as late as 1969, RF/PF units were receiving only 30 percent of the Vietnamese-fired artillery support, and half of it consisted not of support during a contact but of small barrages at suspected VC/NVA locations or preplanned fires against likely VC/NVA routes of attack.

Finally, the RF/PF, for much of the war, simply had poorer leadership, training, and arms than their VC/NVA counterparts, so they could not hold their own, particularly without support. The U.S. improved the situation by furnishing M-16s, mortars, radios, training, etc., to every RF/PF unit. However, even this was not enough to redress the imbalance between casualties inflicted and casualties absorbed.

However, the territorial forces performed well in helping to counter the VC/NVA offensive in 1972. The shift to large-scale, mainforce combat put the RF/PF in the position of supporting mainforce units in battle, and in many cases they fought VC/NVA regular units by themselves.

A review of RF/PF operations during April-July 1972 suggests that they made a major contribution to the war effort. The data even suggest that they temporarily redressed the imbalance between casualties taken and casualties inflicted, which may mean that they were surprised by the VC/NVA fewer times and received more combat reinforcement and support. However, this is conjecture.

Whatever the case, the RF/PF accounted for 28 percent of the RVNAF combat deaths, and claimed 37 percent of the VC/NVA combat deaths. Their kill ratio (VC/NVA to RVNAF) was 2 to 1, the same as for the regulars. This all suggests that the Vietnamization effort paid off handsomely in the 1972 offensive, when the RF/PF apparently fought about as well as the regulars, at least in terms of casualty exchanges.

Adding cost data to the assessment of effectiveness suggests that the RF/PF, dollar for dollar, were the most effective large force in killing VC/NVA troops in South Vietnam. The figures indicate that the RF/PF accounted for 30 percent of the VC/NVA combat deaths inflicted by RVNAF forces, but for less than 20 percent of the RVNAF program budget costs. More startling, the territorial forces accounted for 12-30 percent of all VC/NVA combat deaths, depending on the year, but for only 2-4 percent of the total program budget costs of the war.

These are macabre calculations, because they purport to equate dollars and deaths, which is nonsense, but they do serve to point up the incredibly unbalanced allocation of resources within the allied war effort. The attrition objective alone would seem to have called for more resources and emphasis for the territorial forces. If 30 percent of the VC/NVA casualties can be had for only 4 percent of the resources, what might have happened if the allies had allocated 10 percent of the resources to RF/PF? The potential effects might have been staggering. And the RF/PF role in establishing territorial security has not even been put into the calculation yet.

The primary mission of the territorial forces was to protect and secure the population, particularly in the rural areas. The HES data suggest that about half of the population relied on the RF/PF for the security of their hamlet. Other data indicate that the RF/PF killed or captured more of the VC/NVA clandestine infrastructure than any other force.

There is no doubt that the RF/PF contributed to the increasing security of the countryside. It is tempting to give them all of the credit for the gains, but that is probably not the case, because the situation is more complex than that. Many other forces and programs had a role in the pacification effort, and surely had some effect. Nonetheless, it is interesting to note that the RF/PF increased 58 percent during 1968–69, while the secure population increased 74 percent. And most of the security gain came in 1969 and 1970 after most of the RF/PF buildup was complete.

Comparing the growth of RF/PF with the progress of GVN rural control in 1970–71 yields the interesting statistics that about 60 rural inhabitants came under GVN control for each RF/PF soldier added during the period. From mid-1969 to mid-1970, the increase of 807 new units in Military Region IV closely parallels the pacification gain of 801 hamlets in the secure category.

However, relying on the foregoing data to make the case for RF/PF can be misleading, because analysis of the April–September 1968 period yields the dismaying finding that the security ratings of the population not protected by the RF/PF improved about as often as the population they protected. This clearly suggests that other factors were also working to improve population security ratings.

The same analysis indicates that RF/PF working together had the best effect on HES security scores, followed by PF operating alone. RF alone tended to be associated with security regressions, except in Military Region IV, where the RF/PF were the primary RVNAF combat forces.

The findings are reasonable. The RF were considered to be a flexible, mobile force which could take part in large-unit operations with regular forces, replace ARVN battalions providing territorial security, and provide a security umbrella for PF and other GVN personnel tied down to hamlets.

Thus, RF/PF working together provided both mobile and static defense and could be expected to have a favorable impact on HES scores. About 80 percent of the PF units were recruited primarily from their own or adjacent villages, so they could not appear on the scene until the RF and regulars had established enough security in the area to allow the GVN to recruit PF. Logically then, one could expect to find improving security where PF appear. On the other hand, RF units were the mobile units which were supposed to show up in trouble spots to counter VC/NVA actions, which drag down HES scores.

Results of public-opinion surveys in South Vietnam suggest that the people were more impressed with RF performance than with PF performance, and equated it with ARVN performance. Forty percent thought the PF were effective, and 70 percent thought the RF were effective. Seventy percent of another sample thought the ARVN were effective. Thus, the RF seemed to rate as well with the rural population as the ARVN.

It seems clear that the RF/PF, by their combat performance, and by their permanent presence in the countryside, had a profound and perhaps decisive effect on improving the security of the rural population. Yet they consumed less than 5 percent of the total costs of the war. There can be little question that the Regional Forces and the Popular Forces were the most cost-effective military forces employed on the allied side. However, until the big pacification effort began in 1967-68, they were consistently neglected by both the GVN and the United States.

Chapter 15

Was Failure Inevitable?
Some Concluding Perspectives

At the time of our deliberations the war in Vietnam had not ended, though there were few optimists among our number; the assumption of failure was implicit in the papers and discussions, and little editing was needed after the debacle to take into account the new facts. Yet there was nothing inevitable about the outcome even then, any more than anything in a world of contingencies is inevitable. The lessons of the war must not be read as a process of inevitability working itself out, except insofar as the result is seen trivially, as the outcome of the particular variables of policy chosen. As one of the editors has argued elsewhere,[1] the avoidance of two quite discrete mistakes in the spring of 1975 would at the very least have made a negotiated settlement possible for the Thieu regime, and averted the ignominy of total defeat that did occur. In this chapter, some of the variables that fed into American policy are debated, by participants and critics alike. A brief summary by Robert Pfaltzgraff points the way to the important work ahead in analyzing further the lessons of this war.

Professor Earl Ravenal:
I would generally agree with the comment that war is an art form. Mistakes, progress, and lack of progress are not subject to absolute determination by quantitative measures. However, that does not excuse

---

[1] See W. Scott Thompson, "The Indochina Débâcle and the United States," *Orbis*, XIX, No. 3, (Fall 1975).

us from making a *logical* determination whether what one is doing is sufficient. In other words, whether the lessons that we are learning are sufficient conditions to remedy the shortcomings of what happened before. There is an implicit presumption here, in all the "lessons" people have enumerated that we should have learned from the Vietnam situation, to the effect that, had we learned those lessons, the campaign might have been more successful; and were we to learn these lessons we would avoid certain kinds of mistakes in the future. That is a presumption that is very, very far from being established by anything that I have heard, partially valid though almost all the observations might be.

First of all, whether we win or lose a war has a good deal to do not so much with the objectives that we hold for the war, as with something that goes beyond objectives. That is, not *what* we are trying to accomplish, but, in a larger sense, *why* we are trying to accomplish it. When we begin to ask the question in that form, it seems that we are not yet clear about Vietnam. Although we could articulate objectives, we would not yet be clear about the national purpose. Therefore, it was even impossible for us to tell, at the point at which we withdrew in 1973, whether we had won or lost the war. There seemed to be, for instance, a prevailing opinion that the war in some ways had been lost, and secondly, that it was lost because we made certain mistakes, and thirdly, that we could replay it or do it over again, either in retrospect in the past or in the prospect in the future, and do it better. I could refute every one of those opinions.

Firstly, in the essential sense that I was talking about—the question of "why"—we had probably won the war at that time. Secondly, it was not a question of mistakes. There were no remediable mistakes as if in what we were doing there was a set of variables that we could really change. Give or take a few factors that we could have remedied, there always were other factors that we would do just as badly. Therefore, what we have are not remediable mistakes, but the constant noise, chaos, and confusion that we will have in fighting any war, since each one is a special case—a series of special cases. Third, the basic *choices* that were made were almost inevitable, disastrous as they might have been in terms of cost. And, fourth, though the war, in many senses of the word, was won, nothing like that should ever be done again in the future of the United States. So, in every one of these four senses, I would draw absolutely opposite conclusions.

Another point of great interest is Khe Sanh and whether this represents a model of the sort of thing that could be done in the future. Khe Sanh, in one way, was a unique situation, and, therefore, does not prove very much about the possibilities for conducting the Vietnam War better. It was a case where we finally found a target for the kind of effort which we are most capable of executing. So far as Vietnam itself is concerned, it was a very special case. But there is a wider lesson, it seems to me, from the Khe Sanh sort of situation: There is such a thing as the American way of war, and it is not really all that bad. But it requires the appropriate target. So when we look at the future, at the kinds of situations that will be amenable to the kinds of military force that we, organizationally and temperamentally, are capable of brilliantly marshaling and deploying, that is the kind of lesson that begins to emerge.

Ambassador Robert Komer:
I am not going to address why, as Earl Ravenal asked, we ever got involved in Vietnam in the first place. I am not going to address objectives—national, Vietnamese, or otherwise. I am not going to address our policy and strategy, though I must say that, as we were reminded, we did have a strategy and it was called "attrition." Instead, I would like to talk about a different dimension of our Vietnam experience that has not yet been addressed directly, although Earl Ravenal did get close to it.

To me, any conference on the lessons of the Vietnam War must focus on performance as well as policy. I think that all of us here could agree that, whatever the reasons we intervened in Vietnam, and even if the ultimate outcome had not been a disaster, the results achieved would hardly have been proportionate to the immense human and material costs incurred. Almost 50,000 U.S. and several hundred thousand Vietnamese deaths; 150 billion dollars over almost twenty years; the rending of the Vietnamese socio-economic fabric; and all of the violent impacts on the United States at home and abroad. So I think it is quite important in seeking lessons, especially military lessons, to ask ourselves a basic question. Why did such a cumulatively enormous effort have such limited impact for so long? Why did it involve such disproportionate costs and tragic side effects? Now, many reasons have already been given, and many of them have been alluded to. Among them, of course, was the unique and highly unfamiliar conflict environment in which we found ourselves; another was the sharp contrast between the enemy we faced and the regime we were supporting—an ideologically determined, centrally directed, tough-minded regime in the North, with a revolutionary apparatus in the South, against a weak, traditionalist regime in an only half-formed nation in the South. Third, people have pointed out (and if they have not, they will later) our frequent misjudgment of the enemy, especially of his ability to frustrate our tactics by evading and to counter-escalate against us at every stage up to 1972, when he finally reached the end of his rope, at least for a while. Lastly of course, as General Keegan mentioned, there was the incremental nature of our response: the practice of successive Presidents of doing only what was minimally necessary at each stage.

But I think that even these reasons are insufficient to explain why we did so poorly for so long, despite all the cumulatively enormous effort we and our Vietnamese allies expended. Now this question has bothered me—it has bothered me ever since I left Vietnam—and I would like to advance some supplementary hypotheses on the question of why we did what we did.

Others have already suggested that we *could not* win the Vietnamese War, at least not in any meaningful sense and at any acceptable cost, because of the way we fought it. But this still begs the question of why we fought the way we did. I think the answer lies in an as yet neglected dimension of the Vietnamese War—the impact of institutional factors—bureaucratic constraints, if you will—on the American and Vietnamese response. In effect, both Governments attempted to cope with a highly atypical conflict situation through institutions designed for quite different purposes. The typical behavior patterns of these organizations influenced not only the decisions made but also what was actually done in the field—performance even more than policy. They also influenced the very way in which our response was managed and even led to reshaping that response itself from what was originally intended. Bureaucratic inertia—another institutional factor—made the Government organizations involved—American and Vietnamese—very slow to change these ingrained behavior patterns.

In other words, there was a whole set of real-life constraints inherent in the way the great departments and the great agencies, which made up our two Governments, operate, which made them unable to *adapt* sufficiently to the unique and unfamiliar conflict environment of Vietnam. Though by no means the whole story, these factors did much to help render the American and GVN response unduly conventional, wasteful, and slow to adapt.

One result is what I would call the gap between policy and performance: the sharp discontinuity, for example, apparent in *The Pentagon Papers,* between the mixed counterinsurgency and military strategy that U.S. and GVN policy called for, and the overwhelmingly conventional and military nature of our actual response. I don't buy the thesis that we did not know what we were getting into.

I will go further and say that, to a great extent, American policy makers listened. You can't read the actual operational policy documents in *The Pentagon Papers* or the cables from Ambassador Lodge without getting the feeling that they call, at various times, for just about everything that the critics say we should have done operationally in Vietnam —even the JCS papers include a whole series of sensible proposals on the political and economic, as well as on the military, front. But *The Pentagon Papers* also show starkly the immense contrast between what policy called for and what we actually did. As Maxwell Taylor commented afterward in his book, one of the facts of life about Vietnam is that it was never difficult to decide what should be done, but almost impossible to get it done, at least in an acceptable period of time.

Why was this? Why was it so hard to get things done? Why is there such a sharp discontinuity between the policy in NSSM 288, if you will, and what we actually did on the ground? I think it is largely because the great departments or agencies charged with carrying out the policy were incapable of carrying it out. Instead, what did they do? They did their thing. They played out their traditional, institutional repertoires. Now, be very clear that I am not saying this critically. I am trying to explain what I regard as a typology—a typical characteristic of bureaucracies, of institutions. Every organization has its own institutional repertoire, its own typical behavior pattern, and every institution does best what it is trained and equipped to do and does less well what is atypical or what is beyond the range of its organizational mission and experience. In the Vietnamese case, this was most strikingly evident in the approach of the Vietnamese and U.S. military. Not because they were dumber than the civilians—but because from the outset they dominated what the Americans, at any rate, did in Vietnam. From the outset, their preponderant weight tended to dictate a militarized response. And what kind of response? Our military responded by doing what they were trained and equipped to do.

After World War II, we sized, equipped, and trained our general-purpose forces—Army, Navy, and Air Force—primarily to compete with the Soviets on the plains of Central Europe. That was not foolish. But what we did not bear in mind was that, having trained them for the scenario, they would turn around and do the same thing in the quite different circumstances of Vietnam. Instead of adapting to the unique Vietnamese situation, we fought the enemy our way at horrendous costs, and with some tragic side effects, because we lacked much capability to do otherwise. In effect, we imported the American style of war to Vietnam. It was our style, it worked in two world wars, we did the same thing in Vietnam.

As in other wars, we Americans found the attrition strategy a natural institutional response of forces immensely superior in firepower and mobility which could not bring an elusive enemy to decisive battle in the classic manner. So we fell back on attrition, as Professor West put it, "on grinding them down." To me, these are simple facts. I am simply trying to point out that organizations will do what they are trained and equipped to do, and will not do other things anywhere nearly as well.

Molding the Vietnamese forces in the mirror image of the U.S. forces, which were supplying and training them, was another natural institutional reaction. We organized, we equipped, we trained the RVNAF to fight American style, with American weapons and American tables of organization and equipment, using American ammunition, because this was the only way we knew how. Those who pointed out that this was not quite the answer were up against the ineradicable institutional dynamic which made their advice, however sensible, utterly unacceptable to an organization which was unable to accept that advice operationally, even if it comprehended it intellectually.

Our air campaign against North Vietnam also reflects the way in which an institution prefers to play out its own repertoire. Strategic bombing and interdiction were designed against the Soviets, and we designed and equipped our Air Force to conduct these kinds of campaigns. So when we went to Vietnam and discovered we had to use air power because we did not have enough ground power, and besides, our doctrine called for it, and the Air Force wanted to get into the act instead of leaving it all to the Army and the Marines, the Air Force did what it was trained and equipped to do. I am not blaming the Air Force for it. I am simply pointing out that, when the argument about using the A-1E versus the jet came up, the Air Force kept saying that jets are better at close air support than these slow prop-driven planes. The Air Force did not believe that—what the Air Force really meant was that if we buy prop-driven planes for dealing with guerrillas in Vietnam, we will end the war with an inventory of prop-driven planes when what we need is jets! Because against the Russians prop planes are hardly the answer. The only thing I accuse the Air Force of on this score is that they did not level with the civilians, particularly the systems analysts, who were all saying that the Air Force did not know what it was talking about.

Consider also the critical intelligence inadequacies which plagued the Vietnamese and American efforts, despite the huge resources invested. In fact, we probably spent more on intelligence alone, on our side, than Hanoi spent on the whole war. But the critical inadequacies here were also largely the result of institutional factors. The massive U.S., MACV, CIA, and ARVN intelligence empires focused mostly on what they were familiar with—on the classic role of intelligence as it developed in World Wars I and II. What is it? It is order of battle. It is the identification and location of the main enemy units so that we can target them and clobber them. They did this—they did it rather well within the limits of the possible—but to the total neglect of the guerrillas and the so-called Viet Cong infrastructure, the political-military apparatus that was really running the war. In fact, we tended to see the enemy in our own image, which is one reason why we so often thought that we were doing better than we were.

The civilian agencies also focused on dealing with that with which they were most familiar. The State Department always impressed me as clinging to a traditionalist view of dealing with a sovereign country, even though that country was so much on its back that sovereignty was about the only thing it had left! State's concept of institution building was to encourage the American democratic form—a kind of mirror-imaging on the civilian side that was rather hard to apply to a quite different society like that in Vietnam. AID was also quite conventional. It focused on conventional nation building, even in the midst of guerrilla war. However, the bulk of their money, thanks to the Defense Department and Secretary McNamara, quite properly went into an anti-inflation program to prevent the enormous economic impact of the war from driving the Vietnamese economy totally into the ground.

Why did we not change faster? Why did we not learn more? I will again cite institutional factors. To me, the greatest obstacle to change was "institutional inertia," the inherent reluctance of large organizations to change their preferred ways of functioning except slowly and incrementally under outside pressure. When the preferred way does not work—as it did not in Vietnam—their instinct is not to do things differently but to do more of the same—to pile on more coals, to bring in more troops. This is precisely what happened in Vietnam.

There was also a shocking lack of institutional memory. There were skewed incentive patterns. The military operated, and, I might add, also the civilians, on the basis of their own internal goals, rather than in terms of any concept of overall national, as opposed to parochial, service requirements. Like all organizations, the great departments involved in Vietnam had a thorough distaste for evaluation of their own performance. At the Harvard Business School, there is a standard rule—never allow self-analysis. If you think that General Motors is doing a lousy job, don't ask General Motors to evaluate that proposition.

Next, there was no unified conflict management to pull the disparate aspects of a complex political-military conflict together. This lack of unified management led to an over-militarization of the conflict by facilitating military predominance, just because the military were more effective in deploying resources to Vietnam than the civilians. In fact, the military were effective and the civilians were non-effective, so it is almost an absolute rather than a comparative point. The lack of unified conflict management had all sorts of adverse impact in Vietnam. It led to a proliferation of overlapping programs, and a competition for scarce resources to the point where everybody was getting in everybody else's way. Meanwhile, counterinsurgency fell between stools. It was everybody's business and nobody's, because there was no vested interest, no great department charged precisely with this function. I think that this was what contributed more than any other single factor to the failure to carry out any kind of a pacification program on any scale commensurate with the need for so long.

The lack of any combined command over the Vietnamese and the Koreans—by the way, a stark contrast to normal military practice, as we learned the hard way in World War I and as we practiced in World War II—led to the Americans and the Vietnamese fighting largely separate wars. Above all it deprived the Americans of any institutional framework for getting better performance from the Vietnamese.

Why did the United States and the Vietnamese settle for such a diffuse and fragmented management structure, which was in such striking contrast to the highly centralized enemy effort? Again, institutional constraints bulk large: not just bureaucratic inertia, but the inherent preference of any agency to operate autonomously, the reluctance of agencies to change the traditional dividing lines, for example between military and civilian. The State Department never wanted a unified command, nor did the military! As a result, we never had one. The same factors also operated on the Vietnamese side.

True, there were political obstacles to a unified command. There is no question that it would have smacked of colonialism, and this was the argument that General Westmoreland always advanced when I raised the point. I finally said to him, "Hell, with half a million men in Vietnam, we are spending twenty-one billion dollars a year, and we're fighting the whole war with the Vietnamese watching us; how can you talk about national sovereignty?" He took the point, but we didn't make the change.

Nor do I want to leave the impression that there were no adaptive solutions in Vietnam. Many of them were tried. But they were usually small-scale innovations and, in the military case at least, most of them were either technological or in the tactical exploitation of new technology. For example, the new helicopter tactics, the C-130 gunship. The sensors, which were first designed for use in the so-called McNamara Line, and were then used much more extensively. These were very innovative, and innovative in a tradition which is very congenial to us Americans—*technological* innovation. But on organizational innovation, on institutional innovation, there was very little.

There were a few things: There was the Joint U.S. Public Affairs Office (JUSPAO)—the first time we ever pulled the military and civilians together under one organization with one chief, Barry Zorthian. Another one was CORDS, of course, the unified civil-military pacification organization. Then, of course, there were the parallel GVN changes that the Vietnamese made because they wanted to follow our example. Most of these innovations tended to prove their worth, but most of them were what the analysts call "sub-optimal." They were on a far smaller scale than was sufficient to really change the stripes of Vietnam, as McNamara used to say.

Despite these innovations, the most notable characteristic of our Vietnam effort was still its sheer conventionality. In an atypical situation that cried out for adaptive response, a series of institutional constraints made this all too hard to achieve. Instead, Vietnam really represented, as Herman Kahn, I think, put it very aptly, "a business-as-usual approach."

The resulting lessons from what I have said are fairly obvious in hindsight. The way I would summarize it is that atypical problems demand a specially tailored response, not just the playing out of existing repertoires. What this means to me, and the thought is by no means original, is that it is as important to avoid mis-lessons of Vietnam as to draw lessons from Vietnam. We modeled our earlier responses much too much on our Korean experience, and it is very important that we do not model any new responses too much on Vietnam. But adaptive response is easy to talk about in general; it is just very hard to achieve in practice. It demands a great deal more follow-through than we Americans have ever demonstrated to prevent that gap between policy and performance that cost us so heavily in Vietnam. Maybe Earl Ravenal is right—maybe we just cannot adapt sufficiently. And the answer is to stay out of Vietnams. I hope he is wrong, because I do not think that that kind of absolutist reaction is a good prescription for the future either, but I am afraid that unless we change our ways of doing things, unless we open up the system, unless we change the incentive pattern to generate adaptive response, he may be proved right after all.

Professor Ithiel de Sola Pool:
May I try to answer the Ravenal-Komer thesis that, given the character of the American institutional structure, the mistakes we made were pretty much determined—Ravenal would say inevitable. In Ravenal's extreme formulation we have a particular kind of political-military system that we can use for certain types of war, and for no other. Komer raises the question in more cautious form. He asks whether it is inevitable that bureaucracy must "do its thing." He does not assert that the American Government is incapable of ever behaving innovatively, but

only that heavy constraints toward mindless conventionality stemmed from institutional biases. These constraints are so heavy as at least to make one wonder whether Ravenal's pessimism is not justified.

With Komer's formulation I generally agree, yet I would like to tone it down a bit. I would like to argue that the potential for avoiding mistakes in Vietnam was greater than he suggests. Fate was not binding on us; we were more culpable for our errors because we had greater freedom to act better.

Komer argues that our errors arose out of institutional constraints, not out of ignorance. He argues that we knew it was a political war right from the beginning; we understood that we had to win the "hearts and minds" of men; we knew that attrition would be counterproductive. Thus, he seems to reject the view that our errors were corrigible by still greater knowledge. That is in part so, but only in part. Robert Sansom rightly talked about a "learning process" that took place during the war. The degree of understanding at the beginning was extremely shallow. It improved, but even by 1968 you will not find much sophisticated analyses of Vietnamese politics and society in *The Pentagon Papers*. Such analyses are few and far between.

In the course of the discussions here, we have been presented with some very dramatic illustrations of failures of knowledge during the war. Paul Nitze commented on how badly Secretary McNamara was shaken by reading about Ben Suc. That does not mean that he did not previously understand that the war was hurting civilians whose support we were trying to gain. But the fact that the events at Ben Suc could have come to someone in his position at that date as any kind of revelation of what was going on in the field means that the level and penetration of understanding of the realities of Vietnam were deplorable. I also take it as an intellectual failure in our government that it took until 1969, as Colonel Donald Marshall has described, to redefine our statement of objectives.

There were, of course, a few people—Sir Robert Thompson and General Lansdale and others, such as Gerald Hickey, George Carver, Million Sachs, and Douglas Pike—who really understood something about Vietnamese society, who knew its politics, who knew the social structure, and who expressed opinions as to how the counterinsurgency effort should operate. They were a very thin layer, and while their views were known in a general way they were not brought into the control structure. The people who made the decisions were intelligent generalists whose expertise was in American political affairs and American organizational management. They were not driven by acute analysis of Vietnam.

If one asks "why" we were incapable of acting more perceptively, the answer is indeed in part that bureaucracies "do their thing." But does that mean, as Ravenal asserts, that the outcome was inevitable? It does mean that except under one circumstance.

The political system provides one major counterweight to the bureaucracy and that is the President. If the President does not himself decide that he is going to force the bureaucracies to do things differently, then he has got to accept the fact that they will go on in the conventional way. To build an atom bomb President Roosevelt had to create the Manhattan Project; the Department of the Army could not have done it. To put a man on the moon President Kennedy had to create NASA; no department could have done it. If the President does not supersede the normal decision makers and put appropriate and dedicated specialists in charge, then Komer's thesis will prove right—bureaucracy will "do its thing." If the conventional way isn't good enough, then Ravenal's conclusion of "don't get into it in the first place" is right also. It is sound advice unless the President himself is willing to use his power to force an unconventional approach.

Professor Robert Pfaltzgraff:
It is difficult to assess the military lessons of Vietnam as they may affect the future conduct of war. The technologies and doctrinal innovations spawned by the Vietnam War will be available for use by both sides in the future. We have already seen the utilization of new technologies in the October 1973 Middle East war. However, the general military lessons from the Vietnam War include:

1. The need for a more comprehensive understanding of the rela-

tionship between military power and the development of an adequate indigenous political base and effective psychological operations in a country which is threatened by an insurgency such as faced Vietnam. The effective conduct of military operations rests vitally upon a political infrastructure which is capable of attracting sustained popular support and minimizing the need for heavy reliance upon outside forces such as those provided by the United States. The United States must not be more willing to defend an ally than the ally is willing to defend itself.

2. The need to understand the close relationship between domestic politics and foreign policy, especially in a country such as the United States. The implication is that the United States cannot support over a long period a large-scale U.S. military intervention unless direct American national interests appear to be vitally affected and can be demonstrated as being vitally affected. Those who evolved U.S. policy in the decade after World War II were conscious of the difficulties in assuring sustained popular support for extended U.S. overseas commitments.

3. The existence of gaps in historical experience, culture, and the nature of respective goals makes essential more broadly based understanding of the country in which military operations are being conducted than was evident in the United States' understanding of Vietnam, at least in the early stages of the conflict. The lack of such understanding leads to the development of policies, strategies, and capabilities based largely upon a U.S. experience rather than that of an adversary whom we confront or an ally whom we seek to assist. It also leads potentially to a miscalculation as to the other side's willingness to absorb losses, a problem which is inherent in the calculation of the costs to the opponent of a "war of attrition."

4. The need for a more accurate assessment of the nature of military requirements for the effective conduct of conflict or how to avoid committing too little too late for the wrong purpose.

5. The need to define more precisely the nature of U.S. goals. U.S. goals appear never to have been adequately defined in such a way as to be understood and accepted by a substantial segment of the U.S. population. As Earl Ravenal suggested, the lack of an adequate definition of goals led of necessity to a lack of understanding of the

nature of "victory" or "defeat." The criteria for judging U.S. success or failure in Vietnam were not fully developed, enunciated, or understood at the popular level. For many years to come it will be difficult to reach a broadly based consensus as to the nature of the defeat suffered by the United States in the Vietnam War. This problem arises in large part from the lack of understanding about U.S. goals in Vietnam.

6.   Last but not least, the conflict was a war, decisions about whose conduct were centralized to an unprecedented extent. While new technologies have made possible instantaneous communication, and thus the centralization of decision making, the need for flexibility in the field remains. Bureaucratization in Washington led to the development of plans by persons who had little of the needed expertise or direct acquaintance with operational needs. The authors of several chapters have commented upon the problems created during the conflict by lack of adequate coordination among commands, as well as the need—perhaps the excessive need—to refer decisions to Washington. In thinking about the conduct of future wars, the United States must reconcile more effectively the need for centralization with the need for flexibility in the field.

Closely related is the problem of unity of command. According to Ambassador Komer, the need for unity of command was honored more in the breach than it was in the practice. The U.S. war effort in Vietnam suffered from the lack of unified conflict management. There is need for both unity of command *and* consistency of command.

The military lessons of the Vietnam War, while numerous, are by no means either self-evident or instructive about wars of the future. If the United States succeeded or failed in Vietnam because of its inability to adapt quickly to the circumstances of Vietnam and its penchant for conducting the war in Vietnam with capabilities and doctrines developed and tested in conflicts elsewhere, similar problems may arise in the wars of the future. Therefore, a learning of the military lessons of Vietnam, without regard for the unique characteristics of the Vietnam War and future wars, will serve American policy in those potential conflicts no more adequately than did the strategies and capabilities utilized in Vietnam.

Afterword

A final point seems pertinent. The war is over, the cost was enormous, and the side which the United States backed lost. But there is great irony in the fact that the North Vietnamese finally won by purely conventional means, using precisely the kind of warfare at which the American army was best equipped to fight. In the early 1960s it was a truism among the New Frontier's spokesmen that our lack of a counter-insurgency capability represented a huge gap in our readiness. Yet the argument presented in this book convinces us that we won the unconventional war in that the South Vietnamese and American joint effort had largely eliminated the Vietcong as a serious contender for power by 1972. Thus the North Vietnamese army swept down in conventional formation in the 'Easter offensive' of 1972 but was beaten back. In the ensuing year we traded our withdrawal for the return of our prisoners by Hanoi, at a time when the North Vietnamese occupied substantial portions of South Vietnam. Thus in 1975, the North Vietnamese army again swept across the internationally recognized line to finish the conflict. In 1975, when the North Vietnamese army planted the flag of victory atop the presidential palace in Saigon, its spokesman made clear that it was they who had won the war. In their lengthy battle accounts that followed Hanoi's great military victory, Generals Giap and Dung barely mentioned the contribution of local forces.

Index

Abrams, General Creighton W., 54, 79-84, 142, 176, 188, 189, 229-30, 244, 245, 254
Air Force, U.S. *See* U.S. Air Force
Air interdiction. *See* Interdiction, strategy of
Air Operations, 18, 46, 51-52, 58-60, 67, 80, 105, 125-171, 243-44, 269; ineffective use of, 184-85, 193, 200; reconnaissance, 138, 141, 179; U.S. dissatisfaction with, 128-44; Vietnam War compared to Korean War and World War II, 129-30. *See also* Bombing operations; Gradualism, strategy of; Guided bombs; Helicopters; Interdiction, strategy of; North Vietnamese Army; U.S. Air Force
Ambush. *See* Guerrilla warfare; Insurgency; Viet Cong
"Americanization" of the Vietnam War, 241, 268-69
An Loc, 84, 104, 105, 158, 162, 227
Antimilitarism. *See* United States, backlash against the military; Vietnam War, public attitudes in America toward
Army of the Republic of Vietnam (ARVN), 34, 45, 48, 52-53, 58, 60-64, 66, 79-80, 81, 82, 92, 153, 156, 158, 160-62, 207, 208, 216, 219, 227-30, 247, 261-62, 270; Development of the Vietnamese army, 241-45. *See also* Casualties, Army of the Republic of Vietnam

Army, U.S. *See* U.S. Army
Attrition, strategy of, 10-11, 15, 57, 60, 65-66, 73-93, 136, 146, 152-54, 231, 260, 265, 268, 274, 276; used by Viet Cong/North Vietnamese Army to liquidate civilians, 77-78. *See also* Gradualism; "Search and destroy," tactic of

Base-security strategy, 58, 59
Ben Suc, 65, 274; *Village of Ben Suc*, 199
Binh Dinh province, 26, 32, 34, 45, 79, 179, 221, 228
Blockades, 96, 129, 167
"Body Count," 19, 22, 77, 192, 194. *See also* Casualties; Civilian casualties; Computers
Bombing operations, 54, 58-60, 67, 99, 101-02, 104, 127-36, 139, 145-50, 158, 163-70, 200; cost of, 146-50; expectations too high, 129-32; Linebacker campaigns, 143-44, 165-67, 170, 177; napalm, 126, 138; objectives of, 130-32; policy of restrained bombing, 128-31, 133-34; psychological and political aspects of, 127-28, 130, 133; "Rolling Thunder," 154, 165; tool to bring about negotiations, 130, 132. *See also* Air operations; Attrition, strategy of; Guided bombs; Interdiction, strategy of; Peace negotiations
Bundy, William, 10, 130, 134

Cambodia, *vi*, 97, 102-03, 144, 153, 155,